LETTERS FRO

THOMAS HODGKIN

LETTERS FROM AFRICA 1947–56

Edited and annotated by
Elizabeth Hodgkin and
Michael Wolfers

HAAN ASSOCIATES • LONDON

Copyright © Elizabeth Hodgkin and Michael Wolfers 2000

First published 2000 by HAAN Asscociates Publishing
P.O. Box 607, London SW16 1EB

ISBN 1 874209 93 6 (cased edition)
ISBN 1 874209 88 X (paperback edition)

Phototypeset by M Rules
Printed and bound in Great Britain
by Hobbs the Printers Ltd., Totton, Hampshire

Contents

Introduction

Perspectives on Africa changed slowly but inevitably in the wake of the second world war. Among those who observed the dying colonialism was Thomas Hodgkin, the author of these letters written from tours of Africa to his family in post-war Britain. The collection reveals the interest an intelligent and sympathetic observer took in the factors for change. It reveals his growing awareness of an emergent African nationalism that was over the next decades to replace colonialism. Thomas Hodgkin was in the vanguard of the quest for an understanding of the African dimension of the continent's politics and history.

Thomas travelled to Africa in 1947 with an anti-imperialist sensibility encouraged by his experiences in Palestine in the 1930s. This had included service in the British administration from 1934 to 1936 when he resigned in protest over oppressive policies. That break is shown in a selection *Thomas Hodgkin: Letters from Palestine 1932–36*, London, Quartet, 1986, edited by his brother E.C. Hodgkin (ECH), to which this volume is in part a companion. After Thomas returned to London he joined the Communist Party, and continued to be a member until 1949, when he resigned over attempts by the party to influence his work in the Oxford University Delegacy for Extra-Mural Studies.

The Palestine letters were mainly to Thomas's mother Dorothy Forster Hodgkin (DFH) (one of nine children of A.L. Smith, a historian and Master of Balliol College from 1916 to 1924), and Thomas's father Robert Howard Hodgkin (RHH) (a historian and from 1937 to 1946 Provost of Queen's College, Oxford). Thomas in 1937 met the x-ray crystallographer Dorothy Mary Crowfoot, daughter of educationist and archaeologist John Winter Crowfoot (JWC) and textiles expert Grace Mary Hood (GMC). Thomas and Dorothy were married on 16 December 1937. Her achievement as a scientist of world renown is recounted in a biography, *Dorothy Hodgkin: A Life* by Georgina Ferry, London, Granta, 1998. Although occasional letters in this collection are to parents or children most are to Thomas's wife Dorothy (DMCH); some are in a diary form that Thomas used to assist the journalism that helped finance the later journeys in this series.

By the time Thomas made the first of many journeys to Africa there were three children: Luke Howard Hodgkin, born in 1938 who became a mathematician, Prudence Elizabeth Hodgkin (Liz or PEH), born in 1941, a historian and co-editor of this collection, and John Robin Tobias Hodgkin (Toby), born in 1946 who became a plant geneticist.

This collection is not presented as a portrait of Thomas's own life. A full biography is in preparation by Michael Wolfers, co-editor of the collection, and covers Thomas's family background, upbringing and varied interests in the politics of the Middle-East, Africa and Vietnam.

It must be noted that Thomas's earliest travels in Africa were brief episodes of the years in which he lived and worked in Oxford as secretary from September 1945 of the Oxford University Delegacy for Extra-Mural Studies. We have omitted from this collection the domestic and family concerns that feature in many of the original letters. We have highlighted rather an engagement with Africa that led Thomas to relinquish the security of his Oxford University appointment in 1952 to spend great parts of each year on independent travel in Africa. This led to his seminal work *Nationalism in Colonial Africa*, London, Frederick Muller, 1956, and later to other books beyond the frame of this small window on his African experience (Thomas's travels in Africa continued for a further quarter of a century).

Thomas came late to Africa – he was aged thirty-six when he took the first journey. In childhood and youth he made an accomplished progress through the Dragon School, Winchester College, and Balliol College to a First in Greats in 1932. In the hope of going to Palestine, he applied on graduation for a job with the Colonial Office responsible for the mandate administration.

He was offered instead an appointment in the Gold Coast, and after much troubled thought turned it down. He explained to one of the Balliol dons in a letter of 13 September 1932: 'All my interests and affections are here or in The Near East: the more I read history, the more I am certain that it would be impossible to give up friends and sociabilities unless one could continue learning, and forming relationships in that way – and one couldn't do that in The Gold Coast – a country with no past and no history – and no present either – only perhaps a promising future – and that at a Kindergarten level.'

Thomas went to Palestine as a trainee archaeologist. He then had spells of adult teaching to the unemployed in Cumberland, and to Manchester University students, before going again to Palestine, this time as a civil servant. On his resignation and return from Palestine he enrolled for a teaching course, and endured some difficult months of trial teaching to boys in London elementary and secondary schools. He decided not to pursue the course, and from April 1937 he was again in Cumberland and engaged in the more congenial task of adult education.

He was rejected on medical grounds for military service in the Second World War. In September 1939 he became a Workers Educational Association tutor in North Staffordshire, where the future Labour politician George Wigg was district secretary. Thomas spent the war years conducting classes with civilians and armed forces personnel, and in this context wrote (as a WEA Study Outline) *The Colonial Empire: A students' guide*, London, WEA and WETUC, 1942.

It was with the stimulus of George Wigg and with Colonial Office interest that Thomas began in 1947 to initiate extra-mural work in the Gold Coast and Nigeria. The trajectory of this work can be seen in this collection. The extra-mural tutors appointed during this period from Britain and Africa were a gifted crew. They included many who remained involved in African adult education and political studies over the next four decades: such as Dennis Austin, Lalage Bown, Helen and David Kimble, Ayo Ogunsheye and Bill Tordoff. Thomas met many of the exponents of the new politics in Africa: such as Nnamdi Azikiwe and Kwame Nkrumah, future presidents respectively of Nigeria and Ghana.

The first visits to Africa were to draw Thomas more deeply into the continent, the neglected African pre-colonial history, and the political reawakening of its countries. His journey to the Gold Coast in February 1947 was a turning point in Thomas's life as he first learned of the kingdoms of the western Sudan and recanted his error of fifteen years earlier that the Gold Coast had no history. He was drawn in because he loved the people and the places, and secondly because his own sensibility was something that few outsiders were bringing to this historically interesting time.

After further journeys to Africa he wrote for the periodical *West Africa* in 1950 (and again in 1951) a long series of topical and scholarly articles on the background to African nationalism. He went also to Sudan, to countries under French colonial rule, and along the trails of Islamic influence in Africa.

A few words should be said about Thomas's character and methods of travelling. Money tended to be tight, but even without that he had a natural love for the means of transport used by the local people: lorries, buses, trains (with third and fourth class preferred to first and second). Elizabeth Hodgkin recalls doing a similar journey around 1959 to the one Thomas describes in 1951 – from Lagos to Ibadan, taking seven or eight hours to cover 120 miles, travelling fourth class (in 1951 it had been third class, but he explained that a fourth class had not been running then). Thomas would travel more comfortably when tired or when he found that status (presumably for meetings with politicians) demanded it: he describes a journey second class in October 1952 as 'a compromise between pocket and remaining reasonably bien vu'. On the whole he believed that the delays in out of the way spots might be as interesting as the journey; he describes a delay in March 1951 as 'one of these periodic hitches that make life in Africa jolly'.

As a traveller in Africa he had to be prepared to take whatever transport became available; there is a wonderful camel ride to and from Walata from Nema, described in a diary letter of November 1952. Such methods of transport, and the inevitable delays that accompany them, meant that he was invariably late in his schedule and having to change his programme. For the journeys of 1954 with travel uncharacteristically by air, first-class train or private car, the letters are less dramatic, and Thomas notes being teased about 'the advantages of foreign journalists who travel in luxury motor cars'. Thomas's more usual means of transport involved waiting for long periods for lorries to arrive, or for passengers to assemble, and letters were often written in these gaps or even when travelling – in a letter of January 1950 he apologises for his writing in a truck going along the road at about 60 or 70 miles an hour.

Thomas's letters home were rarely typed and most often were written in his own characteristic style: a neat, small, somewhat italic hand, leaving a wide margin, the space left then usually filled in by turning the page on one side. Often they are on air-mail letters, sometimes on pads from home; they are often difficult to read, many letters complain of biros drying up, and letters written in pencil have become, over the years, even more difficult to read. Often letters were carried about and then added to, becoming more and more scuffed up, or marked by Thomas's great standby of oil (from sardine tins) and biscuit crumbs. He would stay in cheapish hotels or where possible he would stay or eat with friends, acquaintances, or people picked up along the way, who might be Africans, colonial planters, or French non-commissioned officers.

It may be asked what is the importance of these letters to a reader some half a century later? They give a vivid picture of some aspects of Africa in a historically interesting period, the decade between the aftermath of World War II and the independence of the Gold Coast as Ghana in 1957. The letters do not focus on particular events but provide a distinct feel of this period. The letters show Thomas meeting historically important leaders, but he was by nature a populist and a democrat: equally happy to find just as interesting the ordinary characters he found along the way. He was gregarious and generous.

In a letter of November 1952 Thomas notes an interlocutor who 'is one of the hundred or so whom I have already invited to come and stay with us' at the family's home near Oxford. Fortunately perhaps they did not all come, but those – and others – who did were not turned away. When Thomas suffered a heart attack and died on 25 March 1982 (on vacation in the Greek Peloponnese resort village of Tolon after a winter in Sudan) *The Times* obituary said he 'did more than anyone to establish the serious study of African history' in Britain. Thomas lies buried in the Tolon cemetery overlooking the Aegean sea, where his epitaph records alongside his scholarly achievements that he enjoyed cooking for his friends.

Elizabeth Hodgkin
Michael Wolfers
London, June 2000

LETTERS FROM AFRICA 1947–56

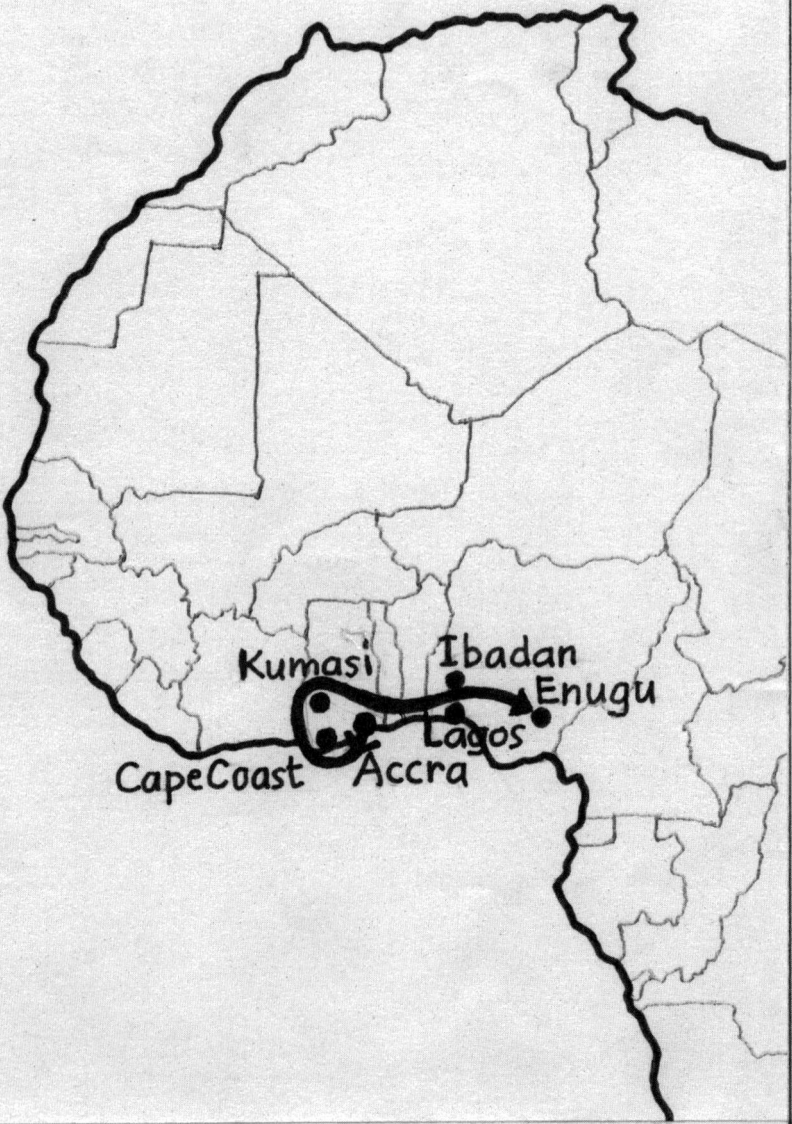

first African journey

First African journey:
to Gold Coast and Nigeria
February–March 1947

The election in Britain in 1945 of the first majority Labour government opened the way to gradual changes in colonial policy. These would bring independence to a partitioned India in 1947, to Sudan in 1956 and to sub-Saharan African colonies from 1957 with the independence of the Gold Coast as Ghana.

George Wigg in the 1930s was District Secretary for the Workers Educational Association in North Staffordshire and was an advisory member of the interview panel that appointed Thomas Hodgkin to become a WEA tutor there in September 1939. Thomas had links with the Workers Educational Association dating back to the 1930s. The family connection was much older. After the WEA was founded in 1903 Thomas's maternal grandfather Arthur Lionel Smith (1850–1924) was nominated in 1907 to the joint committee of WEA and Oxford representatives to examine how the higher education of working men could be implemented in Oxford. Smith was Master of Balliol College, Oxford, from 1916 to 1924. In the second world war Wigg served in the Army Education Corps and took particular interest in West Africa; he became a keen advocate of colonial mass education. Wigg was elected to Parliament in 1945 and shared his concerns over African education with A.D. 'Sandie' Lindsay (Lord Lindsay of Birker), Master of Balliol College and chairman of the Oxford University Delegacy for Extra-Mural Studies where Thomas had become Secretary in September 1945.

From March 1946 Thomas, with Lindsay's support, lobbied the Colonial Office with a proposal for an experimental scheme of extension courses in West Africa. The proposal went to the Advisory Committee on Education in the Colonies and to the colonial administration in the Gold Coast and Nigeria. After nearly a year of soundings, Thomas was authorised to travel to the countries to consider the details of secondment by the Delegacy of two experienced staff tutors – one to Nigeria and one to the Gold Coast to conduct study-courses of weekly meetings with adult students.

Thomas, on his official mission, discussed the scheme with some sixty colonial officials and educationists in the Gold Coast alone between 9 and 24 February, and went on for similar meetings in Nigeria. The mission was successful: from Nigeria Thomas put in hand arrangements for sending the first tutor to the Gold Coast. Recruitment for a Nigeria post followed. Thomas's schedule was largely determined by the official purposes of his mission. However he was keen to meet as wide a range of people as possible, especially 'chaps', meaning to him men and women outside official colonial channels and certainly including Africans. In preparation for the journey he made contact with the West African Students' Union in London and met Africans studying in Britain.

This journey had an unexpected side-effect. A conversation with one of the Achimota teachers stirred in Thomas an interest in the African history of the kingdoms of the Western Sudan. He was recommended to read E.W. Bovill's book published in 1933 *Caravans of the Old Sahara*. Thomas read the book and this led him on to become in time a leading exponent of African history and politics.

To DMCH
[7 February 1947]

Bathurst [The Gambia]
My darling,
    Have just sent you a 5-shilling cable. Hope you get it all right. Have got to this pleasant rest house and have got out of hot English clothes into one of Edward's[1] suits. It really is nice and warm here. Not oppressive at all – rather like Jericho in spring really. We've entered the part of the world where there are lots of 'boys' who do things for you. Demoralising and slightly embarrassing.
    I was pleased at Port Etienne – there were a lot of Arab chaps – not at all negroid – and obviously talking Arabic – so I introduced

---

1 Edward (ECH), born 1913, Thomas's younger brother, in Jerusalem at the time of the writing of this letter.

myself to them, and we started chatting. I was surprised how much we were able to understand one another. We exchanged courtesies and quoted bits of the Koran, and I had to dish out cigarettes. It was nice to be among such people again – (Berber) Beduin from the Sahara they were. A sign of the terrific spread of Arabic culture.

To DMCH
[8 February 1947]

Freetown – Saturday ?about 10 a.m. – Sierra Leone
We have now been flying for several hours (some of which I fear I have slept through) from Freetown, and from the fact that we are climbing down now I should guess we are getting to Takoradi – very nearly at my destination, in fact. As usual in such cases – or at such stages – I find I get cold feet a bit and wonder whether any result one may get will be worth all the effort – or whether I've really cooked up this idea in order to give myself an excuse for an air voyage, etc. But such questionings are inevitable and I don't think matter much. Once one has started it'll be all right. One thing I think I must do as soon as I arrive is fix a definite date for returning (and see about a seat in a plane) otherwise one may find the whole business drags on more than it should

Freetown I was telling you about – it seemed surprisingly green and fresh – and the hills at the back in particular made it more homely. We had a second breakfast of sausage and eggs and pineapples there (having had a first breakfast of pineapples and egg and tomatoes at 6.30 at Bathurst! – It's surprising what one can manage).

I've got talking to quite an interesting chap among this party: a mining engineer, going out to visit his company's concerns. He is one of these intelligent technicians who believes in efficiency and enlightenment and tends to mistrust Socialism but is open to conviction if things turn out differently from what he expects. Interesting to talk to on his own stuff. Is somewhat sceptical about education!

Have now arrived safely (!) at Accra. Staying at Achimota.[2] Have a large room to work in. Everything OK. Will write more soon.

---

2 Achimota was founded as a multi-purpose educational institution by

To ECH
12 February 1947

Accra [Gold Coast]

Until today things have been extremely hectic seeing chaps all day and talking too much (and listening quite a bit). A good deal of scepticism about this project of doing adult education – some of it just official, but some of it sound. Still it's an interesting part of the world, and even in 4 days one has begun to learn a bit. It's a lovely climate – just the right temperature, so that one never feels too cold and not often too hot. Test is that one feels no discomfort when having all one's clothes off. I should say that today it's been like a nice summer day in Jerusalem. At its hottest (and dampest) more like Beirut.

The pleasant oriental practice of fairly frequent drinks – even mossulmanes offer you gin or whisky. The Africans are many of them extremely beautiful – I hadn't realised how good they were – both men and women – very regular clear-cut sort of faces. In some ways this place seems almost Mediterranean – partly perhaps because of the buildings Europeans having been building here since the 15th Century – a number of good castles I gather – only seen the one here (which is Govt. house and is pictured on the stamps) so far. Unfortunately I can't get hold of any decent guide book. Also the people wear marvellous cloaks, extremely bright, wound round like togas. Altogether I feel this would be a good place for a holiday. Only there seems a dearth of cafes – having to write this in the YMCA drinking Army tea.

To DMCH
12 February [1947]

Accra Wed

Actually I seem to have no expenses beyond cigarettes (which I share with my friendly driver) and Paludrin (which I am taking

___

the Gold Coast Governor Sir Frederick Gordon Guggisberg (1869–1930) and educationists, including Dr James Emmanuel Kwegyir Aggrey (1875–1927). The foundation stone was laid in March 1924 and the school was officially opened as Prince of Wales' College and School in January 1927, six months before Aggrey's death.

because you can buy it and not quinine). After a pretty hectic couple of days I've got a bit more time today to breathe, and think (I hope) and get some of the dozen or so interviews of the last 2 days written up. Yesterday I seemed to be talking (and listening a bit!) from 9.30 a.m. till 10.30 p.m. Education Dept. Then H.E.,[3] then Mr Yankah[4] (Teachers Union). Then lunch with Marshall[5] of the Education Dept. and his wife and two charming daughters aged nearly 6 and 3.

Carrying this on after lunch – taken in the best hotel. Just been meeting Oswald Kitching ex-WEA-Labour Officer.[6] He's pretty sceptical about the whole project. But I'm seeing him again at Sekondi on Sunday, when we'll be able to discuss things more fully. These last 3 days have been so crammed with chaps that I hardly know where I stand – alternate encouragement and douches of cold water. I think something will come of it all, but I wouldn't bet on it.

To DMCH
[14 February 1947]

Friday. Cape Coast [Gold Coast]
Here I am staying with Methodists at Mfantsipim School[7] – very friendly and kind but rather Methodist. (One difference between

---

3 Alan Cuthbert Maxwell Burns (1887–1980), joined the colonial service in 1905 and was Governor of British Honduras from 1934 and knighted in 1936. He was Governor of the Gold Coast from 1941 until August 1947. He became UK representative to the Trusteeship Council established by the United Nations in 1946 to govern the former League of Nations mandates. He was compiler and author of several books.
4 J.N.T. Yankah, Gold Coast Teachers Union, was later involved in a report of 1956 on the use of English as the medium of instruction in Gold Coast schools.
5 John Russell Marshall, born 1903 and educated at Glasgow Academy, Glasgow University and Pembroke College, Oxford, was a former master at Achimota College from 1928 and was appointed senior education officer in the Gold Coast from 1945.
6 Oswald Kitching, a senior labour officer in the Gold Coast administration, was later extremely helpful over the setting up of classes, especially for trade unionists.
7 Wesleyans opened the first high school at Cape Coast in 1876; another school was opened in 1905; and an amalgamation soon after took the name Mfantsipim.

C. of E. mission schools and Methodist, I gather, is that the former go in for alcoholic drinks and the latter don't). This morning I've got a bit of time largely because the morning didn't work out as planned, and I only saw 2 of the 3 people I meant to see – the other I'm having tea with this afternoon. Even so my conscience is a bit guilty – and I'm wondering if I ought to be seeing a Catholic headmaster or someone of that kind. Here again I'm very comfortable and well-looked after – have a bungalow to myself (where I'm now writing) and meals with this kind family – the Sneaths[8] (H.M. of the Methodist School). I think there should be quite a good prospect of getting a course going here – meeting some members of the Eureka club (a 'literary' society, mainly teachers) to discuss things this evening. Now in 10 minutes I have to go and chat with the senior boys of this school.

To DMCH
18 February 1947

Kumasi [Gold Coast]
Am staying now at the Wesley Teacher Training College – with the Principal, a very nice chap called Beetham,[9] one of the best I've met so far: extremely helpful. It rained like anything yesterday evening – so feels quite cool now. I'm having a slack morning till 10 a.m. – both Driver and I (particularly he) having had a very strenuous day yesterday. Left Sekondi at about 6 a.m. and got through here at about 3 p.m. – driving a good deal of the way along baddish roads, with dust flying, goats and chicken scampering out of the way – like the early days of motoring. It wasn't a very exciting journey. One of the disadvantages of driving through primeval forest with no hills to speak of is that you seldom see farther than half a mile ahead. No views. And all bits of forest very like every other bit. Forest itself is quite beautiful, with these tall smooth-stemmed grey trees – not beginning to produce branches and leaves

---

8 Rev. Alec A. Sneath was headmaster of Mfantsipim from 1911 to 1919 when he was invalided home, and again from 1945 until his death from a heart attack in 1948.
9 Rev. T. Allan Beetham, Principal of Wesley College founded 1905, became Africa Secretary of the Methodist Missionary Society.

until a long way up – clearings here and there where cassava and bananas and other things have been planted – and villages every 3 or 4 miles with children playing around – houses being plaited together and then covered with mud.

I had a nice time in Sekondi. The Inspector of Education there, a friendly Scotsman called John Wilson,[10] who was taught Philosophy at Glasgow by A.D.L.,[11] took me in hand, gave me all my meals, and introduced me to people. I was somewhat lazy – it being a week-end, and feeling like easing off a bit myself: also not wanting to make any definite commitments there. However I managed to see quite a few people – a nice African (woman) teacher, a good Railway engineer who runs a study-circle for Railway clerks, a not very effective Social Centre warden, his Friend, a teacher (with the name of Welbeck!)[12] who is active in the (Consumers) Co-op movement that is just beginning, and the chaps (English) in charge of technical education, who gave us an enormous meal on Sunday night. (One of them had met Wigg[13] when he was out. I asked what he'd thought of him – this chap thought a moment and then replied "Well, he wasn't what I'd call a good listener"!)

How much all this is achieving, or likely to achieve, I don't know. I think there's no doubt a lot could be done – it'll take quite a bit of time though. There are quite a lot of practical difficulties to be got over – particularly in regard to accommodation and travelling. If I can't find ways round these it may be easy for those who

10 John Wilson, born 1903 and educated at Irvine Royal Academy and Glasgow University, was inspector of schools in the Gold Coast from 1929, seconded to the information department during the Second World War, and senior education officer from 1945. He later became the principal of a teacher training college from 1948.

11 Alexander Dunlop Lindsay (1879–1952) , Master of Balliol College from 1924 to 1949 and Lord Lindsay of Birker from 1945, had succeeded Thomas's grandfather A.L. Smith as Master and was influential in several of Thomas's career decisions.

12 Nathaniel Welbeck, born 1914, of the Gold Coast Teachers Union, was an original member of the central committee of the Convention People's Party (CPP) and later held various ministerial posts in the governments of the Gold Coast and Ghana.

13 George Edward Cecil Wigg (1900–83) campaigned for army education during the Second World War and visited the East and West Africa Commands. He continued to press the case for mass education in Africa when he was elected as MP for Dudley at the end of the war. He was later Lord Wigg.

are sceptical anyway to do me down. However, you know the way I tend unnecessarily to take a gloomy view, usually because I haven't yet got my own ideas straight – and I feel sure that these relations with chaps out here will turn out to be useful. I am very much impressed with Africans, most of them (those whom we haven't made a bit soft through the wrong kind of education) – e.g. last night, visiting this night-school for illiterates conducted by Old Achimotans,[14] where they learn English and Vernacular (Twi) and Arithmetic. Terrific enthusiasm – particularly for English (I was told they are a bit suspicious of Vernacular, as a poor substitute – to prevent them from getting on). All the time, of course, one's feeling is that there's a lack of the kind of organisation to which this enthusiasm, desire for knowledge, etc. can be harnessed. Leonard Barnes'[15] points in *Soviet Light on the Colonies* seem sensible. Let's pray for the day when Wigg becomes Col. Sec.!

To DMCH
20 February 1947

Akropong (Aquapim)[16] *[Gold Coast]*
Spent the morning saying goodbye to chaps in Kumasi, Yaw Adu,[17]

---

14 Former pupils of Achimota College in the wake of the Second World War took the initiative of organising and conducting evening classes for Kumasi workers.

15 Leonard Barnes, author of several books that Thomas drew on in his adult education work, was a member of the sub-committee on 'Education for Citizenship' initiated in 1946 by the Colonial Office and the Advisory Committee on Education in the Colonies. Barnes helped bring Thomas together with a group of Nigerian and Gold Coast students in London in January 1947 when Thomas was preparing for the first African journey.

16 Akwapim was a very early mission station; the first where missionaries survived for more than a few weeks because it was on a hill (they moved to escape the 'miasma' of low lying land, wrongly blamed for malaria).

17 Amishadai Larson Adu (1914–77), known as Yaw, was appointed assistant district commissioner in the Gold Coast in 1942. He became Commissioner for Africanisation in the public service in 1950 and head of the Ghana civil service in 1959. Later he became an international civil servant and served as Deputy Secretary-General of the Commonwealth from 1966 to 1970.

Peter Ady's friend,[18] who has been very helpful all through, and people at the office of the Ashanti Pioneer,[19] who gave me and our scheme an excellent write-up, and Beetham himself, at Wesley College, who is certainly one of the very best educational people that I have met here. Then I set out about 11.30 and arrived about 4. Since then I've been talking to some of the staff here – the younger ones in particular. They're good, I think, a bit dour on first acquaintance, but very learned in African matters and sane. I feel I am beginning to find out a little about the habits and customs of the various denominations – Presbyterians obviously take their job and its relation to the African environment very seriously. We've been chatting since supper, partly about African races and languages, and partly about my stuff.

Back in Accra now. Got here from Akropong at about 11 a.m. – then went to Mr Yankah at his school to talk about this evening's meeting (to discuss plans for a course at Accra) – then to Educn. Dept. Then to Secretariat when I found Peter Canham[20] feeling rather ill (he said from an overdose of Paludrin!) – however we confirmed an arrangement to dine together tonight – which will be nice if he can face it. He's one of Peter Ady's friends. Now back here (Achimota) for lunch – Neill[21] is unfortunately ill with lumbago, poor chap. Next 2 or 3 days I must spend getting my report written and trying to get decisions taken – that may need quite a lot of effort. However it may be quite fun. It's been a very good and useful week, I think. This morning I had to address the boys of

18 Peter Honorine Ady was an Oxford economist who had worked in the Gold Coast and suggested names of possible contacts to Thomas, including Adu, John Tsiboe and Modjaben Dowuona. She was author or part-author of several books on economics and statistics.
19 The *Ashanti Pioneer* newspaper was founded in 1932. Thomas met the editor John Tsiboe.
20 Peter H. Canham, born 1914 and educated at St Paul's School and Pembroke College, Oxford, was appointed colonial service cadet in the Gold Coast in 1930, and later in his career worked on the Africa desk at the Colonial Office. He was secretary to the government in the Gold Coast and Ghana from 1955 to 1958. He was later at the Institute of Education, Ahmadu Bello University, Zaria, Nigeria.
21 H.C. Neill taught at Achimota in the 1930s and left for military service in the Second World War. He returned and was school headmaster from 1946 to 1949, and at the time of Thomas's first visit was also Acting Principal of the whole institution.

Akropong Teacher Training College – about adult education as usual. As usual there were several who said that it was a luxury and nothing mattered but mass education. But I got some support from one or two of the African masters. I liked the place – stuck up on this hill – with more air and sense of space than many places. I was telling you a bit about Kumasi I think (I haven't got the first half of my letter here). I liked the folk there a lot – and it should be a worth while place for classes. Beetham took me to see Asantehene (did I tell you), King Prempeh II,[22] ex-storekeeper (Elective monarchy!). I don't know that he really got hold of the idea, though he was polite about it.

I also spent two evenings visiting these night classes – Monday at the literacy classes run by the Old Achimotans (which I thought was a very good show) and Tuesday at what they call the Post-Primary classes – for literature – mainly with School Certificate in view, of course. I took a group in English history as their proper tutor hadn't turned up– the whole thing was clearly being run too much on school lines – but it was creditable that the chaps them-selves should have got it going at all.

To DMCH
25 February [1947]

Accra – Tues.
I'm feeling a bit browned off actually – in the common undignified position of waiting for a plane. It should have taken me on to Lagos this morning but I gather in fact it's still weather-bound in Lisbon – and is now not going till Thursday a.m. anyway. That is a bore as I've really completed my work here now. Of course one can always fill in time quite usefully in various ways – seeing chaps, writing letters, etc. I might even go a trip out into the bush and see how things go there. But of course I'm really anxious to be pushing on as quickly as possible – so as to get this job done as quickly as possible.

---

22 Asantehene Sir Osei Agyeman Prempeh II ruled from 1935 to 1970 and was supportive of adult education. His successor Nana Otumfuo Opoku Ware II (1919–99) was a former extra-mural tutor. Nana is a title meaning chief.

I've tied up most of the ends here quite satisfactorily, I think – or hope. That is to say I seem to have overcome – with the help of Peter Canham (Secretariat), Dowuona[23] (Achimota) and others the desires of some here to postpone indefinitely, and it looks now as though we can go ahead and bring a tutor out here in April, and that there will be courses for him to take. I got this report written with a good deal of sweat on Saturday (half Saturday night – but one can't work all night in these warm climates – in fact I am being extremely good about going to bed – it's less bother to take clothes off when one has so few to take!) and Sunday, and managed to rush it round to the people concerned on Sunday evening. Then we had various tying up meetings yesterday – and this morning. So really, as I said, my job here is done, and I'm simply marking time meeting people, etc.

Now I'm waiting for my car to arrive. It seems to have got stuck. In this curious pink-gin mad-dogs-and-Englishmen Avenida Hotel.

To DMCH
26 February 1947

Accra

Please do tell me what things you would most like me to bring back. There are many things which I could buy in Lagos (or here) which I know are hard to get at home – marmalade, silk stockings, any other kinds of clothes, rice, household goods, etc. Just say the word and I'll do what I can.

Nothing much further to say just now. Have not yet been able to discover whether my aeroplane is still on the way.

---

23 Theophilus Albert Modjaben Dowuona was educated at Achimota and in 1931 was awarded the first Achimota Council scholarship for further education in Britain. He went to the recently established St Peter's Hall at Oxford and after taking his degree in 1934 he returned to Achimota as a teacher. He was Academic Registrar at the University College of the Gold Coast (UCGC) from its foundation in 1948 to 1952 and Registrar from 1952 to 1961 when the university college was becoming a full-fledged university.

To DMCH
2 March [1947]

Ibadan [Nigeria] Sunday
I'll start this letter here, though probably won't finish it. I have to
go out in a few minutes to begin the day's work – visiting people
at the Govt Secondary School and Training College – then attending a meeting of the Ibadan Progressive Union Study Circle[24] –
which sounds a healthy organisation of the kind I feel at home in!
A paper on 'Physiology' is to be read by one of the members – the
Headmaster of a school here (private enterprise, and very successful, I'm told). I've just come back from spending two and a half
hours with some of the people at Govt College (2ndary School
here) and with the Ibadan Progressive Union. Feel a bit sleepy in
consequence, and may drop off for half an hour. Ib. Prog. Un. gave
me beer for one thing. I avoided dropping off then though. It was
fun – first thing of the kind that I have met – a kind of Mutual
Improvement Society – mainly clerks, govt. officials, teachers, etc.
They get one of their members to read a paper – followed by questions. About 20 there – they meet every other Sunday. Combine it
with a big lunch in the middle. I had actually had lunch already –
also I remembered what Wigg said about dysentery – so kept off
the great hunks of white and grey yam, etc. provided (all looking
rather like suet). It seemed a bit unsociable, but they didn't seem
to expect me to join it. This cheerful schoolmaster read a paper –
or rather delivered a very effective address – on Physiology. I
learnt quite a bit (I don't know how correctly!). After that I
explained what I was after, and we had a quite useful discussion.
They are nice chaps – and wear beautiful clothes – turbans, with
various types of dressing gown – also lovely woven slippers. I must
try to buy some of these things.
    A lot of babies and small children running around, as usual.
Some of them looking very ill – swollen tummies and ribs showing
and suchlike. Some of them nice and bright and cheerful. One very
little one kept on calling me 'Aybu'[25] (= 'European', I was told).

---

24 The Ibadan Progressive Union was founded about 1930 and was
   opposed by the Ibadan Patriotic Association, reflecting political rivalry
   between the people of Ibadan and Ijebu. In the 1950s the political platform shifted to the Action Group and the United People's Party.
25 Aybu or Oyibo, a Yoruba word for white person.

We all had our photographs took after the meeting – sitting on the street – like a College Society. Nice if it comes out.

They seem much more African here than in the Gold Coast – I don't quite know what I mean by that – less Europeanised, closer (of course they are) to a completely different past, and fortunately quite glad to be. I like them.

Found a nice chap called Carpenter[26] waiting for me at Lagos – Mass Education Officer. We found, after a certain amount of mutual suspicion, that we had quite a lot in common – he having done Army education in the W. African Forces during the War and being interested in discussion groups. We chatted a bit, and made plans, he introduced me to the British Council – then had lunch together – after which he packed me off to Ibadan – as meetings had been arranged here for me which it seemed a pity to miss. Since coming here I had a large, excessive, dinner with Butler,[27] the British Inspector of Edcn (5 kinds of drink, I'm ashamed to say) – then a useful meeting with various interested African chaps.

To DMCH
6 March 1947

Lagos [Nigeria]
Just a scribble while spending a few minutes waiting for a chap, in the shade. The chap is called Ojo[28] – Chemistry Master at the Govt Secondary School here. I hadn't the heart to break up his Chemistry lesson, so am waiting patiently till he finishes. I want to see him as he is President of the Civil Service Union here, and well spoken of.

---

26 Arthur John Carpenter, born 1907 and educated at Dean Close School and Merton College, Oxford, was appointed to colonial service in 1930, and returning after the Second World War had been in charge of mass education (mostly literacy campaigns). He was author of *A West African Nature Study* and *Reading and Writing for All*.

27 Frederick Karl Butler, born 1904 and educated at Haileybury and Trinity College, Oxford, was appointed to colonial service in Nigeria, and served as a senior education officer. He was director of education in the Western Region from 1954 to 1958.

28 Akintunde Ojo, president of the Civil Service Union, went on to become a professor of chemistry.

To DMCH
[7 March 1947]

Enugu [Nigeria]
I hope it's going to be worth while spending this week in the Eastern Provinces. So far I don't think much of the chaps (British) here – and they show no signs of being interested or prepared to take much trouble. In fact I have not a very high opinion of most of the chaps on the official side whom I have met so far. Conversation tends to turn to a large extent on (a) other officials, (b) cricket, (c) cars, (d) food and drink – availability of, (e) Africans (occasionally) – troublesome habits of. Still it would be nice if they were a bit more alive. No doubt the climate saps people a bit – but some of them were clearly sapped before they started.

Now let me tell you something about the last few days in Lagos. It's been interesting and I think quite useful. One very helpful thing has been that I've been staying with Gillian, the new Principal of the Technical College at Yaba – an excellent chap – our sort. WEA background and all that. His wife I like in some ways even more – plenty of guts and good sense. Also WEA background – you may know her – she was Chairman of the Cambridge Univ. Socialist Club when John Cornford[29] was Secretary – Elsie Wilks[30] her name was. At Girton in your time there I should think. So they've been an excellent couple to stay with, as you can imagine. A change from the Christian background of Achimota. He is finding things pretty difficult I gather – struggles with authorities of various kinds – problems arising out of the creation (at some future date) of the new University College at Ibadan – acute shortage of staff, etc. etc. If you know any good person who wants a job *immediately* – as a lecturer in Classics, Geography, Eng. Lit – for courses up to tutor-standard let them know about Yaba. (I don't know who does the recruiting – Cox[31] at the C.O. I should think.)

---

29 John Cornford was a Cambridge Communist activist who travelled to Spain in August 1936. He returned home later that month on a recruiting mission and travelled back to Spain in October with seven recruits. Cornford was killed in action on 28 December 1936. Thomas had met him for a few hours twice during that year, on the boat when Thomas was coming back from the Middle East and on the boat-train when Cornford was returning from the Aragon Front.
30 Elsie Wilks graduated from Girton College in 1934.
31 Christopher William Machell Cox (1899–1982), was educated at

Gillian (and wife) have been very helpful – letting me bring people to the house – arranging for me to meet students etc. Late at night we argue politics – he's a bit like Wigg in his willingness to argue almost indefinitely about anything, and in his slightly aggressive approach which compels one to disagree with him even when one is 90% in agreement! My nominal guide has been this chap Carpenter, the Mass Ed. Officer – nice but ineffective. Also whenever possible he feels it necessary to come round with me – while I stress my unofficialness and try and encourage him not to. He's quite friendly to talk to and well-disposed but the Lord knows what is going on in his mind. Fish[32] (Lt. in the Pay Corps – pal of Wigg's) has been extremely helpful – fixed meetings, introduced me to people etc. He's excellent – very sane and knows people. Also I've met some very nice young Africans – Tokunboh,[33] a Labour Officer, fresh from LSE – very good looking and intelligent – politically interested. He introduced me to a lawyer friend of his H.O. Davies,[34] with a pretty very light wife. I spent an hour drinking beer with them yesterday. Davies seemed

---

Clifton College and Balliol College. He became a Fellow of New College in 1926 and director of education in the Sudan in 1937. He was educational advisor to the Colonial Office from 1940 to 1967, receiving a knighthood in 1950, and later in the Department of Technical Cooperation and Ministry of Overseas Development.

32 Captain Noel Fish was in the Command Pay Office in Lagos. Thomas in preparing his first African journey corresponded with him as a possible lead to Africans outside official circles.

33 Matthew Ayodele Tokunboh, born 1916, was general secretary of the Railway Station Staff Union in Nigeria from 1942 to 1943 and the first secretary-general of the Nigerian Trade Union Congress from 1943. He was at the London School of Economics and active in promoting links with other trade unionists in West Africa.

34 Hezekiah Olagunju Oladapo Davies (1905–89) was educated in Lagos at Methodist Boys' High School and King's College and was at the London School of Economics from 1934 to 1937, taking a B. Com. pass degree. He was usually known by his initials H.O.D. and founded and managed the Daily Service press from 1937 to 1941. He was a founder and one time Secretary of the Nigerian Youth Movement. In a 1941 split Davies backed the journalist Ernest Sesei Ikoli (1893–1960) against the Zikist candidate for a by-election. Davies returned to Britain to the Middle Temple and to study law from 1944 to 1947. He attended the Pan-African Congress in Manchester in 1945. After Nigeria's independence he served the government on sensitive international tasks.

much the most intelligent chap I've met here so far: asked extremely pertinent questions. The evening before (Wed.) was quite interesting. I went with Tokunboh to drink beer for an hour in a hotel of a simple type – while we were there a large crowd poured down the street from a large public meeting organised to protest against an (alleged) act of colour discrimination on the part of the Manager of the Bristol Hotel (a very complicated story – impossible to find out what really happened – the chap said to have been discriminated against was a Colonial Office official! on a visit).[35] The crowd began throwing stones etc. at the hotel – then the usual happenings. Police appear – try to clear the street – hit about them with batons a bit – crowd moves off – then gathers again – more efforts to clear the streets – with batons. Police reinforcements arrive – jeers from the crowd etc. Not very pleasant, but interesting. I was able to watch it all from our hotel window close by. Then walked down the street – with an African on each side! Most Europeans here don't take this sort of thing seriously – but it's like the kind of thing that has happened elsewhere. I had quite an interesting talk with Azikiwe[36] – who is regarded as the leading nationalist (corresponds to the Mufti[37] – more or less). Very pleasant to meet. He seemed in favour of our scheme – in general anyway. The TUC chaps were much more suspicious – and particularly wanted to know what was Oxford's *motive* in suggesting sending out a tutor. A bit difficult to explain. My effort to say that Oxford was interested in pioneering in adult education, and had that kind of tradition was interpreted as meaning that Oxford liked to do things first and claim the credit for

---

35 This was Ivor Cummings (1913–92) who from 1935 was Warden of Aggrey House, opened in London in 1934 as a hostel for African students, and on the outbreak of the Second World War was appointed to a Colonial Office post as liaison officer to colonial students and workers. Cummings was a British-Sierra Leonean, born in West Hartlepool to a Sierra Leonean father and British mother. He was denied pre-booked accommodation in the hotel in Lagos (allegedly as an African and by the Greek proprietor). See also letter of 29 December 1949.

36 Benjamin Nnamdi Azikiwe (1904–96), popularly known as Zik, founder and president of the National Council of Nigeria and Cameroon (NCNC), nationalist political party; President of Nigeria from 1963 until the military coup of January 1966.

37 Thomas would have meant the Mufti of Jerusalem.

it! – which perhaps in some ways is not so wide of the mark! They are a far more politically conscious lot of chaps here than in the Gold Coast – and of course there's a more developed national movement – more of a feeling of tension, more distrust of Govt. etc. In a way more interesting – but a tougher problem, I think, from the point of view of my particular job. We had a meeting of the Lagos World Affairs group, which is or has been a pretty lively body of intelligent and politically minded young men yesterday. At one critical moment in the discussion a nice young chap called Ogunsheye,[38] assistant Secretary of the N.U.T. here, whom I'd met and talked to before, tried to put in a good word for me, by talking about my Study Outline on 'The Colonial Empire'. As Carpenter (representing Govt.) was there I wasn't too sure that this was a good idea – However!

Just had a friendly word with the nightwatchman. He walks round with a bow and arrow in case of thieves! I suppose it may be effective but I should have thought they might be better armed themselves!

To DMCH
10 March 1947

Enugu
I go on to a meeting at the Reading Room to discuss the practical possibility of a course in Enugu – then go with my audience, I expect, to attend a lecture by a chap called, I think Ejitrai,[39] well thought of by the Administration – then go back home with a very

---

38 Fidelis Ayo Ogunsheye had a youthful interest in Marxism and was Assistant Secretary of the Nigerian National Union of Teachers. Through his union he was awarded a scholarship to the London School of Economics in 1947. He became a leading member of the West African Students' Union (WASU). In the 1950s he shed his Marxist and communist connections and became director of Extra-Mural Studies at the University of Ibadan.

39 Mazi Mbonu Ojike (1912–56) studied journalism and political science in the United States and returned to Nigeria in 1947, soon becoming vice-president of the NCNC and general manager of the newspaper *West African Pilot*. He was charged with sedition in 1950 and fined. He wrote an autobiography and cultural memoir entitled *My Africa* and published in the United States in 1946.

nice very able half-African half-Scotch Doctor called Savage[40] and
some people whom he has promised to pick up. Things here are
interesting. It's a purely administrative-cum-mining town. (I
wanted to see the mines – but haven't unfortunately had the
chance). Very strong political feeling, and general scepticism about
any offers coming from the whites (so-called). However they don't
yet throw stones at one, still less bombs. But they bitterly resent
the colour-bar – which in fact means the combination of European
political and economic control and the separate social life and superior standards of the European community. (Compare the European
club with its elegance and drinks and boys and all the rest and
African club with a few old chairs and an almost useless billiard
table – also living quarters and pretty well everything else.)

To ECH[41]
19 March 1947

Over Liberia ?
That's where I imagine we are – but I haven't a map at the moment,
so I may be wrong. Only it looks much like what one would expect
Liberia to look – large empty spaces covered with bushes (or bush!)
and only very occasionally a reddish kind of road running across the
country – and very few villages or houses to be seen.

Thinking of Liberia made me think of you – mentioning that
you used to be keen on Liberian stamps – or at any rate the 3-cor-
nered ones – weren't you.

Later. Arriving at Bathurst –
I've got hold of the map which has been interesting. Passed by a
place called 'Hamdallahi'[42] – nice to think that Arabic culture
should have spread here.

---

40 Dr Richard Gabriel Akiwande Savage, born 1903 and educated at
   George Watson's College, Edinburgh, and Edinburgh University, was
   appointed as a junior African medical officer in Nigeria in 1927 and
   became a senior specialist in 1943.
41 Letter addressed to Lt. Col. E.C. Hodgkin, Near East Broadcasting
   Station, Jaffa, Palestine.
42 Hamdallahi (in modern Mali) was in the 19th century capital of the
   Fulani Empire of Massina and the birthplace of a revival of Islamic
   culture. A Fulani pastoralist Sekou Ahmadou undertook to Islamise the

Further evidence of Arabic culture here in Bathurst. Found the 'boy' who tidies my room reading Arabic and tried to open a conversation with him in the language – but he clearly only understands the purest Koran – and my Palestinian dialect (even when I tried to insert case endings, etc.) was quite unintelligible to him.

region and to settle the nomadic pastoral Fulani. He founded the holy town of Hamdallahi which lasted only from 1820 to 1864 as the capital of his empire.

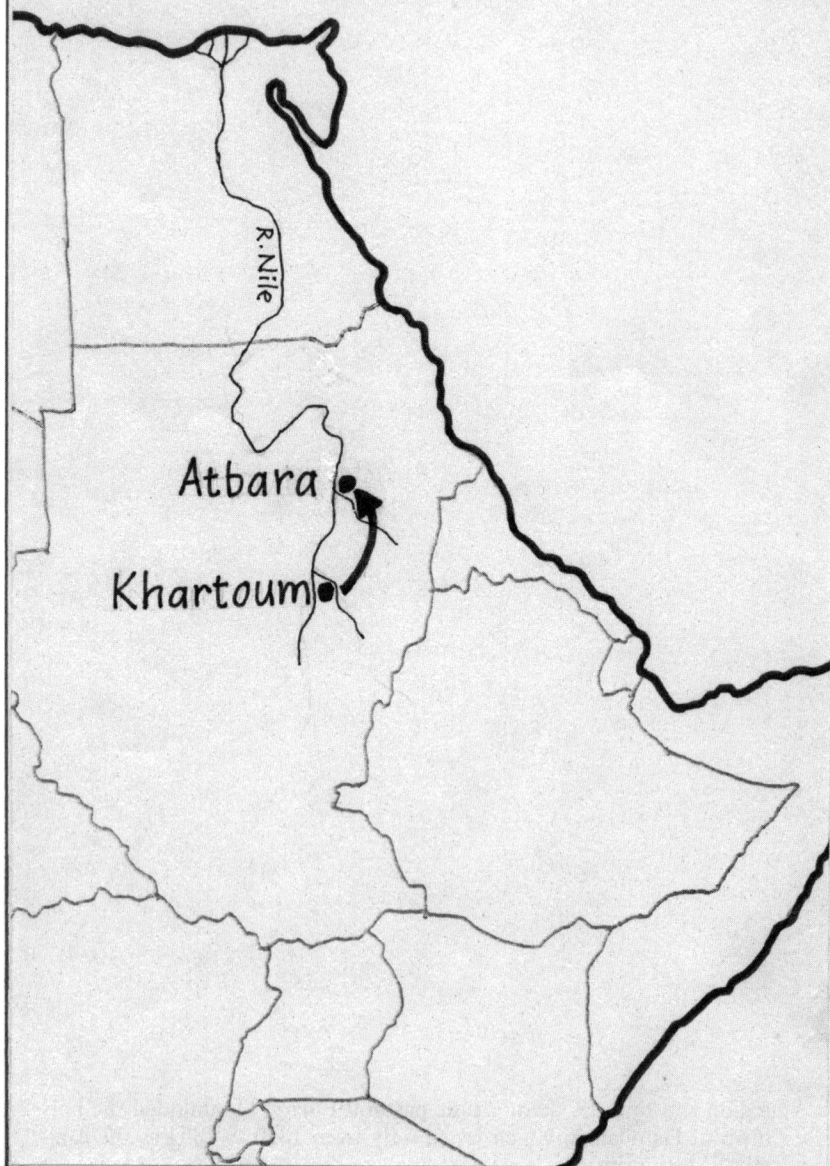

second African journey

R.Nile

Atbara

Khartoum

Second African journey:
to Sudan
March–April 1948

The venture in adult education in West Africa promoted by the Oxford University Delegacy for Extra-Mural Studies made a swift start in the Gold Coast in 1947 since a suitable tutor was already waiting in the wings. The assignment to Nigeria was delayed until April 1948 when an experienced tutor could be spared from extension work in Britain.

The Oxford Delegacy's initiatives in West Africa had been noticed in Sudan. Thomas's second African journey was to Sudan to advise on the possibilities of extending adult education in that country. This was to be on a different footing. The scheme would not be under Oxford auspices but promoted by and financed by Gordon College, the forerunner of a University College then University of Khartoum. Thomas was invited by the Principal of Gordon College to advise whether the College should provide opportunities for extra-mural study.

Thomas reported favourably on the prospects for tutorial classes in Khartoum, Omdurman, Wad Medani and Atbara. He heard concerns expressed from Sudanese about the objectivity of extra-mural work and from expatriate staff at Gordon College about the demands and utility of such work. Expatriate staff argued that extra-mural work would unwisely dissipate the efforts of raising standards in a newly-established university. College staff would not have time for extra-mural teaching in addition to the existing tasks of internal teaching and research.

Thomas argued that the university had to play a part in the whole of the society and that extra-mural teaching was an essential element in university development. However the Academic Board of Gordon College rejected the recommendations and Khartoum University's extra-mural studies did not take off until the early 1960s.

To DMCH
17 March [1948]

Khartoum [Sudan]
Forgive this rude postcard (not quite the worst, I may say);
bought for me by Robin and Elizabeth[43] (on my suggestion). Here
things are going quite well – fairly crowded days. Had lunch
today with Ibrahim Ahmed[44] (Vice Principal of G.C.) and Judge
Shingeiti[45] – the latter said he remembered climbing mountains
with your mother[46] to collect seeds while John stayed down below
collecting potsherds – when he was a young sub-ma'mur. I find
warm recollections of them wherever I go (and a not [?] very good
bust of John in this college). Starting for Bakht-er-Ruda now for
5 days.

To DFH and RHH
23 March 1948

Khartoum
I had meant to write before – days have been full, as you can imagine, and I've not really been able to keep properly track of what I
have been doing – These fairly continuous discussions, parties,
visits, etc., tend if one's not careful to become a rather blurred

---

43 Robin Hodgkin, born 1916, Thomas's first cousin, the son of his
   paternal uncle George Hodgkin (1880–1918) and Mary Wilson
   (1880–1972), who as a widow married Thomas's maternal uncle Arthur
   Lionel Forster Smith (1880–1972). Robin was headmaster of the
   Teachers' Training College at Bakht-er-Ruda on the White Nile and
   had recently married Elizabeth Hodgson, Principal of the Girls'
   Teachers' Training College in Khartoum.
44 Ibrahim Ahmed, Vice Principal of Gordon College (later the
   University of Khartoum) As an inspector of schools he had been a
   friend of Thomas's father-in-law, John Crowfoot (1873–1959), inspector of schools, then Director of Education in Sudan from 1914 to 1926
   and later Director of the British School of Archaeology in Jerusalem.
45 Muhammad Saleh Shingeiti, activist in the Sudan Graduate Congress,
   Judge of the High Court and first Speaker of the Sudan Legislative
   Assembly.
46 Grace Mary Crowfoot (1877–1957), Thomas's mother-in-law, expert in
   weaving and flora, wrote *Flora of the Sudan*.

impression – and I have not really been good this time about taking notes as I've gone along.

I've been staying most of the time with Robin and his nice wife Elizabeth. This house is only 5 minutes walk from the Nile – a lovely river – with lots of birds – ibises, kites, geese, cormorants, etc. I've not yet seen a crocodile – said to be scarce in these parts). We strolled down there yesterday at tea-time. Apart from the time here at Khartoum I've spent the rest at Bakht-er-Ruda – this very interesting Teachers' Training College about 140 miles further up the White Nile – Robin drove me there and back, by the kind of desert road that is almost impossible to find if one doesn't already know it. Just brownish sand going on for miles, with bushes (like Dead Sea Fruit), and occasionally strips of irrigated land (growing cotton, etc.) when one gets near the Nile. Really I think it's what they call semi-desert, since when it rains things do grow (like the J'lem–Jericho hills – only better). To get to Bakht-er-Ruda we crossed the flooded Nile in a barge – rather like Port Meadow[47], with the tops of trees standing up above the water – and again lots of birds.

. . .

Today is Gordon College Sports and Diploma giving – a kind of Speech Day. I gather I am supposed to go – and anyway it may be a way of meeting people I want to meet. One gets up with the sun here (about 6), works till 2.30 – lunches – sleeps a bit, has a cup of tea, works again – dinner usually 8.30 to 9 – bed 11 to 12. Not a bad rhythm.

To DMCH
5 April 1948

Atbara [Sudan]
Writing, or beginning this in some spare time while I am waiting for Khalifa Abbas to come into this (Railway) office. These 4 days here have been quite interesting, though in some ways a bit frustrating. The political situation (strike, etc. followed by the arrest 3

---

47 Port Meadow, in Oxford, then frequently flooded.

days ago of Suleiman Musa,[48] secretary of the Workers' Affairs
Association – the Trade Union which includes all the workers in
the Railways and Railway workshops) has made contacts a bit difficult. S.M. was jugged (on account of a speech in the mosque) just
before I could see him. However in the circumstances I haven't
done too badly. I visited a couple of schools and talked to the masters – took one form (the boys) for their English lesson, and
discussed my plan with them a bit. Had tea with a nice Railway
chap called Khalifa Abbas, who had been a clerk and then had 3
years at Gordon College, with some of his friends (some of them
unfortunately wouldn't or couldn't come on account of the arrest
of S.M. and all that).

I also had an evening at the Sudanese officials club – nice oldish
men several of whom again were friends of John's. (The nice thing
about this relationship with John is that people, lots of them, are
obviously very glad to be reminded of him, and were really fond of
him and your mother – and usually have stories of some kind to
tell about him – one of them for example told how John succeeded
in getting him to Gordon Coll. from the elementary school,
although the H.M. of his school tried to do him down in favour of
an 'Omda's[49] son who had no real claims!) I also spent a couple of
very pleasant and interesting evenings in the Old Boys' Union.
This is a club for workers who have 'graduated' from the
Technical College – intelligent, but most of them only Arabic
speaking – so conversation got a bit difficult at times.

(Switching over to pencil – this pen isn't very good). The first
evening we mainly discussed the possibility of classes in the club –
I think in fact classes of a WEA type would go well there, if taken
in Arabic, since the chaps I met were in many ways very like their

---

48 Artisans of the mechanical department of the Sudan railways trained at
   Atbara Technical School formed the Workers' Affairs Association in
   1946 which was the precursor of the Sudanese trade union movement.
   The dispute in 1948 was over pay; a three-day token strike in January
   had brought traffic to a standstill. The arrest of Suleiman Musa on 2
   April 1948 was linked to a strike called for 18 April. He was sentenced
   to a fine and to 15 days' imprisonment. The strike was called off following the recommendation for higher wages made by the Report of
   the Committee of Inquiry. Soon afterwards, in May 1948, following a
   riot, Suleiman Musa was dismissed.
49 The Omda is the head of a village or town.

opposite numbers in Whitehaven or Stoke-on-Trent – although all on strike and having a tough time, very friendly and quick to see jokes. They fed me on lemonade and tea. The next morning I went along partly to see their literacy class, partly to hear from them about the causes of the strike – they talked quite freely about this, and I learned a lot. We drifted by degrees, in a thoroughly WEA way, to discussion of Trade Union questions in England, the Marshall Plan (and might it be applied to the Sudan?), Communism (of which they did *not* approve) and Islam (of which of course they do), etc. They very nicely saw me back to the Rest House both evenings. This led on to supper at about 9 after which I read Russell lazily (have now got ¾ way through Hume) and went to bed – sleeping out of doors and waking at 5.45 or 6. Nice to watch the sunrise and listen to the cooing of innumerable doves – in immemorial banyan trees, of which there are a lot in this (British) quarter of the town. Now I am back in Khartoum – the journey (190 miles) taking just over 1 hour! I'm staying at Wilcher's[50] – he kindly met me at the airport. Since then I've been talking with him and Sir James Irvine[51] – who really is a very nice old chap.

My birthday actually wasn't too bad! – it so happened that a couple of American geographers were passing through, staying in the resthouse, with a young Egyptian geographer – the older American was a Professor from Ann Arbor University, Michigan – both thoroughly liberal types – v. little use for Truman and much concerned about civil liberties – they had a bottle of whisky which we drank together – while discussing Sudanese and world affairs. Nice they were. I also met on my way back from Wad Medani (this is going back some way in history) a girl – now wife and mother – who used to be called Mary Cross, worked in the

---

50 Lewis Charles Wilcher (1908–83), from Australia was a Rhodes Scholar at Balliol College from 1930 to 1932 and contemporary with Thomas. He was Principal of Gordon Memorial College and subsequently of the University College of Khartoum in the period from 1947 to 1956 when he became Warden of Queen Elizabeth House, Oxford, from 1956 to 1968.

51 Sir James Colquhoun Irvine (1877–1952), Vice-Chancellor and Principal of the University of St Andrews, was chairman of the Inter-University Council for Higher Education in the Colonies from its establishment in 1946 until 1951.

Biochemistry Dept. at Cambridge when you were there, and knew you, as well as Joseph,[52] etc. of course – now married to a chemist at the Gezirah research station. Nice person. Our car kept boiling – so we had to stop about 9 times on the journey and didn't get in till 10 p.m. – she had an 8 months child with her who behaved like an angel.

. . .

52 Joseph Needham (1900–95), Sinologist, Professor of Biochemistry at Cambridge, author of *Science and Civilization in China*, and Dorothy Crowfoot Hodgkin's colleague and friend.

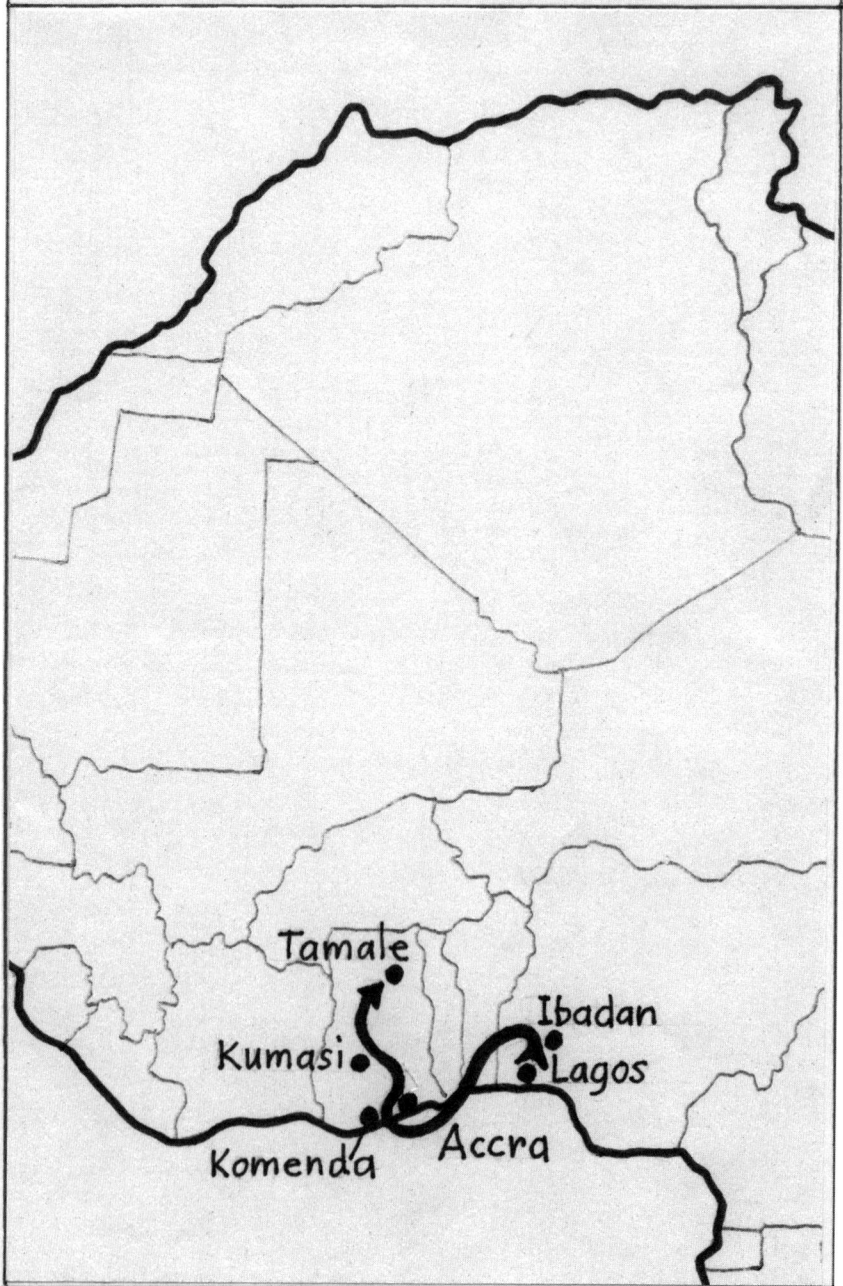

third African journey

Tamale

Ibadan
Kumasi
Lagos

Komenda
Accra

Third African journey:
to Nigeria and Gold Coast
December 1949–January 1950

The African adult education programme of the Oxford University Delegacy for Extra-Mural Studies was well established by 1949 with skilled and dedicated tutors in place in Gold Coast and Nigeria. Responsibility for the extra-mural work in the Gold Coast and in Nigeria was transferred to the University College in each country and to full-time directors of extra-mural studies.

Thomas felt it was time for the Delegacy to extend into other West African territories of British influence, such as Sierra Leone, and to the colonies and protectorates of East and Central Africa, including Northern Rhodesia and Nyasaland. He canvassed these ideas through fellow educationists and through George Wigg who put them to the Secretary of State for the Colonies, Arthur Creech Jones.

Thomas's ideas for expansion were coldly received in the Colonial Office since officials and advisers believed the Delegacy was including too many Communists among its tutors. Furthermore experiments that might be tolerated in the trading colonies of West Africa were unacceptable to the colonial governors of the settlement colonies on the other side of Africa. Thomas's third African journey was at the invitation of David Kimble to help in Gold Coast with residential courses for part-time tutors and for others willing to work in adult education. He took the opportunity to see how extra-mural work was taking shape in Nigeria.

Wigg put Thomas in touch with the editor of *West Africa* magazine, David Williams, for whom Thomas agreed to write a series of articles on the national movement in the Gold Coast. The scholarly and topical articles were published as 'Background to Gold Coast nationalism' in the period from 9 July to 2 September 1950 and reflected Thomas's much deeper involvement in Africa. Later in 1950 he and Basil Davidson, the General Secretary of the Union of Democratic Control (UDC – founded in 1914 by E.D. Morel and other democrats), organised a pioneering conference at Haywards Heath on 22 and 23 October for Africans and Europeans to discuss the 'crisis in Africa'.

To DMCH
29 December 1949

Lagos [Nigeria]
Sitting drinking beer in the cool fairy-light-illuminated creeper-grown garden of the Bristol Hotel, which when I was last here I saw having stones thrown at it by an angry mob because it had refused to take in a high-up black official from the Colonial Office – since then management has changed, I gather, and it behaves reputably. Anyway Mr Esua,[53] the Secretary of the NUT (Nigerian Teachers Union), an extremely nice man, booked me a room here. It's a low kind of dive – soft music and a drunk man making between them rather a row. The drunk is now come to sit opposite me – I fear he may want a heart-to-heart conversation. Obviously he does. I am not taking part. My present plan is to leave for Ibadan at 8 a.m. by the only train of the day. It takes about 7 hours to go about 100 miles – everyone whom I've told so far that I'm going this way has expressed surprise, ending up by saying – 'It will be an experience'. Things have gone quite well so far. I haven't tried to go to Enugu – I doubt if I could fit it in anyway – with Ibadan. I was met at the airport by Esua, who took me back to his home and gave me beer while we talked. He then drove me over here – I'm afraid this letter is getting somewhat interfered with by the conversation of the drunk who makes more or less incoherent remarks at irregular intervals. I must say it was nice to find oneself here again – with the sunshine and the vultures (or kites probably) and the palm trees and the women in bright clothes with pots of water on their heads and babies on their backs – and the babies themselves – or little ones of Toby's age –

---

53 Eyo Eyo Esua (1901–73) founder member of the Nigerian Union of Teachers and the first full-time general secretary from 1943 until his retirement in 1964. He became chairman of the Federal Electoral Commission in 1964.

with their very bright eyes and teeth dancing about in the road – and young men with shiny skins on bicycles – and the lagoon with all the boats moored in it that one crosses on the way to Lagos. I've rung up Foot[54] (of Nablus) and Crofts[55] (whom we once met in a train – ex-Birmingham tutor), and have fixed to see them before I go off. I'll be going off to bed soon since last night was rather interrupted – called at 3 a.m. to board the (now mended) aircraft – saw the sun rising over the Sahara – a beautiful mixture of blue and red light in the sky and pale golden on the land – then I slept for quite a while. We reached Kano at about 12 – and that was the first real taste of proper sunshine.

To DMCH
2 January [1950]

Lagos
I am having a restful morning after a fairly energetic 3 days – sitting in my bedroom in this fairly horrible hotel looking out on the ships and the harbour and the slums and the large blocks of Western buildings – shops and banks and missions. In rather less than an hour I am going over to Yaba (a suburb) to call on Mr Esua again – but that should give me time to tell you most of my story.

I left Lagos earlyish on Friday and took the train to Ibadan. It was meant to leave at 8, and left in fact a bit after 8.30. I bought a 1st-class ticket – mistakenly – and was later told that there only 3rd-class carriages on the train, and had to bribe the booking office clerk to let me change to a 3rd-class ticket – a little weak perhaps.

---

54 Hugh Macintosh Foot (1907–90) was educated at Leighton Park School and St John's College, Cambridge. He was appointed as an administrative officer in Palestine in 1929. He and Thomas had been colleagues in the Palestine administration when Foot was serving in Nablus. Foot became Chief Secretary in Nigeria in 1947, and was Acting Governor from 1949 to 1950. Later he was Governor in Jamaica and Cyprus and as Lord Caradon was the UK permanent representative at the UN.
55 Probably Reginald Alfred Crofts, born 1912 and educated at Dover County School and London University. He was in the commerce and industries department of the Nigerian colonial service from 1946 to 1954, and in 1948 was appointed deputy director of the marketing and exports department.

I enjoyed the journey: the train went incredibly slowly – 7 hours to cover about 120 miles – yet we didn't stop at any station. It was pleasant to see so much of the country – mainly palm–forest, with patches of cassava and yam and banana grown in spaces that were partly cleared. The seats were hard and one's behind got sore – also one got hungry – however I relieved hunger by eating Nigerian biscuits (bought at a station) and oranges and ground-nuts – bought for me by a friendly student who was sitting opposite. We had a long conversation – mainly about politics – in which a chap in khaki with a moustache also joined – both were Ibos, and therefore pro-Zik, but the student was a Catholic and held strong views about Communism which the khaki-chap vigorously contested. (The student was at the Univ. Coll. – doing a teacher training course.) There was a nice incident at one station when a man climbed into the carriage with all his household goods – chairs, tables, screens, pots and pans, a year's rations of yams, and crate of hens, etc. The guard indignantly told him to put his stuff in the van, but he paid no attention and went on piling it up at the entrance to the carriage making it impossible to get in or out. It was a nice sociable journey – mothers with their sleepy children, gayly dressed Yoruba men, livestock – beggars and men selling things dropping in at stations (including a man selling a kind of soap which would cure all diseases including cancer and T.B. – about which my friends were rightly sceptical.) Eventually we got to Ibadan and I found Mellanby's[56] car and driver – went back with him – had a meal – talked to M, – a somewhat inscrutable man of a somewhat cynical type, who dislikes serious conversation and is obviously not much interested in Extra-mural studies – however Gardiner[57] seems to

---

56 Sir Kenneth Mellanby, born 1908, first Principal of the University College of Ibadan, from 1947 to 1953, and then head of Wye College, University of London.

57 Robert Kweku Atta Gardiner; born 1914, educated at Adisadel College, Cape Coast, Fourah Bay College, Freetown, Selwyn College, Cambridge and New College, Oxford and in 1942 married to Linda Charlotte Edwards. He moved from being Vice Principal of Fourah Bay College, Sierra Leone, via the UN Trusteeship Council, to be director of Extra Mural Studies in Ibadan from 1949 to 1953. He was head of the Ghana civil service from 1957 to 1959. He left Ghana to have a distinguished career in the UN, including serving as Executive Secretary of the Economic Commission for Africa in Addis Ababa from 1963 to 1975.

get on well enough with him. I had dinner with Gardiner – he has a nice gay Jamaican wife (Gold Coast himself) with an American intonation: also 3 nice children. Gardiner had 3 friends there – one the Secretary of the local Ibadan extra-mural Cttee – one a tutor – and one a charming Dahomeyan – exiled by the French for 7 years for 'subversive' journalism (in spite of having fought with De Gaulle from 1940 to the end of the war!)

Mainly political chat – quite interesting and useful. Gardiner taking a sensible line, I thought. Then on Saturday I went over with Gardiner to Abeokuta (half way between here and there – we had lunch with the Ransome-Kutis[58] – he the Principal of the CMS Grammar School – his wife very young and charming (in spite of having grown-up children) and extremely active in the women's movement in the province, having built up a strong organisation that was largely instrumental in getting their corrupt old Alake (= King!) sacked after 28 years misrule.

Again a long lunch – African food – which I'm not awfully good at – it's so very hot – including ground-nut stew. Back to Ibadan in the evening – out to supper with Mellanby (with whom I was staying) with English members of his staff, Harris[59] by name – he's

---

58 Rev. Israel Oludotun Ransome-Kuti (1891–1955); Principal of Abeokuta Grammar School from 1932 to 1954 and founder and first president of the NUT from 1931 to 1954. His wife Olufunmilayo Ransome-Kuti (1900–78) founded many women's organisations including the Egba Women's Union and campaigned for women's rights including the right to vote. In 1968 she was awarded the Lenin Peace Prize. She sustained severe injuries when thrown off a second-floor balcony in 1977 by soldiers storming her son Fela's house – he was a world famous musician and a strong critic of military rule. The other children include Professor Olikoye Ransome-Kuti, a paediatrician, and Beko Ransome-Kuti, a doctor and human rights activist. Both Fela and Beko were imprisoned under Sani Abacha's rule.

59 John Harris, born 1903 in New Zealand, was educated at Christ's College and Canterbury University in New Zealand, and at University College, Oxford, and University College, London. He and Marguerite Darby married in 1943. He was at Ibadan from 1949 to 1968, and became Deputy and then Vice Chancellor of the University of Ibadan. He was Vice Chancellor of the University of Benin from 1972 to 1974. Marguerite Harris was the first manager of the Ibadan University bookshop opened in 1949. 'Against the advice of most experienced European residents of Nigeria, Mrs Harris insisted that customers should have free access to the books on the shelves. Contrary to her advisers' misgivings thefts were completely negligible': Kenneth Mellanby, *The Birth of Nigeria's University*, 1958, page 213.

librarian and she runs a book-shop, a nice vigorous progressive
N.Z. woman – also a pleasant Dane (you wouldn't know it),
Professor of English, called Christopherson[60] – and a couple of
Zoologists called Webb[61] – she in particular seemed a soft and silly
creature – dislikes Africa – thinks her students bad Biologists (as no
doubt many of them are), etc. We argued hard once Mellanby had
gone and the majority view was strongly on the side of the
Africans, as people who were just as capable as anyone else of
developing a good civilisation. Back after 1. Next day I went to the
College Church! – because R. Gardiner and family were all going –
then off to Ijebu-Ode where we had lunch, at about 3, after paying
a ceremonial call on the local chief (Alajala[62] or something he's
called). He gave us beer and presented with his signed photograph.
I was a little muddled about all this, since I had an idea that we
were visiting Gardiner's local Branch Secretary, not a minor potentate.

Being New Year's day everything and everyone was very gay –
walking, or dancing, through the streets of Ijebu in beautiful new
clothes – these lovely Yoruba robes – singing and drumming –
groups of men and groups of women, sometimes together but usually separate. We again had lunch with the Principal of the
College – another Gold Coaster – also with a charming wife and
family. Then at 4.30 Gardiner took me this long drive back here –
very generously – and I managed to keep a dinner engagement I'd
made with Hugh Foot – we had a very nice evening – talking more
about children and suchlike than about politics – he was flying to
England today and they both had upset insides, so I didn't stay
fearfully long (still it must have been getting on for midnight). I
liked meeting him again – he approved of the work we're doing
here.

---

60 Paul Christopherson published *The articles: a study of their use in
   English*, 1939.
61 J.E. Webb published on 'The ecology of Lagos Lagoon' and other
   papers in *Philosophical Transactions of the Royal Society of London*,
   1958.
62 The Awujale was not a minor potentate but chief of a territory of 2,456
   square miles and 647 villages. Daniel Adesanya Gbelegbuwa II who
   reigned from 1933 to 1959 was thought by his people too close to the
   British.

To DMCH
6 January [1950]

Komenda[63] *[Gold Coast]*
I'm just waiting to go off to Accra with David[64] and Helen.[65] In some ways I am sorry not to be staying in this beautiful place for the day. It really is a marvellous place – with the sea just 50 yards away and the noise of the waves breaking all the time – a bit like Bamburgh[66] or Athlit[67] in some ways: also a bit of open country just beside with all sorts of bright flowers (unidentified by me) growing.

Imagine this pool – called Pupa[68] (I don't know why) at the end of a pretty derelict village – with a grove of palm trees just beyond, and beyond that a lagoon: vultures sitting in the palm trees, and every now and again flapping out and flying across the pool to another tree. David + 40 students from the College[69] spent 4 or 5 days working with the village on draining the pool, cleaning it out,

---

63 Thomas had been invited to the Gold Coast for a New Year School for adult education students and a training course for part-time tutors in adult education at Komenda College from 7 January 21 January 1950.

64 David Kimble, born 1921, was a staff tutor in Berkshire, Buckinghamshire and Oxfordshire for the Oxford University Delegacy for Extra-Mural Studies from 1945 to 1948 when he was sent out as the first resident tutor in the Gold Coast. In 1949 he became director of Extra-Mural Studies, a post he held until 1962.

65 Helen Rankin (later Kimble), born 1925, was in Lincoln from 1945 as the first of Thomas's postgraduate tutor trainees in the OU Delegacy for Extra-Mural Studies. She was an extra-mural part-time tutor in the Gold Coast from 1950 to 1960, and lecturer in Economics Department of the University from 1960 to 1962 when the Kimbles left Ghana. They launched the Penguin Africa series of books and the *Journal of Modern African Studies*.

66 Bamburgh by the sea in Northumberland, where the Hodgkin family used to spend their summer holidays.

67 Atlit in Palestine where Thomas had been several times in the 1930s to see the Crusader castle.

68 The school was preceded with a village project, arranged after consultation with the Chief, but not his subjects, to improve the brackish water supply, polluted by goats and people and known as Pupu (not Pupa). The aim was to ensure clean drinking water.

69 Volunteers included adult students – mainly teachers, who could afford to take most of the Christmas holiday off -with students on vacation from UCGC and the local teacher training college.

building a wall round it, putting a filter of stones round the edge, etc. Quite a big job. By the time I got there it was nearly finished, and people were slacking off a bit – there wasn't the same lead from the students either. But yesterday evening it was a marvellous sight – several hundred people – women in gay clothes with babies (many of them) on their backs, carrying pans of various kinds on their heads full of water from the pool – mixed with men (mostly naked from the waist up) – breaking from time to time into song and drumming – getting more and more energetic as it became evening and the pool became nearly empty and they felt they were near the end of the job.

Meanwhile the chief – Nana – sat quietly by under the shade of a palm tree – a man of low intelligence and little initiative. The real work of organising and stimulating the people was done by a charming elderly man called Mr Sam,[70] educated, an MBE, who had once been Regent and had got 6 schools going in his State where there had been none before. He took things very seriously – got worried when people didn't work as hard as they should – and constantly had passionate arguments with David which began with denunciations and ended with withdrawal on both sides and reconciliation. There was also a Secretary whose main job seemed to be to produce drinks when it was all over. (This pen of Margery's[71] is becoming a bit tricky to manage – I don't know whether it's me or it). Also a village policeman who looked like a character in a French musical comedy, waved his arms wildly and shouted and ran round hitting the women (not very violently) with a palm branch. The greatest excitement occurred when the men began to fell palm trees which they thought were overshadowing the pool (I've just gone and bought another pen which I hope will work a bit better). They felled it *very* skilfully and with great excitement. When each tree finally collapsed there was a terrific rush of

70 Edu William Afyi Bampon Sam, born 1900 and educated at Seaford College and University Tutorial College, London, was inspector of plants and produce in the Gold Coast from 1928 and assistant registrar of co-operative societies from 1945. He was decorated with the OBE.
71 Margery Fry (1874–1958) penal reformer. Thomas was her third cousin once removed. At her house in Holland Park in 1937 Thomas met Dorothy Crowfoot who had been an undergraduate at Somerville where Margery Fry was Principal from 1924 to 1931.

everyone around to pick up the coconuts – we sat in the shade and drank coconuts (à la Swiss Family Robinson). It was quite exhausting work in the hot sun, carrying large pans of water or earth, or shifting large stones, or digging out the mud.[72] Good practice for gardening when I come back.[73]

There was supposed to be a general strike starting today – but it seems rather doubtful whether it's starting. An interesting state of affairs; I'll try to write more about it next time.

To DMCH
10 January 1950

Komenda
I'm very sad to think I haven't got a letter off for 3 days – it's this frantic rush which I'm living in now that this course has started. I won't let it go on this way – but will try to leave more to David, Lalage[74] and Dennis Austin[75] (the other full-time tutor who works in Ashanti) in future. I'm not even being able to enjoy this beautiful country, and bathe – which I keep meaning to do. Of course it's

---

72 The volunteers broke stones, built a dam at one end with sand to filter the sea water and a containing wall around it to keep out the goats. and children. Some weeks later the Kimbles revisited the pool and found fences broken down, children and goats paddling, and the water thoroughly polluted. This had been a top-down project, discussed mainly with chiefs and elders and labour was provided under the chief's orders rather than through community involvement [Helen Kimble].

73 Thomas was not an enthusiastic gardener or accustomed to physical labour.

74 Lalage Bown, born 1927, was a postgraduate tutor trainee in the Oxford University Delegacy for Extra-Mural Studies and one of the first extra-mural tutors to come to the Gold Coast, 1949–55; resident tutor, in Uganda from 1955 to 1959; assistant director then deputy director in Extra-Mural Studies in Ibadan from 1960 to 1966; director of Extra-Mural Studies and Professor in Zambia, from 1966 to 1970; then Professor in various universities in Africa and finally the first woman Professor of Adult Education in Britain, at Glasgow University, until she retired.

75 Dennis Austin, born 1922, was a resident extra-mural tutor in the Gold Coast and taught in the UCGC (and University of Ghana) from 1949 to 1959. He was later Professor of Politics at the University of Manchester.

partly that – as well as the actual programme (2 courses at the same time) being fairly heavy, chaps naturally want to see one and talk about this and that (and I to see them too) – and I've got this study-group started on the G.C. national movement – which should turn out to be quite interesting and worth-while. Before I go back to telling the story of the last few days I'll just chat about things at the top of mind which I'd like to tell you of. First there's the strike: we here of course are entirely isolated, so I've seen nothing of it – but occasionally information seeps in from the outside world – thro' straggling students who turn up late, etc. I gather that it's got going on quite a substantial scale – railways stopped, PWD,[76] shops shut, etc. I want to try to get in to Sekondi to see what's happening if we can manage it, fairly soon. Still I really so far know about as little as you probably about the actual situation.

To DMCH
12 January 1950

Komenda
Well, we went over to Sekondi yesterday. That's the main indus-trial centre, and centre of the strike movement.[77] Everything there seemed dead – shops all closed – nothing moving. Men walking about the streets with bows and arrows – which they don't seem to have actually used yet but keep in reserve in case things happen. I've been told they are poisoned arrows, and they look pretty nasty instruments – so it isn't as primitive as it sounds. Everyone quite friendly to us. We must have looked an odd party – about 9 Africans and 5 Europeans, piled into a College lorry – and dressed somewhat oddly – Lalage in an enormous straw hat. As soon as we came into Sekondi we were accosted by a huge Senegalese, who talked French, of a kind not very easy to understand. He carried a large wooden club, and appeared to be acting as a kind of picket. He seemed to think that the British ran strikes in a very tame way as compared with the French who, he said, shot, and people 'fall

---

76 Public Works Department.
77 Positive Action – a campaign of strikes, boycotts and non-cooperation unless the British declared immediate self-determination – had been declared from midnight 8 January.

asleep without getting up again'. We then went and called at the Post Office where David engaged the postmaster in conversation – the latter was obviously worried, his branch of the Union having decided not to strike and having just been instructed to strike by the Central Office. After him we called on a wealthy lawyer called Awooner Williams[78] – a friend of Kwa Hagan's[79], vice-President of the U.G.C.C. (the 'moderates' – United Gold Coast Convention). He was friendly but most reactionary: bitterly opposed to the strike and complaining that the Government ought to use stronger measures – arrest Nkrumah and other leaders, and use tear gas agst the strikers if need be. He was obviously a Girondin of the most property and class-conscious kind: spoke in contemptuous language of the 'mob' and the 'rabble', etc. Most interesting. When talking of Kofi Konuah[80] who is associated with Nkrumah's[81] CPP (Convention People's Party – the Radical organisation which is behind the strike) he said how shocked he was that 'a Durham man' should associate with such people. He talked to us very much

---

78 R.A. (Francis) Awooner Williams, founder member and treasurer of the United Gold Coast Convention (UGCC) and identified with the conservative wing of the party.

79 A democratic People's Educational Association (PEA) was founded at Aburi in February 1949 to support adult education and practical community action; Kwa O. Hagan became National Secretary. Hagan was in the first group of four adult education organisers recruited in the Gold Coast in 1949; in his case for the Cape Coast region. He was later senior resident tutor at the Institute of Adult Education in the University of Ghana and wrote a thesis at Oxford on the growth of adult literacy and adult education in the Gold Coast from 1905 to 1957.

80 Kofi Konuah, reportedly inspired by Aggrey's example, became a teacher and in 1931 founded the Accra Academy, a private secondary school for boys, with the aim of providing good tuition at a reasonable cost for children from less fortunate homes. He turned later to radical politics. The school has continued.

81 Kwame Nkrumah, founded the CPP in 1949 and led the struggle for the Gold Coast's Independence. He was sentenced in January 1950 to three years' imprisonment for leading an illegal strike but was released in 1951 (see below). In 1952 he became Prime Minister, President in 1960, and was deposed, in a coup d'état during his absence in China in February 1966. He was allowed haven in Guinea, and died on 27 April 1972 in Rumania where he had travelled for medical treatment. After lengthy negotiations it was agreed that the body should go to Ghana for burial honours complete on 9 July 1972.

as one University man to others! – expressed in the course of conversation very little liking for the Labour Govt which he also
thought let the rabble have things too much their own way. After
chatting to him we drove on to Takoradi – the main industrial
town, about 6 miles away – looked at the situation there, and on the
way back called on the offices of the CPP, where a nice fat cheerful leader of the Railway Workers Union came out and chatted for
a little about strike prospects, while a friendly and interested
crowd – mainly of children – gathered round. Then we came back
at breakneck speed – a most dangerous and frightening drive – I
haven't been so frightened since our trip to the Farnes[82] – we sat
about on the floor of the lorry holding on to one another and to the
sides – being thrown up high into the air whenever we got to a
bump – which was pretty frequent. My behind was pounded into
a sore and jelly like state by the end. It was a mad sort of ride, leaving one feeling utterly limp. In fact the whole journey was pretty
mad – since David gave us no idea what he was proposing to do,
and we simply wandered, in a casual way from point to point, various members of the party getting lost or left behind from time to
time.

About things in general. It is a very nice, though pretty strenuous life. Food is odd – it's the African kind; palm-nut stew,
ground-nut stew (I can't tell the difference – they both taste to me
of red-pepper and little else), yam (which I quite like) plantain (a
large kind of banana, cooked, which I don't like), kenki (a kind of
cold porridge, used as a vegetable),[83] + a fair amount of bread,
butter (at breakfast) and jam – fruit salad (at lunch – with paw
paws in it and pineapples – both excellent). All this is supple-
mented by occasional bits of European food of varying quality
prepared by David's cook, Joe. The total effect is that one is far
from being starved, yet is always slightly hungry – a curious kind
of state, which is probably quite good for one (physically I mean).
At any rate I feel very healthy and vigorous. The course itself is
going quite well. I think the stuff they are getting is quite good –
one is never quite sure how much is getting across, but there is
plenty of discussion (sometimes about 20 people talking at once!).
David runs things very well. I think – an incredibly energetic and

---

82 Farne Islands, off the coast of Northumberland.
83 Made of pounded, fermented cornflour.

vigorous chap. The best choice I ever made, I suspect! He's developed a lot – far more power and decision and drive than I ever realised (sometimes a bit too much, possibly, but people here obviously like and respect him a lot, and he's done a remarkable job in an incredibly short time). He's got an excellent team working with him, and they know what there are after: in fact, it's already a movement which can I hope play quite a big part in shaping the future of the G.C. – and it's popular unofficial character is as clear as daylight. It's nice too finding the best elements in the Oxford tradition transplanted here and flourishing in this new soil.

To DMCH
15 January [1950]

Sunday Komenda
The strike has meant no posts for the last 3 days or so – but I gather the Postal workers are not going on with the strike – so maybe letters will begin coming through again tomorrow. It does make one feel rather cut off – but I feel sure all is well with you – at least I have the mixture of hope and faith that prevents one from being worried. And in spite of distance one can feel quite close – somehow being beside the sea makes one feel nearer – it is so like all the other seas we've lived beside. One thing I've resolved on is that next time I come to Africa we must really come together. You would love it – I wish in a way I'd made more effort to bring you this time. I'd have loved to have you here for the singing of African songs in the evenings – and the general nice friendly atmosphere – the jokes and the arguments and all of it.

We're half way through the course now – and I think it has gone quite well so far – we're all fairly exhausted but I think we can collect a second wind for the second week. This Sunday I (wisely!) left free on the programme. It's been a typical kind of Sunday. Late breakfast (at 8 a.m.!) – staying on talking after breakfast with a nice vigorous man from Togoland called Dumoga[84] and Dowuona – joined by David, Helen and Lalage later. Now it must be nearly 11.

---

84 Probably John Winfred Kodzo Dumoga, who was deputy editor of the *Ashanti Pioneer* from 1950 to 1958 and later editor of the Accra *Daily Graphic*.

It's surprisingly cold. I'm wearing a waistcoat – it's like a definitely cool summer's day in England. That's apparently due to the Harmattan – a cold dry wind from the Sahara that blows at this time of year. This afternoon we're planning to go into Sekondi again and meet some people. The strike is still going on – but it sounds as though it was losing momentum a bit. It's a rather confused kind of situation: no one is altogether clear what the strike is about. There's an industrial issue (the dismissal of about 60 meteorological workers employed by the Govt. who came out on strike) mixed with a political issue – the question of self govt. – or 'Dominion status' as it's called – *now*. So far there haven't been any major demonstrations or clashes – apparently – though about 150 people have been arrested and some have been beaten up for breaking curfew. There are Emergency Regulations in force – which means more summary powers for the Govt. – and one of Nkrumah's papers has been closed down. It'll be interesting to see how things develop – it certainly isn't as yet an effective general strike – partly I should guess because people aren't altogether clear about the issues. I am trying through this study-group here to get as clear as I can about the situation and its background – but it is complicated. Nkrumah has clearly a good deal of backing in the towns – among unemployed and casual workers and probably manual workers and small salary workers generally – also among the poorer cocoa farmers and fishermen. I went along to the village – Komenda – on Friday and had a talk with fishermen while they were making nets – or rather Windful[85], who can talk Fanti, ran the discussion, and I chipped in now and then. They were clearly pro-Nkrumah – felt he was the champion of the poor and oppressed. It was nice meeting these fishermen – those of them who talked were clearly vigorous people, alive and full of jokes and with a strong sense of belonging together and being used to a hard life – like fishermen everywhere, I suppose. David's idea (or one of his many ideas) is that the P.E.A. (= People's Educational Association) in the G.C. ought to run discussion-groups for illiterate farmers, fishermen, workers, women, etc., on their own local problems – in the vernacular. I think this is sound – tho' it will be a pretty terrific job.

85 Herbert Winful, born 1916, engineer, part-time adult education tutor and a housing director.

To DMCH
18 January [1950]

Komenda
I am writing this while Mr Asyem[86] – a nice intelligent Agricultural
officer – gives a practice talk about Middlemen in Agriculture.
Quite a good one. Unfortunately I'm feeling rather sleepy and
finding it difficult to taken an intelligent part in things.

Very little contact with the outside world since Sunday – bits of
news come in though through visiting lecturers, etc. I gather 2
African policemen have been killed in a row in Accra. That is likely
to embitter things a good deal more I'm afraid. And the Govt.
seems to have started arresting 'leaders' (including the Chairman of
the Accra Branch of the Postal Workers' Union, who should have
come on this course.) We had an interesting time in Sekondi on
Sunday. Met the Propaganda Secretary of the CPP in the street –
a nice and able man called Welbeck whom I'd met in Sekondi 3
years ago when I was here. Then went on to call on the Chairman
of the CPP, dressed in a skin robe: later the editor of the local CPP
paper (the only one not yet suppressed) came in – and we had a bit
of talk – in fact we talked quite hard for about one and a half
hours – at the end a somewhat snake-like and obviously left-wing
young chap came in, who I gathered had just come back from
England.[87] They all tended (unlike Welbeck) to regard us with a
certain amount of suspicion, so we didn't learn as much from
them as we might have. However it was interesting and useful.
They were hopeful about the strike going on. They seemed to think
Sekondi/Takoradi was quite solid. The Govt has ordered all
Govt servants to return to work this week or be dismissed – Govt

86 A.K. Asem came from Tsito and trained in tropical agriculture in
   Trinidad. He and his father with H.K. Addae and S.Y. Adom (also at
   the Komenda school) were supportive of the Awudome Residential
   Adult College at Tsito. A.K. Asem later became Director of
   Agriculture.
87 J. Kwesi Lamptey from Sekondi. While in Britain he was a member of
   WASU and served as president of the Gold Coast Students' Union. He
   was elected chairman in 1949 of the London branch of the Congress of
   Peoples Against Imperialism. On his return to the Gold Coast became
   acting national vice-chairman of the CPP; see also letters of March 1951
   and notes to letter of 30 March 1951 below.

servants including many of the strikers – particularly Railway workers, Post Office and Public Works. They didn't think it would have
a great deal of effect.

After leaving them we met a friend of David's in the street, local
Chairman of the Postal Workers' Union – and we stayed and chatted with him in the street. This caused a bit of a fuss in the street
since people seemed to think that we were trying to put pressure on
him to go back to work. One man shouted at us but we carried on.
A man called Dadsi[88] came by whom Kwa Hagan introduced to
me, rather offensively, as 'a *nominated* member of the Leg. Co.'[89]
who was also drawn into the discussion. We then went on and
called on Quarshie,[90] the Labour officer, and found Roberts,[91] the
British Education officer, sitting there. They seemed to be discussing our course and seeing how far Komenda could be regarded
as a centre of subversive influence! David in his engaging way
invited everyone we met – CPP officials, Education Officers, etc. –
along to visit the course on Tuesday. (In the end they fortunately
didn't all turn up at the same time). There hasn't yet been any
major clash in Sekondi – apart from the beating up of a chief who
supports the strike.[92] He had his men out drumming, breaking the
curfew; the police came and told him to stop they beat him up and
smashed up his home – apparently (His followers ran away). He
was taken to hospital – and arrested. It's interesting that there is
this radicalism among some of the chiefs.

---

88 Kofi Amponsah Dadzie was a Cape Coast trader and later a sympathiser
to the Ghana Congress Party formed in 1952 to oppose the CPP. He
was an independent candidate in 1953 in a legislative assembly by-election opposing N.A. Welbeck, the CPP propaganda secretary at the
time. Dadzie was defeated in the popular vote, but later succeeded in an
election petition on the grounds that Welbeck was not a registered
voter in the Cape Coast municipality.
89 The Legislative Council from 1946 to 1951 contained 6 *ex officio*
members, 6 nominated members and 18 elected members.
90 Richard Abusua-Yedom Quarshie, born 1918 and educated at
Achimota College and Lincoln's Inn, London, became a labour officer
in 1945 and was in foreign service from 1956 to 1961. He was trade
minister in 1969.
91 E.D. Roberts, Education Officer.
92 Possibly Nana Kobina Nketsia IV, chief of Sekondi, who was imprisoned
in 1950 for defiance of emergency regulations and released with
Nkrumah in 1951. He studied anthropology at Oxford, wrote his doctoral
thesis on the impact of Christian missionaries on Akan social institutions.

To DMCH
21 January [1950]

Road from Komenda to Accra
Now the course is finished and we're on our way back. It's sad to
be leaving the place in many ways – a beautiful spot and one
which we must come back to together. The sea usually covered
with a lot of little boats. (I've been eating sardine sandwiches
which have got a bit spread over this page – also had a short sleep.)
These boats are canoes – like the model one I brought back last
time – hewn out of trunks of trees – gayly painted with names on
them in white paint – in English sometimes (like 'Nobody') or in
Fanti – and sails like Chinese junks, which only make it possible to
sail with the wind behind. Yesterday we went out on a lagoon about
2 miles away in canoes – paddling them – paddles very like oars but
the bit that goes in the water shorter and with magical names written on them. We all took a hand at paddling and occasionally
raced each other. The lagoon was full of birds – gulls, waders of
various kinds, egrets, and large heron or crane like birds. When we
landed the children followed us in large numbers and Lalage won
a bit of applause from them by pulling faces. (We are going along
this road at about 60 or 70 miles an hour so writing isn't all that
easy.) After the row we came back and had a bathe in the beach
just below the College. Only the second I'd found time to have
during the fortnight there. An exciting rough kind of sea. The
waves just bash you about – there's a very strong suck out so that
you can only just stand up in it, but as the waves throw you back
on the beach with about equal force, they about cancel out. One
couldn't swim much, it was mainly a matter of letting oneself be
tossed about by the waves. A 2-foot python is said to live in a cave
on the beach – one of the students has seen it – but I didn't. I have
also missed seeing a monitor lizard which was around – a pity. The
ordinary lizards are very nice though – with these golden streaks on
their bodies. They have a marvellous way of nodding their heads
several times with sudden jerks as though they worked by clock-
work.

I'm continuing this letter from Okine's[93] where I am staying

93 Attoh-Kojo Okine, born 1911 and educated at Achimota College and
   Balliol College from 1945 to 1948. He was a tutor at Achimota

Saturday night. Heard just as we arrived that Nkrumah and other CPP leaders were arrested. This will, I fear, prevent me from seeing N, as I had hoped to do. Same misfortune as I had in the Sudan! You'll probably have heard the news of the arrests on the BBC. The strike seems to be a good deal less effective than it was. We were called 'Stooges' in Nsawam when we tried to buy some petrol – otherwise no incidents on the way.

Sunday, Had a long talk with Okine, continued this morning, about his job in which he is unhappy – he teaches at the Training College here). Have tried to encourage him – I don't know if it's had much success. He is perhaps a bit of a frustrated type – like the young Russian intellectuals in the novels of Turgenev. Let me tell you a bit more about the last days at Komenda before I send this off. I got very fond of the place – the view over the bush on the one side and the sea on the other – with the village among the palm trees a mile or so away, and the canoes and the fishing nets along the beach. Little yellow birds and butterflies of the swallow-tail kind and bright flowers. The students I grew very fond of – and though they varied a good deal as regards intellect and ability they all worked extremely hard and took their work very seriously. In some ways time was rather too full for one to be able to give them as much individual attention as one would have liked. But I'm pretty sure they enjoyed it and got a good deal out of it – they almost all seemed to be people who would go ahead and do things of a useful kind in their own places when they got back – and quite a number were already doing such things. We had a nice winding-up social at the end – in which we all put on tribal shows – Gas, Ashantis, Ewes (pronounced 'Evies') and Europeans. Our European tribal drama was a take-off of the course – with Lalage acting the part of David, quite well (and I Creech-Jones[94], arriving to give a lecture on 'the Role of the D.C. in Adult Education' – which I was

---

Teachers' Training College from 1949 to 1951 and later senior warden of the Kumasi College of Technology. He became chairman of the Accra branch of the UP. He was detained by the Ghanaian authorities from 1958 to 1962 and escaped to Togoland. He later taught in Nigeria and again in Ghana.

94 Arthur Creech Jones (1891–1964), vice-president of the WEA. He was secretary of State for the Colonies from 1946 to 1950 and emphasised adult education as a necessary preliminary to self-government.

never allowed to give). The Ewes did a marvellous animal-like dance – contorting their whole bodies – the Gas did part of their Christening (or child-naming) ceremony. They gave me a very friendly and unexpected farewell – including singing 'For he's a jolly good fellow' – which I found somewhat embarrassing – the people of the G.C. being much more warm-hearted and demonstrative than the people of Oxford (University anyway!).

Plans for today a little vague. David will be coming round to collect me some time. It's being a very useful time from my point of view – I've been able to think about one or two questions in the way one can when one gets away from them (about jobs and the like) – and this African diet and country life have made me feel very healthy – I hope I've lost weight, it feels like it!

To DMCH
24 January 1950

Accra [Gold Coast]
This letter I had meant to send off before I left Accra this morning. Now it is night, and I'm writing from *Kumasi* – sitting in a rather sordid rest-house, knowing that I should pull myself together and go to bed, but not feeling very much inclined to do so. We've been having a nice evening – talking about the state of the nation (G.C.) with Casely Hayford,[95] a Cambridge lawyer – African – son of one of the greatest of the national leaders of a generation ago. This one is a nice old fashioned Liberal. Has a great admiration for our dear Queen (Victoria), and strong monarchist sentiments generally – at the same time much disturbed about the present state of affairs – with the arrests, etc. (He's defending the people up here who are on trial for the usual kind of thing – fomenting a general strike intended to coerce HMG.) We had a dusty drive up from

---

95 Archibald Casely Hayford (1898–1977), son of Joseph Ephraim Casely Hayford (1866–1930) who was a lawyer, writer and early nationalist. Archie Casely Hayford was educated at Dulwich College, London, and Clare College, Cambridge and was also a barrister, CPP leader, and later Minister of Agriculture and Natural Resources (see letters of March 1951). He was ironically dubbed "DVB" (Defender of the Verandah Boys) for his defence of the Kumasi CPP leaders.

Accra; I travelled with Newlove Mamattah[96] (Mary's friend – he sends his love!) – no incidents – forest almost all the way with some pleasant wooded hills on our rights. When we got here we met Wm. Boatin[97] and Dennis Austin who took me off – gave me supper – and drove me round the town. It's a nice town – friendly people – built on hills like Rome. Tomorrow we go to Obuasi – one of the gold-mining centres – also call on the Chief Commissioner[98] for the Colony and tell him we mean to have a One-day School on Saturday – taken by me and Dennis on 'The Meaning of Democracy'.

The nicest name I've come across in the G.C. – I meant to tell you earlier (Luke will like it). One of the masters at Komenda College is called Mr. Wonderful Geolampius Chlorofine Dadson – the cause of the name being that he was born to his father unexpectedly in old age. 'Dadson' = simply dad's son – 'Geolampius' presumably = 'the light of the world'. 'Chlorofine' untranslatable (to me) – but it sounds scientific and grand!

To DMCH
28 January 1950

Kumasi [Gold Coast]
Just a quick line this is, while waiting in the office of the Ashanti Pioneer for things to happen. It's been a bit of a scrappy day so

---

96 Newlove MacGregor Mamattah was in the first group of four adult education organisers recruited in the Gold Coast. He had probably met Thomas's first cousin Mary Cowan, born 1914, a daughter of his maternal aunt Lucy Margaret Smith (1890–1974), at a party given by the Hodgkins for the Gold Coast organisers during their training course in Britain in July and August 1949. See notes to letter 12 January 1950 above.

97 William Boatin, also among the four Gold Coast recruits of 1949, became the adult education organiser for the Kumasi region (his father Chief Kwamin Boatin had been secretary to the Asantehene Prempeh I and William had been born during the Asantehene's exile in the Seychelles from 1901 to 1924.).

98 Thorlief Rattray Orde Mangin (1896–1950), educated at Marlborough College, became an assistant district commissioner in the Gold Coast in 1919. He was appointed chief commissioner for the colony in 1945 and knighted in 1949.

far – mainly trying to fix things for the future. Seeing some Trade Unionists at tea and then going with Joe Annan,[99] a very nice able African Labour Officer, to visit his class in a neighbouring suburb, taking him back to Dennis Austin's for supper and chat. I am staying with D.A. – in a primitive bungalow he has temporarily – sleeping, quite comfortably, on cushions on the floor. The main difficulty here is that so many people have been arrested. And others are naturally careful and a bit suspicious of Europeans – a situation that by now I am not unused to. Since I started this letter we have actually had a bit of bother – the Pub. Reln's Officer[100] demurring about announcing the subject of my lecture 'Problems of Modern Govt' on the Radio. Could you imagine anything much more innocuous? Especially absurd since we had spent half an hour yesterday morning with the Chief Commissioner discussing the whole thing, and had made concessions to his point of view. However I imagine we shall carry the thing off in the end. It is at the same time amusing and frustrating – this colonial society – and depressing too.

Had a nice time yesterday, driving out to Obuasi – a gold-mining town. A curious mixture of Durham slag heaps and overhead travelling cages and Austrian Alps – or the foothills of the Alps. Lovely wooded hillsides all round. On the way back I was dropped off at Bekwai, where I gave a lecture (on Economics God help me) to a nice small group of chaps, the real tutor having got sent to England. After the lecture I was taken care of by a cocoa-broker (African), who gave Dennis and me 4 poached eggs on toast each, 4 Hamburger sausages, Whiskey and coffee – a marvellous meal. Came back here and talked from 10 to 11 in a

99 J.S. Annan, born 1914, was educated at Achimota College and took an external London Bachelor of Science degree in engineering. He worked as an electrical engineer for Gold Coast Railways and went to Edinburgh in 1941 for post-graduate work. On return he became a trade union organiser and was a delegate to the Pan-African Congress in Manchester in 1945. He was attached to the Ministry of Labour and a part-time extra-mural tutor in economics. He became Permanent Secretary of Labour in Ghana and in the 1960s went to the Food and Agriculture Organisation.
100 Possibly Major Victor James Alexander Lillie-Costello, born 1907 and educated at Malvern College; after military service from 1939 to 1946 he was appointed Public Relations Officer for the Gold Coast in 1948.

somewhat sleepy condition to Nancy Tsiboe[101] – a charming, beautiful and intelligent African – whom I had met here last time – wife of the Manager of the Ashanti Pioneer, in whose office I am now sitting.

To DMCH
28/29 January [1950]

Kumasi – Sat

I'm writing this waiting for this one-day School that Dennis and I are doing to start. So far no one here but me. Doubtless though some people will roll up some time. Africans are not over-punctual, usually. Not a lot has happened since I last wrote. Yesterday we reached an amicable settlement with the P.R.O. (about this school) and concluded by inviting him out to lunch. Not a very impressive man, and a bit anxious to impress. Still it was quite useful talking to him. We also had an interesting time visiting the trial of two Trade Union leaders – charged with encouraging participation in an illegal strike, designed to coerce Govt, etc. It reminded me strongly of similar events in earlier British history.

Damn, this never got finished. I'm now standing in the sun on Sunday morning waiting to start for Tamale. The School went off all right – only about 50 there. But quite a lively discussion. 3 British officials turned up – one the quite nice P.S. to the Chief Commissioner. I hope they were impressed. They ought to have been. After the school was over we went on and had drinks with lawyer Casely Hayford (who is defending the Trade Unionists) and with John and Nancy Tsiboe – ending up with champagne! – in which we drank one another's healths. Result I was extremely sleepy and dropped off twice during supper.

---

101 Nancy Tsiboe stood unsuccessfully for the Ghana Congress Party (GCP) in Kumasi South in the 1954 election. She was national treasurer of the United Party (UP) formed in 1957 and crossed to the CPP in 1960. She was married to John Tsiboe (1904–63), owner manager of the *Ashanti Pioneer*, founded in 1932.

To DMCH
31 January 1950

Tamale [Gold Coast]
It's before breakfast, sitting in this rest-house, looking out over open dry grassy country: very different from the South. In many ways I prefer it. One gets tired of this perpetual forest. It's a feudal kind of country here: every one touches his hat to you like mid-19 Century England. We had a pleasant drive up here on Sunday, the forest gradually thinning out and drying up and becoming what I think they call savannah in the geography books. We stopped and bought a nice red water pot which I shall be bringing home at a village, Yeji,[102] on the way. Yesterday we also shopped a bit in the Tamale market, a good one, with the goods being made in the booths where they were on sale – cloths and embroidered trousers and caps and hats of various kinds and leather work (nice red leather they use). I bought one or two odd things, including one of these nice N.T. hats, though later I decided that there were others more beautiful than mine. I want to bring you one of these beautiful Kita cloths, but they cost quite a lot and there may be duty too. At 4.30 I had my lecture. I wasn't altogether satisfied. It went on too long for one thing, so discussion was too short. The chief with a retinue of elders, all chewing cola nut, came along (David had asked him that morning at an interview where we were given yams and a live guinea-fowl) – as the poor old boy can only speak Dagomba I don't know how much he got out of it. Had a pleasant chat with some of the lads afterwards who seemed interested and keen. The main problem up here is finding a tutor. Today we go on to Yendi, after one or two calls – that's the capital of Dagomba.

Have just seen Chief Commr. – quite friendly – now going to Yendi.

---

102 Yeji was the ferry crossing point for the Volta, and travellers who had to wait some time would buy goods.

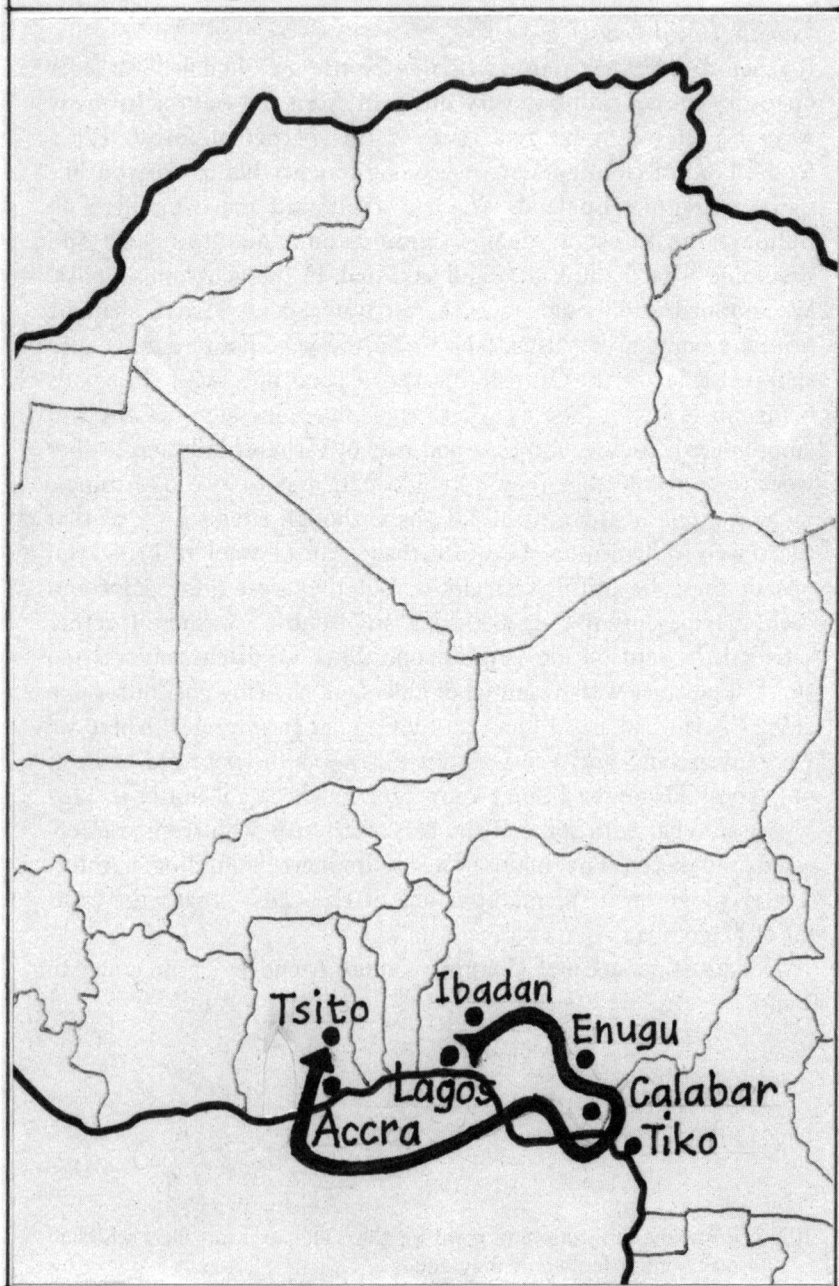

fourth African journey

Tsito
Ibadan
Enugu
Lagos
Calabar
Accra
Tiko

Fourth African journey:
to Nigeria, Cameroon and Gold Coast
February 1951–March 1951

Thomas had been enchanted by his first journeys to Africa and by late 1949 was thinking of how he might disengage from the Oxford University Delegacy for Extra-Mural Studies (although achieving this as an amicable break was a slow process). He wanted time to see and learn more of Africa in order to write about the continent. Thomas's fourth African journey brought him into contact with university teachers but was motivated by a request by David Williams for a series in *West Africa* on Nigerian nationalism.

The gap was widening between Thomas's interests and enthusiasms and the motives of the Colonial Office and the educational establishment in Britain. An enduring friendship followed Hodgkin's meeting in Accra in March 1951 with Kwame Nkrumah, then recently released from colonial imprisonment to lead the Gold Coast government (and eventually independent Ghana). The UDC in August 1951 published a sixpenny pamphlet by Thomas *Freedom for the Gold Coast*, in which he urged British support for 'an enthusiastic self-confident and democratic movement for national independence and for liberation from the colonial past.' The *West Africa* articles were published as 'Background to Nigerian nationalism' in the period from 4 August to 15 September and from 6 to 20 October 1951.

To DMCH
[25 Feb 1951]

Lagos [Nigeria]
Saturday morning I spent getting transport (a fine large lorry – in which I could take all my wives children camp-followers

equipment, etc. if I wanted – but in fact the one old man who seems to like to come round with us) and talking to the U.A.C.[103] That was quite interesting – in its way. Things are made extremely pleasant and helpful for me through staying with Fidelis Ogunsheye. He lives in a Yoruba house out at Yaba and looks after me extremely well. We spent Saturday afternoon going and visiting H.O. Davies together – after a chat with Mr Esua, a nice old friend and Secretary of the N.U.T. Davies has a nice intelligent wife – he is himself a barrister, ex-N.U.T., and is one of the most, and quite likely *the* most intelligent nationalist out here. A long and useful talk with him, followed by a visit to some of F.O.'s more radical friends. Then back to Lagos to a superior (by Lagos standards) hotel – which means a sort of roof-garden-cum-Night-club, where we sat and drank a little and talked with Davies and others till a late hour (about 1.30). Sunday was somewhat similar – most of the day spent in talk with various chaps – Trade Unionists, a small discussion-group of Ogunsheye's, the Secretary of the Lagos Extra-Mural Committee and lunch with Sabben-Clare[104] who is in the Secretariat here – was at Winchester and acted in a play of mine at Oxford – and whom I came across accidentally: nice also to see again Carpenter, the Mass Education Officer, who took me round last time I was here.

Yesterday too we ended up with a Night-club, of a slightly lower and more interesting kind. Nice to watch white and black dancing uninhibitedly together – Rumbas and Sambas and suchlike. All these very different African types – some like the wood-carvings, some with almost Mediterranean faces, very quick and elegant dancers. One thing about this society is that it is at least civilised in having little colour bar – and this particular joint was pleasant

---

103 The United Africa Company was formed in 1929 as successor to the Royal Niger Company and through merger with other trading companies. It was a Unilever subsidiary and became a commercial colossus in the region of West Africa.

104 Ernest Elwin Sabben-Clare, born 1910 and educated at Winchester College and New College, Oxford, became a colonial cadet in 1935 and was appointed a district officer 1947. He was an editor of *Health in tropical Africa during the colonial period*, based on the proceedings of a symposium held at New College, Oxford 21–23 March 1977. As a history scholar at New College in 1930 he had played the role of Otto, the mayor, in a one-act comic play written by Thomas.

just for that reason – tough-looking British soldiers and policemen dancing away with gay pretty African girls.

It would, I think, be sensible to get this letter off before the news gets too stale. I want to try to see Zik, whom I have so far only been able to say 'hullo' to. Best plan, I think, to call at his home. I'll tell you more later. Today's been fairly quiet so far. More Trade Unionists in the morning – lunch with Rogers – and odd jobs since. Now going to visit Fidelis' class. What I lack most so far is documentary material. I must try to get more of this – on Wednesday I'm going up to Ibadan – for 3 days or so.

To DMCH
[27 Feb 1951]

Ibadan [Nigeria]
Came up here yesterday in this small lorry which we have succeeded in winkling out of the Public Relations Dept. – with a nice young driver (who has only twice disappeared so far) and an elderly shadow who rides in the back – whose function is not at all clear – but 2 retainers are better then 1 for respectability in this country (cf medieval England). I came up here with a nice man, of similar tastes and approximately similar ideas, called Carey,[105] asst. Editor of *West Africa* who has been reporting the G.C. Elections and the Eucharistic Congress at Kumasi (both gorgeous spectacles which the Africans much enjoyed, I gather). For the moment I've exchanged simple life at Ogunsheye's for a high standard of living in a Govt. rest house where one has baths and kippers and such-like. It's not what I'd intended, but it probably will do no harm for a bit – and so far life is fairly economical. It's a beautiful spot here (where I stayed when I came 4 years ago – at much about the same time of year), an open place surrounded by palm trees – one lives in a pleasant hut – with bird noises all round. All this has been fixed by Tokunboh, a charming chap whom I met out here 4 years ago, been since at LSE, now Labour Officer here. He dropped in

---

105 Edward (Ted) Carey was briefly assistant to David Williams, the editor of *West Africa* from 1949 to 1978. Carey moved into administrative tasks for Overseas Newspapers, a part of the Mirror newspaper group that had acquired the magazine in 1948.

last night, and we had a very useful chat. Now going out to see him and people he's fixed up. Handsome he is as well as very intelligent. Had two and a half hours talk with Zik yesterday which delayed us a good deal – but it was very useful to have. A nice man, though a bit of a megalomaniac, I think

. . .

To DMCH
[2 March 1951]

Ibadan
It's a lovely early morning now – with grey sky – quite cool – hens poking about on the grass – pink in the sky where the sun is coming through the mist – and tall beautiful palm trees all round. These last couple of days I've been seeing people hard – under the admirable guidance of Tokunboh – very nice Labour officer from Benin. His idea is that it is a good thing to visit these so-called night-clubs – from the point of view of meeting interesting people: a sensible idea, except that it means getting home at between 1 and 2 a.m. each morning. However I'll have an earlier night, I hope, to-night, I'm going out this morning with Galletti and Baldwin[106] (G. was at Balliol with me – a nice, very serious person – can be heavy going – but useful to find him here) – they are doing an economic survey of some cocoa-producing villages – finding out how much their income cocoa farmers spend on food, funerals, etc. Also having dinner with G. to-night. Went down with Carey (this Assistant of David Williams who is out here – poster of this letter)

---

106 Robert Galletti Di Cadilhac, born 1908 was educated at Cheltenham and at Balliol College from 1926 to 1931 (so part contemporary with Thomas) and was in the Indian Civil Service from 1931 to 1947. He became a Colonial Office research officer in 1948 and was chief research officer and executive officer for the Economic Survey of the Cocoa Producing Areas in Nigeria from 1950 to 1954. Kenneth David Sutherland Baldwin, born 1920 and also educated at Oxford, was an adult education tutor and fellow of the University College of Ibadan. Isaac Odzesanwo Dina (1914–73) took an external London University degree in history and an economics degree at the London School of Economics, and was an extra-mural tutor. They *published Nigerian Cocoa Farmers. An economic survey of Yoruba cocoa farming families* by R. Galletti, K.D.S. Baldwin and I.O. Dina, 1956.

to Abeokuta yesterday and had a useful time talking and having tea with Mr and Mrs Ransome-Kuti. She is a remarkable woman – full of energy and passion – also organising ability, which is a rarer quality here. She's a bit like your mother in some ways – has got a women's union of 80,000 members going – they weave and wear their own cloth (lovely stuff) – run a maternity clinic, and take political action when necessary!

C. goes now

. . .

To DMCH
[6 March 1951]

Enugu [Nigeria]
I am enjoying the delights of air travel – in other words stuck here for the time being on my way to Tiko (Cameroons). We were just about to take off for the next stage when the captain noticed the engine popping and called for a screwdriver. He hoped it would only be a plug but it turned out to be the magneto. So they have sent a signal for a relief aircraft, engineer and magneto. I suppose one should have learned to be patient about such things, but it's rather a bore – and I can't really safely go calling on chaps in Enugu until I hear whether we are moving or stopping.

(AIR). We got going after all – and are now making for Calabar – in fact it was at this point that the young BOAC chap came in and told me to pack my traps and go with him to the airport since the relief aircraft was just coming in. We're now having a cool and beautiful journey – following the left bank of the Cross River. Sky a bit misty – everything a pale colour – forest below, and the curves of the river and its sandbanks running through it. We shan't apparently get further than Calabar to-night – so it's a question where one stays. However I shan't be stranded – since I have many names of students who were in the Oxford extra-mural class (one of the best we had) – and could always scrounge on one of these. Also I have invited myself (if necessary) to sleep with a friendly Catholic Bishop[107] who is travelling in this plane, and

---

107 James Moynagh was Roman Catholic titular bishop of Lambesis and appointed Vicar Apostolic at Calabar on 12 June 1947.

whose home (see?) is at Calabar. He looks very well in purple and
white. Knows Gervase and David Mathew[108] – both of whom I
seem to have missed by about a day. (Gervase, like me presumably,
is not taking term too seriously).

So what with one thing and another this is being a pretty idle
day. Not altogether sorry since I had indigestion (usual kind of
gyppy tummy I suppose) yesterday, and this quiet life is good for
it. Now we are getting into the creeks, a lot of water ahead of us.
I do wish you were on this journey – and enjoying the beauty of
the evening too. (These planes can't land at night apparently – or
else the airport can't take them.)

Nice sunset beginning on our right. Lots of little boats (and
bigger ones) in the river below. Now we are coming down, having
just passed over Calabar – marvellous peach-coloured sky as we
wheel round – close to the trees now and just about to land.
There – we've hit it – without much of a bump.

Thursday. I hoped to finish this yesterday but much has happened and there's not been much chance to write. I've reached the
Cameroons, and am staying in extreme comfort with the chairman
of the Cameroons Development Corporation at Bota (near
Victoria) – my room is just beside the sea – noise of the waves
breaking all the time – and a most beautiful bay – Fernando Po in
the distances across the bay – and lots of little islands (including
one where Roger Casement used to live as consul) spread about –
rather like Perros-Guirec[109] – more likely the Italian riviera really –
with their mountains – little Cameroon and great Cameroon
behind. One couldn't wish for a lovelier place to stay in.

Following on from when I left off, I spent the night at Calabar
with the kind Catholic Bishop (in white mantle with purple

---

108 Thomas began to know members of the Mathew family when he
     was an Oxford undergraduate in the 1920s. Anthony Gervase
     Mathew (1905–76) was educated privately and at Balliol College
     from 1925 to 1928. He entered the Dominican Order in 1929 and
     was ordained in 1934. He was an archaeologist and specialist in
     Mediaeval English, Byzantine and African History. His older
     brother David James Mathew (1902–1975) was educated at
     Osbourne and Dartmouth Royal Naval College, at Balliol College
     from 1920 to 1924. He was ordained in 1929 and was Archbishop of
     Apamea and Apostolic Delegate in Africa from 1946 to 1953.
109 Perros-Guirec in Brittany. where the Hodgkin family had spent a hol-
     iday during summer 1950.

cummerbund and purple socks – and large gold pectoral cross) and
his fraternity of St Patrick – all Irish priests – very friendly – living
well – two or three lively and intelligent and knowing the people
around (the tribes near Calabar are apparently some of them pretty
primitive – hunting peoples, who hardly go in for agriculture at all).
I sent myself to sleep reading 'The Tablet' – which is an interesting – and rather depressing – exercise: an odd world, this world of
the Roman hierarchy. On yesterday morning early to Tiko – where
I was met by a nice young man – Secretary to the CDC[110] who
brought me over here. Fairly active day visiting the wharfs and harbour – going out in a launch on the bay – seeing a palm oil mill,
managed by an ex-Indonesian Dutchman called Sanders (you would
have made much more of it than I – he had a lab, which I regret-
ted I couldn't admire more intelligently).

Afternoon spent visiting new housing estate here – a bit embarrassing being shown round by about 5 high-powered officials of the
CDC at all. Then some talk with a nice welfare officer who is particularly concerned with the Trade Union here – then went round
to visit some of the literacy classes: they have about 80 running in
all – 15 to 20 in each – very impressive, teachers some of them
excellent (though one was teaching English in a phonetic way which
made me fear they might get into trouble later) – everyone enthusiastic and working hard: the last class we visited was at the end of
a long bush path – we walked in the dark – found this shack with
one or two feeble lanterns – some bits of plank to sit on – a black-
board, and that was all. I can't pretend I'm finding out much about
nationalism at the moment, but it's very interesting for all that.

To DMCH
[10 March 1951]

Saturday Leaving Tiko [Cameroon]
I've been staying all the time with Smith,[111] the Chairman of

110 Probably H.R. Cleaver. The Cameroons Development Corporation
    (CDC), established by statute in 1946, was a quasi-public body engag-
    ing in agriculture, trade, industry and transport. Profits were to be
    handed over to the Government for the development of the
    Cameroons.
111 F.E.V. Smith, Chairman of the CDC. The Chairman was manager of

C.D.C., in this most beautiful spot in all Africa – with Fernando Po just across the sea, out of one's bedroom window (we're just passing it now – this is the aircraft for Calabar – on the right is the great Cameroon mountain, covered with thick forest – both are surrounded in clouds now, but in the morning and evening while I've been there they've been beautifully clear). I would have liked to get a ship to take me across as an illegal immigrant to Franco's colony, but found no ship. (There are two nice Hausa boys in this 'plane – going to school at Calabar or Lagos? – just said goodbye to their father, a wealthy looking old trader, wearing a hat like the one I bought from the Northern Territories of the G.C. you know: now we're flying over the sea: sharks and barracudas in these parts apparently – so bathing is risky.) Yesterday evening I sat for an hour or more in front of Smith (my host)'s house with him and some other CDC people (a nice Irish couple from Antrim and a merchant captain from Tyneside) drinking whisky and watching the sun set, with a banana ship steaming out of Victoria harbour, and all the little islands in the bay becoming gradually silhouetted against the sky – and an occasional canoe moving quietly across the bay.

(We're now back in Nigeria, among the flat creeks, away from the mountains: one can see that there is a real barrier here, at the Cameroon mountain – the people to the East of it are said to be of different stock from Nigerian tribes – Bantus like the people to the south of them. It's strange to see villages in these creeks – where nothing grows but mangroves, and there seems to be no communication between them and the outside world except by water; I suppose they must live on fish.)

But I've told you really nothing yet about these last 3 days. They've really been spent sight-seeing mainly – visiting banana, palm-oil and rubber plantations, oil mills, saw mills, rubber factories, brick factories, and such like. It is interesting – this industrialisation – and I've never really seen a plantation economy in operation before. It's not a fearfully hopeful sight with the labour lines – long rows of workers' shacks or huts.

---

the CDC until 1952 when, after the resignation of Smith, the post became part-time and a general manager was appointed.

Calabar. *[Nigeria]* Now arrived here and having tea. Somewhat surprised to find both a PRO[112] vehicle (which I can use for the following week – that's a great advantage – to go about in the Eastern provinces) and a nice young Ibo driver (very bright – more like a District Commissioner than a driver) and accommodation at the Rest House. These were all asked for, but one is surprised when things go according to plan. Going back to the last 3 days. I was able to find Alec Dickson,[113] living at Buea with a nice (female) painter cousin of his – had 2 very interesting hours with him. (You remember him – vigorous highly critical chap – friend of David Kimble's – was Mass Education Officer in the G.C. – he came home for a drink with us late one evening, in the summer some time). A lot of gossip, of course, of a kind that is probably better passed on when we meet! He is starting a training scheme on Thursday on Kurt Hahn[114] – Outward Bound-lines – climbing mountains – going out to sea in canoes – and suchlike – idea being to give Africans opportunities for developing 'leadership': if it were anyone but Dickson one would be a bit sceptical – but he is the kind of person one naturally has confidence in. However he's having great difficulties – no food arrived for his chaps – etc. So I hope it comes off all right.[115] Also visited

---

112 Public Relations Office.
113 Alec Dickson (1914–94) was appointed in 1948 as Social Development Officer for the Gold Coast Government. From 1951 to 1953 he ran community development training based at Man O'War Bay, Victoria, in Cameroons, and aimed at young adults in their 20s. He was married to Mora Dickson, a biographer and illustrator. Alec and Mora Dickson set up Community Service Volunteers, an inspiration for Voluntary Service Overseas (VSO) and the US Peace Corps, to give school-leavers a chance to live away from home on socially useful work in their own country.
114 Kurt Hahn (1876–1974) was born in Germany and founded the Schule Schloss Salem in 1920. He travelled to Scotland and opened Gordonstoun School in April 1934, set up the Outward Bound movement at the end of the Second World War and founded the first United World College in 1962.
115 The experiment had severe difficulties. Two students were lost on the mountain and died in April 1952. Since Mount Cameroon was regarded as sacred, some students felt they would be violating a tabu by climbing it. Recruitment fell off for subsequent courses. Dickson was under administrative pressure to shift the emphasis of training from community service to adventure activities for schoolboys.

Gibbons[116] – the Commissioner – living in a great German Schloss
on the top of a hill, with antelopes heads and a signed photograph
of Von Moltke[117] on the wall. Coming back from Buea (where they
live – right up in the hills) we had a blow-out, and had to spend
one and a half hours or more changing the wheel – jack not working – in the end, being unable to get the car up high enough to get
on the new wheel (having let all its air out) we had to dig out the
road (a new idea to me). Back at 10 p.m. for a dinner of roast duck.
Yesterday I spent the morning seeing things at Tiko – travelling
about in a trolley on this German 20 cm. railway which runs all
over the plantations – going at a great speed, up to 50 m.p.h. –
lovely for the children it would be. (If anything happens the only
thing to do is to jump off, apparently). Then in the afternoon I had
a very useful two and a half hours with Manga Williams[118] (an old
reactionary chief – invented by the Germans), Martin[119] (an intelligent young Education Officer) and Dr. Endeley[120] (formerly
president of the CDC workers Union) – an obviously very able, as
well as charming, chap – and leading person in the Cameroonian
national movement: all members of the Board of CDC – Smith
(the Chairman) is an astute old man – a dictator of, I think, a

---

116 Brigadier Edward John Gibbons, born 1906 and educated at King
Henry VII School, Coventry, and Gonville and Caius College,
Cambridge, was appointed colonial cadet in Nigeria in 1929. He was
appointed Commissioner of Cameroons Province from 1949 to 1950
(he operated under the Lieutenant-Governor for the Eastern Region
of Nigeria). He was author of several reports on African local government.
117 Probably Helmuth Von Moltke (1848–1916), chief of Prussian general
staff from 1906 to 1914 (his uncle of the same name was chief of general staff, but mainly before the colonial period).
118 Chief J. Manga Williams, OBE, was from 1924 sole representative of
Southern Cameroons in the Nigerian Legislative Council.
119 E.K. Martin. The CDC provided primary education (free after 1952
thanks to union action) for the 'true children' of its employees, ran
adult classes (mostly for literacy) and offered some scholarships for
further education.
120 Dr Emmanuel Endeley (1916–88), Cameroonian nationalist and trade
unionist. He founded the Cameroons National Federation (CNF) in
1949, calling for a separate status for Cameroons within Nigeria. In
1951 he was a member of both the Eastern and the Federal House of
Representatives. He opposed reunification with French Cameroon,
but remained a deputy, at one time Minister of Labour.

benevolent, or largely benevolent, kind – all threads are in his hands, and no one can take a decision about anything from night classes to bananas without him.

To DMCH
11 March 1951

Sunday Calabar
Involved in one of these periodic hitches that make life in Africa jolly. I must go across by the ferry tomorrow morning in order to meet Robert Gardiner at Aba. However I find that nothing has been done about booking a place on the lorry [*sic*, ferry] for our car, and without a place we can't cross. So here I am waiting at Elder Dempster's[121] trying to get them to give me a place – truth is it looks from the book as though the ferry is rather full – so it may not be easy. If the worst comes to the worst I will try to go across myself and scrounge a ride to Aba somehow.

Oron. Across the river now. Have picked up a friendly policeman (European) who will take me (eventually) to Aba. There I meet Robert Gardiner.

Port Harcourt [Nigeria] Wed. 14/3/51
Oh dear – This letter has got very stuck – since I found Robert Gardiner yesterday I have been leading a strenuous life again. It's been a very nice and useful time. R.G. is such an extremely intelligent and good person. But I'll try to be a bit historical. Saturday night we had a tornado in Calabar – violent wind and rain. Sunday was spent partly seeing people, and being looked after by a nice Jamaican headmaster and wife called F.E. James – who had friends (the more respectable type of politician) in to see me. But the day was partly messed up by trying to get this car onto the ferry – which should have been done before. It meant a good deal of time wasted going round and making myself a nuisance to various people (waking respectable British shipping officials out of their Sunday aftn sleep, etc.). In the end it didn't work – so I had to leave the car to follow next day and take a lift from this policeman.

---

121 Elder Dempster line – Liverpool shipping line serving West Africa among its principal destinations.

However – apart from spending 3 hours over lunch – that didn't mean much delay – and I got to Aba and met Gardiner by about 4 pm. Since then things have been very nice: he's an excellent person to go round with – and doing clearly an excellent job, though badly handicapped, particularly in this area, for lack of money. I did a lecture for him here in P.H. last night – the usual sort of nice W. African audience – about 150 or more there – almost all young and bright and full of questions, of an extremely leading and relevant kind! I was talking on 'The Origins of Current Ideological Conflicts' (R.G.'s title, not mine!): gave what I thought was a pretty restrained talk – which I think they liked – then Robert talked – and then lots of questions. There was a new European magistrate sitting in the front row of the stalls – however he didn't look a trouble-maker, and so far I have not been asked to leave the country within 24 hours. Robert's idea, I think, is to repeat a similar show at Aba to-night (we return there this morning). On to Enugu tomorrow.

To DMCH
16 March [1951]

Enugu [Nigeria] Friday
Back here again – having a fairly quiet day – seeing Trade Unionists and others. On tomorrow to Lagos. In many ways I wish I could have a bit longer in the East. It's an interesting part of the world and takes quite a lot of understanding. I can't pretend to have got my mind clear about it in a week. Still it's been a good week – and it's been particularly nice to be able to go round with Robert Gardiner – from whom I've learned a lot. He's having a difficult time out here – in the East – I'm afraid: not getting any money – so there are no tutors – which is depressing seeing how keen people still are. I had these 2 nice meetings which I lectured to at P.H. and Aba – the Aba one rather smaller (about 60 people) but extremely lively. We went on till about 9.30 with sheep baaing in the background and a crowd of black heads looking over the wall at us.

Bother. Now Saturday. I haven't been as quick over getting letters off this week as I'd hoped to be. Now sitting in Enugu airport waiting for the aeroplane to take me back to Lagos. At least the aeroplane's here, but it's not due to take off for another 20 minutes. I've had quite an interesting morning so far. Started off with a talk with the personnel manager of the colliery, and learned a good deal from him about what has happened since the shooting over a year ago, (Ojiyi[122] and his lieutenants – who was the Union boss here when I was here 4 years ago – are now in jail on a sentence of 3 years for misappropriating Trade Union funds. The attitude of the miners – or many of them – seems to have been that Ojiyi got concessions for them and if he made 2 or 3 thousand for himself in the process, they weren't worried!) I then went on and had a look at one of the pits – couldn't go far underground, to the coal-face, for lack of time. They are sunk sideways into the hill (adits, I think they call them), not downwards, like British pits – they can get all the coal they need that way at present apparently.

We're now passing over from the jolly open hilly country you have round Enugu and on the way to Onitsha to the forest belt – which I must say I don't find nearly so attractive. Now to go back to recent history – working backwards. I've been staying the last 2 nights at Enugu – in the rest house – great comfort – e.g. hot baths. Nice also because Dr Savage, very intelligent Creole (partly Scotch) doctor has been there, and we've had very long talks after dinner both evenings. He seems to find himself growing more British as he grows older, while I find myself growing more African – or pro-African. He told stories of his ancestors – who came back to the Gold Coast from North America – freed slaves – including his grandfather, a prosperous trader, called Buck Savage, who lived at

---

122 B.O. Ojiyi as secretary of the Enugu Colliery Workers' Union was prominent in November 1949 when Nigerian miners at the Enugu Colliery held a go-slow and sit-down strike in protest over refusal of wage and welfare demands. A confrontation between police and strikers brought police shooting and the death of twenty miners. 'Others, like B.O. Ojiyi . . . himself a hewer, conform more to the traditional chiefly pattern: a 'wizard' who built up a great reputation for himself by the wage increases he won for his miners, and came in time to dominate the mine management as well as his own union; drawing no very clear distinction between trade union funds and his private purse – a paternalist attitude which later led to his imprisonment. "The worthless Ojiyi" is the description given him in the Fitzgerald Report [on the shootings of workers by police]. Yet from the standpoint of the Enugu miners he was clearly worth a good deal.' (quote from *Nationalism in Colonial Africa*, page 137)

Sekondi and used to entertain the local English community on palm oil and champagne. They were very English indeed these immigrant Creoles apparently – went on the grand tour – bought Victorian plush furniture and so forth. Yesterday I also attended a meeting of the Enugu Trades Council – out of doors – on benches under the trees: they were very friendly and welcoming (15 to 20 of them), and I learned quite a bit. I also had a talk with the officials of the new Coal miners union[123] – one of them a nice bright lad called Anakwe – who seemed to be secretary of all the radical organisations in Enugu.

Damn I must be getting sleepy – hence these mistakes. Up at 6.30 this morning – now 1.15 p.m. – so one does tend to drop off later in the day. We are now travelling just beside the coast – white waves beating on the sand. The coast here much broken up with creeks. Flying just above some beautiful low clouds – nice and cool. At Benin there was an extremely elegant chief in long orange robes and cap who'd come just to see an aeroplane – not having seen how they took off. He had a boy with him with golden (brass?) anklets – and round his own neck were great strings of coral beads. Also (going back to history) had a useful chat with a fat man called Stephens[124] at the Secretariat – and found out quite a lot about the new Constitution, and the way in which it is intended to work, from him. It seems to me a rather odd business. On Thursday I said good-bye to Gardiner – left him at Owerri in the pouring rain – it really does rain here when it starts. Came up from Aba with him by car.

I was sorry to leave him. (Now we are bouncing about through clouds). An interesting drive up from Owerri to Enugu – once one broke out of the forest there were grand views from the tops of the hills over the country round – men in those parts more or less naked, just a little belt round their middles.

123 The Nigerian Coal Miners' Union, successor to the Colliery Workers' Union was registered in April 1951.
124 Possibly D.S. Stephens, educated at Sandford Park School and Trinity College, Dublin, and Crown Counsel in Nigeria from 1946.

To DMCH
[27 March 1951]

Accra [Gold Coast] Tuesday
Again I don't seem to have been very clever about writing. But I've
had a very nice useful and full day and a bit in the Gold Coast so
far – driving round with David at the moment, on the way to watch
Achimota play Ibadan University College at hockey (and probably
see some chaps while doing so). I had a very interesting talk with
Kwame Nkrumah[125] this morning, and hope to see him again
before I go. Nkrumah is, I think, an extremely nice and intelligent
man.
   Later. It's now 5.30 a.m. Wednesday morning. I've been waiting
since 3 a.m. for a lorry by which I am supposed to be travelling to
Kumasi. A bit of a bore. It's a newspaper lorry, and there seems to
have been some hitch over the paper. This is the kind of thing that
regularly happens over here. The trouble is that it doesn't look as
though I am going to have much time at Kumasi. Perhaps it's a bit
wild to go but I wanted to see Dennis, William Boatin, Joe Annan,
etc. And this is the cheapest way of doing it.
   Going back to Nkrumah, he seems an altogether admirable
person, with very sound ideas. Also approachable and friendly –
there was a crowd of people there to visit him when I turned up.
The whole atmosphere here is very exciting – sense of things happening rapidly.
   Enormous crowds come to welcome Kwame and the other CPP
leaders wherever they go, 200,000 said to have been at the meeting
at Kumasi last week-end. 1700 Branches or more in the Gold
Coast. CPP has so far as one can make out pretty well become the
real government of the country.
   David has of course been benefiting from this situation – in that
it stimulates the demand for adult education. He's just run one
weekend-course (only it's called a 'conference') on Legislative
Procedure for Deputies and Ministers (and got about 50 there), he's
shortly going to run another on The Budget (just before the Budget

---

125 Nkrumah was elected from prison to the Legislative Assembly in
    February 1951 in the first democratic elections in the Gold Coast.
    Then he was released from prison and 11 days later became leader of
    government business.

session). I suspect it's the first occasion in human history when a University has run an extra-mural course for the Cabinet and MP's. Jolly sensible. And, of course, many MP's are ex-students.[126]

Saw various other people yesterday – Casely Hayford, who clearly much enjoys being Minister for Agriculture and Natural Resources, Dzenkle Dzewu[127] (who may be the next chairman of the Party), Dowuona (who, of course, is on the other side – David says he chose the wrong party), etc.

Now we seem at last to be setting off. Will get to Kumasi some time, I hope. It's being very nice here – everyone most friendly.

To DMCH
[30 March 1951]

Good Friday Accra.
I'm sure you're right in saying that if one is going to do any solid work one will have to settle down in one place for a longish period – but that is for the future. One can see how things work out. Meanwhile I have got some kind of impression of the state of affairs in Nigeria, and even in these 4 days in the Gold Coast one picks up enough in the way of information about recent events to be in a better position to interpret things when one gets back. It is a very exciting country to be in at the present time: there is no question about the strength of support for Nkrumah and the CPP. Wherever one goes are CPP flags, ties, caps, dances, rallies, slogans, etc. This kind of popular movement hasn't, I think, ever happened before in Africa – not on this scale anyway. Wherever Nkrumah and the leaders go there are enormous and enthusiastic crowds – said to be 200,000 in Kumasi last week-end. And though there is still some opposition to them it is at present completely ineffective. Even the Asantehene, who a year ago was hauling Krobo Edusei[128]

---

126 Some eighty out of the 104 Legislative Assembly members had attended extra-mural classes.
127 Dzenkle Dzewu, early leader in the CPP (a former sergeant-major he rallied ex-servicemen to the party) but was one of those expelled from the CPP in April 1952 and joined the GCP on its foundation in May.
128 Krobo Edusei (1915–84), founding member and former secretary of the Asante Youth Association, one of the leaders of the CPP. He was Minister of the Interior from 1957 to 1958. He was reinstated, as

(an Ashanti CPP leader) over the coals for his activities, now receives Nkrumah and the others in state, gives him £25, two sheep and 'a quantity of foodstuffs and vegetables' and says what a good show CPP is (according to one paper he even encouraged his people to join it – most of them have already anyway!) Sir Tsibu Darku[129], a chief who's been member of Leg. Co. for a long time, knighted and all that, finds himself threatened with destoolment by his people and appeals to Nkrumah to intervene and put things right – and so on. 'And so the whirligig of time brings in his revenges'. Even Kwesi Lamptey[130], whom I met in Sekondi a year ago, regarded simply as a bad boy just back from England, is now Under-Secretary for Finance (The Hon. Kwesi Lamptey), and gets reported in the papers when he visits the Dunkwa PEA class and kindly says a few words to them. I spent Tuesday evening with Casely Hayford, the nice liberal lawyer whom I saw quite a lot of in Kumasi last year, now Minister of Agriculture and Natural Resources – obviously very much enjoying his job and impressing his permanent officials. We talked of the changes that had happened over the last year – and he told me that Kwame Nkrumah had the complete loyalty and affection of all of them, and what a wonderful experience it was to be working in this team.

Yesterday I went over to Chito[131] – across the Volta – and saw this residential college which the Chito chief, his Elders and people are building for the Extra-mural Dept. and the PEA – encouraged by Lalage and David. It's all being done by voluntary labour – no

---

Minister of Agriculture, in 1962 and was affected by a scandal over his wife's purchase of a gilded bed.

129 Nana Sir Tsibu Darku was educated at Adisadel College and enstooled as Omanhene of Asin Atandasu in 1930. He was a member of the Legislative Council from 1932 and knighted in 1949. He opposed the CPP and was defeated in the 1951 elections. He abdicated from the stool in September 1951 but remained a territorial member of the legislative assembly until 1954. He was later reconciled with Nkrumah and after independence was chair of the Tema Development Corporation and then of the Cocoa Marketing Board. He was re-elected chief of Asin Atandasu in August 1962.

130 Kwesi Lamptey, CPP leader who resigned in August. He joined GCP and then the United Party (UP). In 1969, after Nkrumah's fall, he held various ministerial positions, including defence, leaving politics after the 1972 coup.

131 This is Tsito; see notes to letter of 18 January 1950 above.

money or work from any official source. The people of the village work 3 days a week – and there's a determination to get it finished as rapidly as possible. It's in a marvellous position – on the side of a hill, looking over the plain and the forest. It's built in 3 blocks – one of two storeys – and will house 40 students. Enormously impressive. All the Chief's war leaders are in charge of squads doing particular bits of the work. We had lunch together afterwards, with Lalage and the chief, a very nice and energetic man – ex-Achimota!

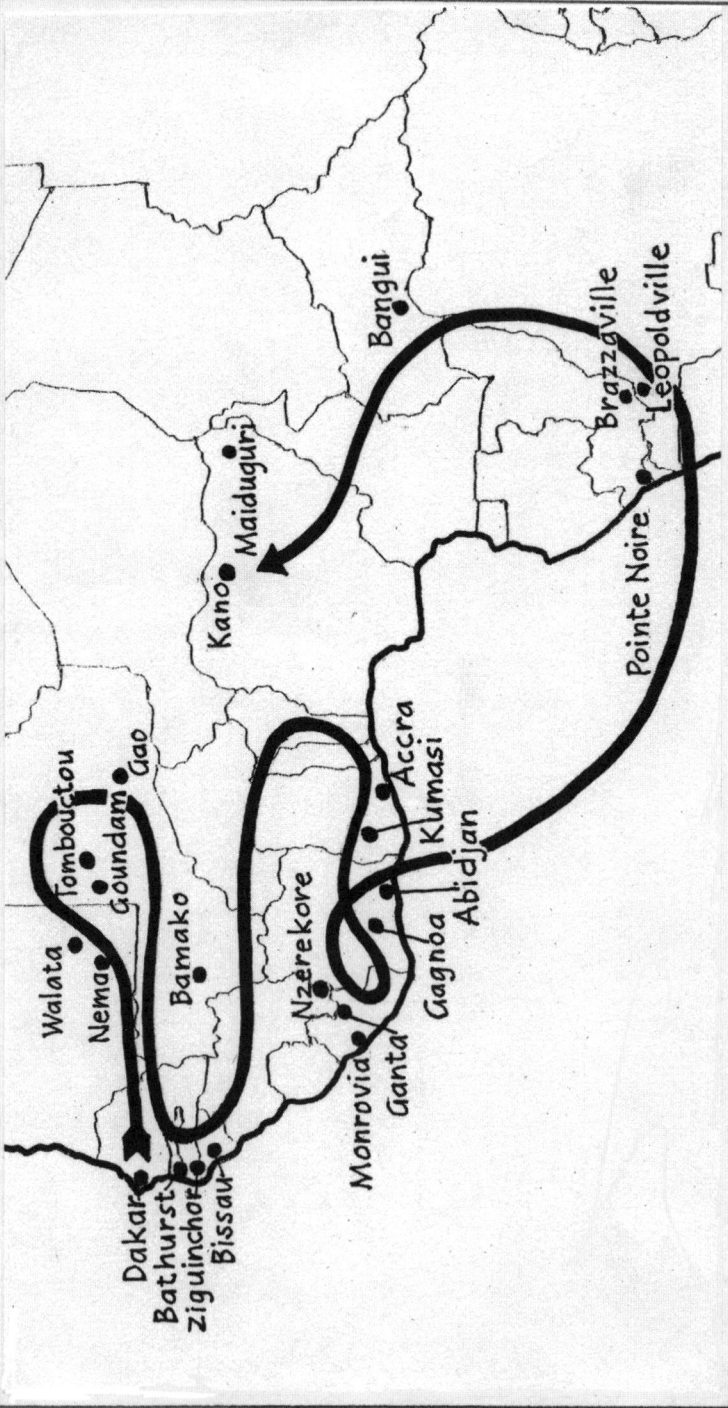

fifth African journey

Walata
Nema
Tombouctou
Goundam • Gao
Bamako
Dakar
Bathurst
Ziguinchor
Bissau
Nzerekore
Monrovia
Ganta
Gagnoa
Abidjan
Kumasi
Accra
Kano • Maiduguri
Bangui
Brazzaville
Leopoldville
Pointe Noire

Fifth African journey:
to Francophone Africa
October 1952–March 1953

Thomas continued his work with the Oxford University Delegacy for Extra-Mural Studies until a successor was found. By May 1952 he was free of the professional obligations in Oxford, and could pursue his interests in African history and politics. He decided to spend several months at a stretch in Africa beginning in October 1952 and returning to Britain and his family by April 1953.

He planned to allocate his time with two to three months in Francophone West Africa and Togo, about a fortnight each in Portuguese Guinea and Liberia, a week or two in the Gold Coast where he could attend a history conference and recuperate with friends and a fortnight seeing the north of Nigeria with which he was fairly unfamiliar. He would then spend a month in French Cameroons and French Equatorial Africa, and three weeks in the Belgian Congo.

This was an ambitious programme and Thomas had little money to spend or to allow for contingencies. The children were growing. The gratuity from his Oxford post went into the travel budget along with journalistic commissions from *West Africa* and from the *Spectator*, whose editor Walter Taplin had been a pupil of Thomas's father. Thomas determined at the outset that he would be using public transport and of the cheapest kind. Trains, buses, lorries, boats and camels rather than private cars or aeroplanes, except in rare cases when the latter were unavoidable.

The articles he had written for *West Africa* after previous journeys – on the national movements in the Gold Coast and Nigeria – had been a success. He proposed a new series on the ancient cities of the Western Sudan and on political developments in French West Africa.

The French colonial federations were formed in the late 19th and early 20th century scramble for Africa and were abolished by

1959. French Equatorial Africa (Afrique Equatoriale Française: AEF) included the Central African territories of Oubangui-Chari, Gabon, Tchad and Moyen Congo. French West Africa (Afrique Occidentale Française: AOF) included the West African territories of Dahomey, French Guinea, French Sudan, Ivory Coast, Mauritania, Senegal, Niger, and Upper Volta.

Thomas had an underlying sense that the pre-European civilisation of the Western Sudan had a bearing on the ideas of contemporary West African nationalism in the 1950s. His long-term intention was to write a book-length study of West African nationalism and knew that it would take some years to complete (the book eventually took a continental rather than regional perspective on Africa).

If Thomas's political views had raised alarm in the Colonial Office they were no more reassuring to the French authorities. Thomas felt himself under watch by French intelligence, and found his pursuit of precolonial history less alarming than too conspicuous an interest in contemporary politics. He discreetly combined both.

Thomas carefully prepared this fifth African journey, securing visas and the sympathetic interest of well-placed academics, diplomats and officials in the colonial administrations. He joined the International African Institute and this opened doors to research institutes in Africa. He made a detailed list of people who would be helpful en route through discussions in London and Paris.

A major hitch in Thomas's plan came in December when he found himself at San Domingos frontier post and was refused admission even though he had a valid visa issued in London in September with three months' validity for a stay of 60 days. The local administration had just received a letter from Bissau instructing them not to admit Thomas Hodgkin to Portuguese Guinea. Thomas's indignation can be seen in the letters below. His only consolation was that the leading Portuguese scholar he was going to meet happened to be in San Domingos and he entertained Thomas, arranged accommodation and drove him back to safe haven in Senegal.

In other ways Thomas's journey was a success, although the recurring warmth of the reception he generally received at all levels was as much due to the attractiveness of his own personality as to any agenda of officialdom. A series on 'Cities of the Sudan' was published in *West Africa* in the period from 21 March to 29 August 1953. He contributed a chapter 'Towards self-government in British West Africa' to a book *The New West Africa*, edited by Basil Davidson and A. Ademola, 1953. Thomas wrote on French West African political developments in 'Background to A.O.F.' in *West Africa* from 2 January to 6 March 1954.

To DMCH
9 October [1952]

4am Thursday Bordeaux [France]
I haven't much of a story to tell since I left you. I bought *Le Soir* and saw about this horrible train accident – took the bus back to the hotel: called at Cheik Diop's[132] address in the Rue des Ecoles, but found him out – looked for our restaurant of the night before – but found another, also quite nice – and had a ham omelette and half a litre of white wine: then took a taxi to the station. A porter cleverly found me a place in a fairly crowded train. There was a nice chap opposite me in the carriage, who promised to wake me at Bordeaux (and did).

To DMCH
14 October 1952

[Dakar, Senegal]
So long as all goes well with you all (which is all that matters) I don't regret this journey – for I think it can be useful – though one can't entirely see ahead what one hopes will grow out of it.

---

132 Cheikh Anta Diop (1923–86), Senegalese historian, joined Rassemblement Démocratique Africain (RDA) in July 1950. He was secretary general of the Association des Étudiants du RDA (AERDA) in Paris from 1951 to 1953. He prepared two doctoral theses on the African origin of Egyptian civilisation for the Sorbonne but no jury could be formed to consider the work. The material was published by *Présence Africaine* in 1954 as '*Nations nègres et Culture – De l'antiquité nègre égyptienne aux problèmes culturels de l'Afrique noire d'aujourd'hui*', providing one of the cultural foundations of the struggle for independence.

Arrived yesterday 4 pm. Met by Consul Pirie[133] at the quay who exclaimed 'Winchester!' and got me through all formalities with the greatest speed – took me off in his car – which he has since lent me (he has another) – driven by a nice Gold Coast boy. Less good is that the arrangements for staying at IFAN have broken down, and Monod[134] is away. Housed last night in a very expensive hotel – from which I will escape as soon as this can be organised.

To DMCH
18 October 1952

Dakar
All's well here. Till lunchtime today I had a fairly strenuous 3 days – seeing people, in the usual way – mainly French officials – but nice and helpful ones. Now I have a breathing space till 7 – when Pirie comes for me to take me out to drinks and dinner with people called Frumentien – he, I gather, is the Director of Information or something of that kind. Both my main problems were solved this morning (in the way such problems frequently *do* get solved – provided one doesn't let oneself get agitated!) – one by the arrival of Mauny,[135] the archaeologist, from his conference at Morocco, whose help I need over planning this journey to the ancient cities of the Soudan; and the other by Pirie succeeding in arranging for me to move from this frantically expensive hotel to the Hôtel du Gouvernement, where I can live bakshish it seems. Both very cheering events. Also I've seen most of the people I've

---

133 Douglas Gordon Pirie, born 1910 and educated at Winchester from 1924 to 1927 as a contemporary of Thomas. He went on to Edinburgh University, served in the Colonial Office from 1947 to 1950 and in the Foreign Office from 1950 to 1953.
134 Théodore Monod, born 1902, former colonial administrator, historian, author of many books on the Sahara and honorary director of IFAN, the acronym in the 1950s for Institut Français d'Afrique Noire but later standing for Institut Fondamental d'Afrique Noire; and see letter of 25 December 1952.
135 Raymond Mauny (1912–1994), was head of the prehistory and archaeology section at IFAN and author of seminal works on African history, including *Les siècles obscurs de l'Afrique noire: Histoire et archéologie*, 1971.

so far tried to see – except Senghor[136], who seems elusive – extremely busy, I suspect. The *Grand Conseil* opens on Monday, and that should be interesting to watch and listen to. I called last night on some friends of Basil Davidson's[137] – Africans – whom it was extremely refreshing to meet – like-minded, and interested in everything to do with British and African affairs. We sat in this chap's shop for a couple of hours, and talked while he counted the cash.

To DMCH
23 October 1952

AFRIQUE OCCIDENTALE FRANCAISE
CABINET CIVIL
Dakar
I have not joined the Cabinet Civil – but am waiting in M. Bolle's[138] office for him to turn up, and this is the pad on which he scribbles notes. So it will do very nicely for a short letter to you. All's going on quite nicely – except that I don't quite see how in the next 48 hours, before I leave for Bamako, I shall get through all the various jobs that I mean to get through. Still I propose to try. About one thing you were (as usual) entirely right – and I was entirely wrong – that is the question of a *watch*. I really am some-what stuck without one. There are no clocks in this place – and one can't always be asking the time – hence I find myself being usually uncomfortably late (or early) for every appointment. Entirely my stupid fault. I wonder if you could sweetly buy me a moderately priced watch, of the kind that will go in the tropics, knock it about a little (so that it ceases to be new) and post it to me by airmail at I.F.A.N., Bamako-Koulouba, Soudan Francais, French West Africa.

---

136 Léopold Sédar Senghor, born 1906, poet, writer, politician and first President of Senegal from 1960 to 1980.
137 Basil Davidson, born 1914, became a writer and historian, especially of Africa. Thomas and he collaborated closely in a conference held in October 1950 at Hayward's Heath to bring together African and British intellectuals and politicians.
138 Conseiller Diplomatique auprès du Haut Commissaire de la République en AOF (Dakar) M. Bolle.

If I can leave Bamako by about Nov. 8th (it rather depends on boats and means of transport generally), proceeding by way of SEGOU, MOPTI, DJENNÉ, I would hope to arrive at Tombouctou (as they call it here) on about Nov. 16th (that again may be over-optimistic): stay there for 3 or 4 days – and that I think had better be the next address after Bamako:-

Chez
HAIDARA MAHAMAN[139]
TOMBOUCTOU
Soudan Francais
Fr. W. Afr.

(He is a friend of Claude G.[140] and said I could stay with him). Well, this chap don't seem to be turning up – so I had better go off and do some other work. Had lunch yesterday with Cornut-Gentille[141] – The High Commissioner – a nice chap, not formal.

To DMCH
25 October [1952]

Dakar
This is just to scribble a line to you before I leave for Bamako. Train goes at 5.10 p.m. – arriving 11 p.m. tomorrow. Watched the waves a bit this morning drinking with an elderly Socialist who was explaining his Party's policy to me, but it takes quite a lot of

---

139 Mahamane Alassane Haidara (1910–82) served as a senator of France from 1942 to 1959, then as a deputy and president for the National Assembly and a member of the Malian government, bringing Mamadou Dia the support of the north where Haidara's portrait was more widely hung than that of the country's President. He was imprisoned from 1968 to 1975.

140 Claude Gérard, left-wing Catholic editor of *Afrique-Informations* in Paris and had a broad range of contacts with the trade unionists and new politicians of Francophone Africa in the 1950s. She provided Thomas with personal introductions to friends in several African countries.

141 Bernard Cornut-Gentille (1909–1992), was in the Resistance Movement in France during the Second World War and was a préfet in France from 1944 to 1945. He became Governor-General of French Equatorial Africa in 1948 and was Governor-General of French West Africa from 1951 to 1956.

explaining, I think. It's rather restful to think of 30 hours in the train – going 2nd – a compromise between pocket and remaining reasonably bien vu. Actually the extra comfort will probably not come amiss.

To PEH
28 October [1952]

Bamako [French Sudan]
A nice little boy has been standing opposite me, as I sit in this cafe, singing quietly. It's a nice town full of trees, built just beside the river Niger, which I haven't yet visited. I believe Mungo Park came here at the end of the 18th Century, and was very pleased to find the Niger flowing from West to East, which he thought it did – people in Europe having previously thought it flowed from East to West, getting it mixed up with the river Senegal. It's a funny sort of river really (as well as a beautiful one) since it almost goes round in a circle. The one thing that seems to be important in Africa is not to be in a hurry – because nobody else is, and if you try to be something is bound to go wrong. Needless to say it's easier to believe this than to act on it. At the moment I am waiting for a car which was supposed to come here to pick me up at 9 – and now it's 9.15, but it hasn't yet appeared. Still, it's very nice to fill in the time writing to you. In the street women walk up and down in gay clothes, carrying large enamel or wooden basins full of fruit and vegetables on their heads – so do quite little girls. Boys come and offer one cigarettes. Men drive carts with rubber tyres, pulled by thin-looking ponies. Here and there are French people, among the Africans. Most of the Africans here are Bambara (which makes me think of Bamburgh, since you pronounce it in much the same way. A man opposite is carrying on his head an enormous load of gourds – big round jars for keeping water in. The men mainly wear long robes – white or blue or green – with sometimes red fezzes, sometimes black ones: sometimes white caps on their heads. Soon – though probably not till Saturday – I hope to start on the journey up towards the Sahara (not right into the Sahara, but up to the edge of it).

To DMCH? (Diary Letter)[142]
13 November [1952]

Douak [French Sudan]
We've stuck a bit, so here's a chance to write. This is being a pleasant journey by camel – enormously to be preferred to horses – from
the point of view of comfort of the saddle, exhilarating, as compared with disintegrating, sensation of trotting, and speed. We left
yesterday a bit after midday, and I have said that we shall get to
Walata tonight, but am inclined to think that is simply an idle
boast – particularly now we've come to rest here at about 8.30 a.m.,
having overshot the water where we should have stopped, and
having to send a lad back by one of our camels to get it. Meanwhile
a couple of women boil a kettle – having wandered here from the
nearby millet field, presumably for another nice cup of tea.

So far this journey is in every way preferable to the last –
camels apart. It's good open country, with this line of rocky hills to
the right all the way; these few fields of millet have been the only
sign of cultivation in what is practically desert – sand and stones –
with a certain amount of camel grass and thorn bushes. But one can
see a long way and that makes a lot of difference to one's enjoy-
ment of things. My main problem is to make my camel trot. I seem
to remember difficulties over that in Sinai in 1936, and, of course,
I am a bit out of practice. I do the kick (more or less) that I've been
told to do, but it only comes off about once in five times. One can't
really hurry enormously in these parts; and though I seem to be
getting a bit behind schedule it can't be helped. I shall have to cut
out Es-Suq, I expect, which is a long way NNE of Gao, and
would mean more camel rides, but otherwise I should be able to
manage with the Niger steamer. But this excursion into Mauritania
(?) is being well worth while – 'The party system in Mauritania in
its relation to the social background' would make a good respectable
academic subject. Actually there *is* a party system in M., the struggle being between the Entente M. and the Union Prog. M.[143], and

142 This letter is a transcript typed by DFH. The original is missing and
    the blanks are in the transcript.
143 Entente Mauritanienne founded 1946 and supporting Morocco-
    Mauritania union; Union Progressiste Mauritanienne-Parti du
    Regroupement Mauritanien founded in 1947 representing traditional

it appears that they compete as to which is the more conservative, traditionalist and 100% Moslem. UPM won the last elections on this racket. It has de Gaulle as its honorary President – he gave them a donation of 10,000 francs. EM is suspected of socialist tendencies.

Camelier with water back, so on we go, having picked up a travelling companion over our tea.

Halt for lunch. Feeling fairly jolted after a morning's trotting. Quite grateful for this pause. Also fairly warm. Lunch of a form of plain biscuits and dried meat – all right. Another round of tea – or rather, the traditional three rounds. Camped under a thorn bush. The way these camels eat these thorn bushes with spines a couple of inches long as though they were strawberries and cream is something surprising. We've picked up various friends for lunch – our travelling companion, and camel, who goes with us all today, a cheerful young Beduin who seems to have sprung out of the rocks and sand and has helped us over lunch, and two little boys – ?brothers. We've been travelling today over much the same country – very like the Aqaba region in some ways. This range of red hills on the right, desert with occasional protuberances on the left, crossing dry wadis now and again. Beautiful in its way. The lad has prepared a marvellous mess of chopped up biscuits, dried meat, sugar and hot water. I don't think I'm hungry enough to face it. I asked the gommier, Mohammed Abdullah, what it was called, and he said with a smile "matbukh" ("having been cooked"). About describes it. I have just told M.A. my name – Touma, owld Rabin, owld Touma, owld Hanna owld Touma etc. (They like good long pedigrees – preferably back to the prophet). We had a nice conversation about England last night. How much do rifles cost? What sort of game is there? How many of the English are nomads? (Answer a few thousands). Are the inhabitants of villages in England black or white? (They are usually black here, in contrast with nomads, who are usually white – i.e. Moors.)

Nov. 14th. KERI [French Sudan]
Dawn; waiting for our early morning cup of tea. Arrived here just as it was getting dark. Thankful to stop. I spoke a bit soon about

---

ruling classes and standing for Mauritanian independence against Morocco's claims.

the comfort of camel-riding. The first day we trotted very little. Yesterday we trotted almost the whole time. It tells on one. Though it is possible to keep going if one keeps oneself as loose as possible, and imagines that one is not oneself but a sack of potatoes that is bumping along, while one is only mildly interested in this sack of potatoes, and is concentrating on admiring the surrounding view. Now we are sipping our early morning cups of tea. There is only one charming and friendly nomad here, with tent and quite a lot of animals. He "disgorged" as they say a sheep for us again last night; (a bit extravagant, I thought, but the boys took it for granted), and produced some lovely bowls of sheep's milk, straight from the sheep with a rich froth on top. The way we kept this trot going yesterday was that one of my two companions always rode behind me, and if my camel ever showed signs of slowing down he stirred it up from behind. This meant occasional fearful bounds forward at a quick trot. (The sun has just risen). We had rather frequent stops in the evening, frequently meeting other travellers; and one always has to stop and talk, about the route and other matters. One party consisted of a handsome gommier from Timbedra, a friend of M.A.'s, who had been away as far as Goundam in the East and in the west, rounding up chaps who hadn't payed their taxes, and was taking them to Nema for judgement. Also we stopped because of the saddles, and for evening prayers etc. I don't think I told you how, when we stopped for the night at the small nomad camp, a handsome boy came out to meet us talking elegant French. Very nice and friendly he was. He was on his way from Walata to Nema for school (term started on Monday), riding on his ox, but was filling in time on the way giving a hand with the sheep.

I am fond of this country – these bare hills – that are partly reddish-pink and partly yellowish-grey, and the feeling that one is scouring a boundless plain.

WALATA [French Sudan] Nov. 15th.
Here in this exciting town. I would put it very high in the list of exciting towns and wish you were here to see it too. Perhaps not quite in the class of Bokhara and Samarkand – but close to it. Well worth two days being bounced around on the back of a camel to get here. Actually we did get here in the 2 days I said I thought we would, leaving at 1 p.m. on Wed. and arriving at about 2 p.m.

(judging by the sun) on Friday. Today we are taking it easy, having a leisurely breakfast – like Saturdays at home (sometimes). I have just drunk a lot of cafe-au-lait, and am about to have my 3rd. round of tea. There is really so much to tell you about that I wish I hadn't left myself with only this miserable little paper that you like to use for the people you don't want to say much to.

We are housed in a guest chamber on the upper floor – all the houses here have 2 storeys, the upper one reached by steps at least a foot deep – so it's quite a climb; next to walled roof garden, also a general feature. The whole wall of the room is painted in dark red paint, with the famous Walata designs, which one finds in every house here (more or less). They are almost too elaborate to copy, but I'll try on the next page. They are done entirely by the women, and ought to be renewed (traditionally) every year. Much else I have tried to copy in my note book. I have also bought, quite cheap, an ornamented leather bag, a pottery doll's house, and 3 pottery incense burners, basket-shaped.

I write during the siesta time. I don't want to siesta much, since I must take more photographs before getting caught up in more entertainment. We have been eating and drinking (quite unintentionally) since dawn. I can best describe the day by giving a programme of meals (times are approximate, as time, in the mathematical clock and watch sense, doesn't exist here).

7 a.m. Rise, cafe-au-lait bought.

7.20. Tea, 3 rounds, till

8. Mantu Idris, our host, appears, and invites us into his house down below.

8.15. Water-melon, chez Idris

8.30. Dates with sweet , biscuits and "ganat" – a sweet drink made from dates

9.15. 2nd. of 3 rounds of tea

9.30. Roast pigeons (I ate 3) and delicious hot batter puddings (round, a bit like Yorkshire pudding), followed by a further glass of tea.

10. 3rd. round of tea.

10.15. We call on Imam el Qadi[144] and his friends

---

144 'Imam' is usually used for the person who leads the Friday prayers at the mosque. 'Qadi' is judge. Thomas met Mohammed Jiddou Ould Mohammed who filled both roles at the time.

10.30. Biscuits and ground nuts

10.45. 4th. round of tea. (During this various children call with various things to sell – see above).

11.30. M.A. comes to say it is time to call on the Marabout ? Master of the Advanced Ecole Koranique. We don't because the Imam won't let us – food in the offing.

11.45. More pigeons (I only ate 2 this time) and lots of kuskus.

12.15. More tea.

12.45. Eventually got to the Holy Man, who has been kept waiting a shocking long time.

1. p.m. 5th. round of tea, chez Holy Man.[145]

1.30. 2 sorts of mutton, cooked in different ways (in the pot or on the fire), kuskus, a sort of spaghetti (2 bowls of it) and a kind of small vegetable marrow.

2. More tea.

And here we are. It's amazing how much one can put away if one has to, and if one hasn't eaten a great deal during the last few days. But the hospitality of this town is amazing. I really meant simply to see these chaps to get information from them. I didn't get a lot of information, owing to the weakness of my Arabic, and of the interpreting services available (not their lack of knowledge) – but this fantastic flow of food and hospitality.

M.A. is out seeing to camels. It's now evening. As always there's a bunch of children in our bedroom. One has a toy gun of a kind that Toby would love (and the rest of us hate). He pushes real gunpowder down the barrel with a ramrod and then puts a match to it. (I have forbidden him to do this in our bedroom). One little boy has been following me about all day and yesterday, ever since I arrived. In many ways he has been a helpful slave, but at times a little wearying. He speaks nice French and so likes to interpret. Also he carries my camera and my notebook, picks the [hairs?] off my clothes, brings me water to drink, heats water for poultices, tells other little boys to say "Good day, sir" (in French or Arabic, according to their capacity) to me properly. At times he produces tall stories, on which others throw doubt. E.g. he said that a rather primitive little tribe nearby, who live mainly by hunting with dogs, probably came originally from France, or else from the country of the Arabs.

---

145 Thomas is referring to Bou Ibn Mohammadi Ould Sidi Othman at the Koranic school.

Nov. 15th. Another halt for lunch. On the way "home", i.e. back to Nema now. A long march this morning, I should guess about 35 km. (5 hours at 7 km. an hour). We rose at dawn – before dawn; sun just rising as we wound down the hill from Walata. We are resting at the water-hole where we spent Thursday night. The boys seemed quite glad to see us back and offered another sheep. M.A. I'm glad to say refused, so we've lunched off dry biscuits and dried meat, not much of which I could face in the heat, and after yesterday's orgies. I've had a bit of sleep, but not much, since M.A. woke me saying he meant to sleep but his heart wouldn't let him, since he kept thinking of the road ahead. However his heart has let him spend the last half hour making tea and cleaning his rifle. Why is it, I wonder, that Arabs can always sit perfectly still, while we always restlessly wriggle, shifting from one uncomfortable position to another? Also, if there's nothing to do they just do nothing, and if they've nothing to say they just say nothing, whereas if we've nothing to do or say we just invent something. We've passed back out of the Ankar – the region of real sand, rippling and blown into strange Picasso like shapes (just like Bamburgh), back into the Hoodh, the region of sandy earth (uncultivable except as here, where there's water, and so a bit of millet) and camel-grass. Also (like Bamburgh) there's almost always a wind in these parts, blowing down from the mountains to the East. We've had a chief drop in for a cup of tea on his way home from Nema. A nice handsome elderly chap, with a lot of grizzled hair and a beard.

When I get back to Nema or Bamako I must write about Walata properly for you. One could make a very nice 3rd. programme broadcast of it: "Une ville qui meurt" as everyone calls it. A mixture of Maryport (as we knew it before the War), Basra, and any Oxford (male) Senior Common Room. Highly civilised donnish characters, whose life seems to be spent almost entirely in food and prayer, and remembrance of things past. I wanted to think that I was the first Englishman to visit Walata, but I'm afraid that this is not correct. Two came, they said, in the 1930's. I wonder who? Possibly author of "The Caravans of the Sahara",[146] which I carry

146 Edward William Bovill (1892–1966), educated at Rugby and Trinity College, Cambridge, published *Caravans of the Old Sahara*, 1933, and rewrote and updated it as *The Golden Trade of the Moors*, 1958.

round with me. (London Library copy). I fear Nowell Smith,[147] the nice young man who let us in after closing time so that I could recover my precious hat, will think it's a bit bent when it returns after several months in a rucksack. But I hope he'll think that adds to its real value). We are starting off again shortly – another 20,000 bumps before nightfall. Fortunately after a while one becomes so accustomed that (for a time) one becomes oblivious, and can hardly conceive of any other sort of existence. So I'll knock off this for the moment.

Nov. 17th. Halt for lunch – about 2 hours short of Nema. We have, I think, done rather well. Though by yesterday evening I was pretty exhausted and eventually refused to move except at the slowest pace. But M.A. was fine and kept us going, and we arrived at the Bedu encampment which he was seeking a little before sunset. And what bliss it is when one gets off one's camel and lies on one's back, and feels one's limbs gradually becoming one's own again, and watches the sky, and sees the stars come out, and the blue get blacker, and watches the lads make the fire, and drinks the first round of tea, and then the beautiful warm foam-covered milk, and then the handfuls of roast mutton. Living such a life one sees a bit more where Islam comes in: one would need a very simple religion which didn't make heavy demands on the intellect, but enabled one to keep going when things were bad, and to express one's relief and thankfulness when they got right again.

This is a nice spot beside a well, under a tree with a lot of orange-coloured berries, with many gay little birds hopping about – a bit like chaffinches, but smaller and prettier, with black and white striped heads. M.A. has been telling me some grim stories about bandits who kill their travelling companions with hatchets, to explain why it is that he doesn't like to sleep in the middle of the day. I have had two short but pleasant naps. (We are just passing on some of our meat to a caravan of 6 chaps, having had a lunch of excellent roast leg of mutton, and now on our 3rd. go of tea). M.A. has washed (with soap) and shaved. I have 5 days of good red

---

147 Simon Nowell-Smith (1909–96), educated at Sherborne School and New College, Oxford, was assistant editor of *The Times Literary Supplement* and served in Naval Intelligence in the Second World War. He was Secretary and Librarian of the London Library from 1950 until 1956 and was a scholar, bibliographer and book collector.

beard, but am leaving it for now. After all, M.A. has a wife at
Nema, but mine is in England.

We had only a 500 franc note (£1) to give in return for our
sheep last night, so M.A. saw to it that we had a fat one for our
money. He thought, though, that the "passagers" who dropped in
on our meal were having too much as compared with us, and said
at one point "You've had the head, the liver, and the lights – It's
about time the Christian and I had something; after all, it is we
who are paying for the sheep".

Nov. 18th. NEMA again [French Sudan]
Waiting for the lorry to take me to Bamako. Although we fixed it
all this morning I have my usual fears of being left behind, so have
just been into the town to make sure that that the lorry is still there
and will call for me. Having lived here now twice (for a day or so
each time) one more or less knows everyone in the place. So one
has a succession of conversations (in French or Arabic according to
the chap) about how we like Walata, and how far England is away
from here, and whether it is further than Mecca, and suchlike.

It really is in many ways quite a beautiful town (Nema) with this
situation on an inlet running up into the mountains; with a great
plain to the west; and these pink and yellow hills on the other 3
sides; and groves of palms here and there; and the orange-yellow
mud houses with their flat roofs; and the stray animals that wander
around (I found a donkey occupying the lavatory – a hard job to
turn him out); and martins and other birds flying all round the
buildings – often into the room and out again. And this great
wind that blows down from the hills almost all the day and night
(like Bamburgh), but particularly in the early morning. A young
ostrich, somewhat the worse for wear, is strolling across the quad
at this moment.

A bit tired today after all this camel – at the same time clean
(relatively), shaved, and in my right mind – only it's a bit full of
impressions at the moment, inadequately digested. And I doubt
whether I'll have time to digest them, unless I have it on the river
Niger, going down to Segou, Mopti, and Timbuktu. I shall have to
leave as soon as I can find transport from Bamako, since I've
already fallen a bit behind schedule; there's a boat, I know, leaves
tomorrow, but I've missed that, since we can't arrive at B. before
tomorrow evening at the earliest. But it's very good to think of

finding letters again, having been cut off from communications now for two and a half weeks. And I'm afraid there'll have been bad gaps in what you've had from me.

We arrived here in nice time yesterday evening, about 5 p.m., and I saw Saint-Gratien for a moment, bought some cigarettes (my last having disintegrated), went to the dispensary and found the nice elderly bearded infirmier there, who (though it was 6 or after) took enormous trouble dressing my boils – only 4, and only one of them at all nasty. (I'll see Vernier[148] again at B. and see if he wants to push in some more penicillin). Then shaved myself, wrote a little, and slept. St. G. called this morning at 7 – off on tour unfortunately, as I'd have liked some further talk with him. Did some odd jobs in the town, and then called on M.A. for dates, sennah, biscuits and tea. Several of his friends around, also (I take it) his pretty young wife. A curious sort of conversation. The cook here was reading a jolly good (Arabic) book and told me the plot. [I leave this out not because it wasn't a good story but to save my time D.F.H.]

We also had one of our usual conversations about current affairs, in the course of which M.A. showed that he'd remembered precisely the figures I had given him earlier for the populations of France, Britain, Germany, Italy, Spain, USA, USSR. This time we brought in also Turkey, the Arab States, and China. They were all struck by the fact (new it seems) that there are more Germans than French or British (or Arabs) and lots more Americans than any of 'em. Russians and Chinese don't interest them much. My general account is a simple one: unshakeable Franco-British friendship since 1915; menace of German aggression still a reality; lack of confidence in American ideas and methods. Reaction of Moors is "Don't worry about the Americans. There may be a lot of them but they are not a fighting race like the British and French". Attitude to Atomic Bomb, however, (of the cook anyway) was deplorably fatalistic. God made the earth and men for his pleasure, and if we are all blown to bits, that is no more than we have the right to expect. It's all foretold in the Koran anyway. However, it's also

---

148 Jean-Frédéric Vernier, born 20 January 1905, trained at the Ecole du Service de Santé Militaire at Bordeaux, became médecin colonel on 25 January 1945 and in 1952 and 1953 was local director for public health in Soudan (modern Mali).

foretold that Mohammed must spend 2000 years under the earth (?) before the end of the world, so by this reckoning we have some 731 years still to run – which gives us a breathing space.

This argument, that the earth and man were created simply for God's pleasure and will all be destroyed when he thinks fit, was supported by the cook's version of the Koran's version of the first few chapters of Genesis – told at great length with a wealth of detail. Some of it, e.g. Satan getting into the Garden of Eden by being swallowed by the serpent and so riding undetected – I remembered from the Koran; but the very jolly bit about Satan playing his guitar as he sat under the Tree of the Knowledge of Good and of Evil, and thus attracting ——, was new to me.

BAMAKO Nov. 23rd.

Now I can return to decent sized paper again. I have been in this pleasant hospital now for almost 3 days, and am beginning to feel a fraud. Fever entirely cleared up. No longer feeling even tired as I was yesterday. Nothing left but two boils which are rapidly getting cleared out. See no reason why I shouldn't go out tomorrow, and begin to organise the next stage. A bit of a bore to have lost half a week in this way, but it's one of the elements of uncertainty in a journey that one has to accept. And I don't suppose 3 days of idleness do one any harm. Now I'll try to fill in the gaps in this diary, so as to send it off tomorrow.

First, WALATA. It really is a remarkable town. It lies just under the brow of a rocky hill, or rather ridge of hills, standing up out of the sandy desert. It's the final habitation on the way north; the next water is 18 days away; the next inhabited place (I'm told) Taodini, the city of salt, 27 days. And for several centuries, from the 13th. on, it was a commercial city of the first importance, the meeting place for the caravans from North Africa and the caravans from the south – black Africa. Gold and silver from the south, textiles, manufactured goods, copper and salt from the north. And now it's a distressed area. Its economic basis was clearly decaying in the 19th. century, since the main trans-Saharan routes ran more to the east. But even when the French came, in 1912, it was still relatively prosperous. Now it's falling to bits. It has no function in the economy of AOF. The population has sunk to about 200. And all the vigorous young have gone elsewhere, to apply their commercial powers where trade now flows – Bamako, Timbuktu,

Dakar, etc. Those who are left depend for their living on cattle, camels, a bit of trade with local nomads, and shops which they own elsewhere, e.g. at Nema. Most of the houses are uninhabited and tumbling down, which makes the place look like one of those Haman towns. But those that remain are very impressive; stone built round a courtyard, with an entrance-hall; rooms opening out of the court; these steep stairs; and an upper story, with a roof garden; and an airy drawing room, where visitors are entertained. On the outer walls these cruciform designs. Wooden doors covered with several iron bosses with patterns on them. The rooms frescoed with these dark red patterns that I've tried to sketch. Niches, for cupboards, inset in the walls, with decorations running round them. Lovely highly ornamented red leather hangings and camel-bags. Incense burners. Doll's houses made of pottery for the children – made on the model of their own houses. And the great variety of interesting foods that I've described. And the few who live there are these highly civilised middle-aged to elderly men, who seem to spend their time (apart from commerce and attending to cattle) largely in meals and prayer. 5 times a day they go down to the mosque to pray. And before the time of prayer they sit on seats in front of the haram – you can meet everyone who matters there. The mosque itself is most exciting. The haram – like all the streets, indeed the whole town – is half-submerged with sand. But the mosque inside is undamaged, reminding one much of the Mosque of Aksa at Jerusalem, or indeed any early Christian Basilica. 4 long aisles, divided by 3 rows of 13 columns, with that kind of pinched ogee arch between broad columns of varying thickness. Said to have been built in the 8th. century (by tradition). I must find out what the authorities say. The plan seems certainly an early one.

I'll try not to write any more about W. now, since I'll have to write it up properly for David and so on. But it's a place to return to. Maulai Idris, our host, looked after us marvellously and refused any return. The grandson of M.Y. (a learned man, much travelled, and the author of several books) called late in the evening, full of apologies for not having invited us to his home, but he hadn't realised till late who we were. By then, I'm afraid, I was a bit tired, and my conversation rather flat; yet he later sent round a women of his household with an Arabic letter, which between us we did our best to make out; a leather ornamented ostrich egg; and a bowl of fresh milk; and Mohammed Bouy, a learned fat elderly man, dashed in before evening prayer with an account – in French – of the History of Walata that he had done.

A word or 2 about camels. Now that I've got reasonably used to it I'm all for camel-riding. My great mistake of course was not to realise that these were trotting camels, and therefore quite different in style from those we rode on Sinai; not that, had I realised this, I could have done anything about it. This means though that one can travel a good distance 40 miles in a day quite easily. What gives out are the legs, and to a lesser extent the back, simply from the strain of going on doing the same thing.

Another problem is getting him to lie down; this is done by dropping the cord, beating his head with a stick, and talking to him gently. (it doesn't always come off). Also the worst crime is to lose one's stick. It's like losing one's oar at rowing. By tradition one is fined a sheep for doing it (I did it 3 times I'm ashamed to say). All in all they are marvellous beasts, beautiful in their own way. There's nothing pleasanter than riding into one's camping place at the end of the day – with a slow stroll – one's feet crossed across the camel's neck – with all the bumps behind one. But while trotting one has several winds, I found. Always for the first quarter of an hour or so the motion seems fantastic and jarring: then one gets used to it and settles down – that's the first wind: then after an hour or so one begins to feel weary of it all, but the weariness goes off and one develops a 2nd. wind, when one begins to feel the camel and oneself one organism, uncertain of where one leaves off and the other begins. And then a 3rd. wind, later on, in which one is more oblivious of the outside world. And beyond this there are 4th., 5th., and 6th. winds – but after the 6th. wind has worked itself out, it's not so good.

A word about Mohammed Abdullah, the gommier who went with me. One couldn't have had a better or nicer man. As Hyperion to a satyr compared with poor C.M. Of course it's notorious that Englishmen love Bedus because they will behave as if they've been to the best public schools. But, even allowing for this, M.A. was a truly admirable chap. He'd never been to Walata before, but he never made a mistake about the route. Whenever he set himself a target he hit it. He didn't talk a lot but his conversation was always interesting. He had a very nice sense of humour. And he looked after me like a mother. He didn't care a rap about money. I was very sorry to say goodbye to him.

Another very good and intelligent Moor was the interpreter at Nema.[149] I learnt a lot from him about local history and a bit about Mauritanian politics, which will all come in useful, but isn't worth recording here.

I won't say much about the journey back from Nema to Bamako. It was, without question, the most unpleasant part of the whole excursion. No-one's fault but my own, for beginning to feel ill soon after it started. Quite rightly the chap who ran the lorry wanted to get back as quickly as possible. So we drove all through the night, and all through the next morning till 12.30, with one hour for breakfast; and one couldn't sleep because of the perpetual bumps on the fearful stony roads, and because, if one did, one fell on to the driver. And one couldn't keep one's leg with the boil on it still. So what with one thing and another it was penible, though it was a friendly crowd to travel with. But by morning one had got beyond enjoying friendly company, and only longed to stop, as eventually we did, having done about 600 km. from Nema, with 140 to Bamako to go. I tottered straight to the nice Commandant whom I'd had dinner with on the way north, and his wife gave me two liberal brandies and water. That and half an hour's chat made a lot of difference. Then 2 hours sleep, and new dressings at the Dispensary. So by the time we left – 4.30 or so – I felt much restored. However, then I made what turned out to be a mistake. S.G., the patron, said "It's getting late, there's a good restaurant at Kati. You eat and stay the night with me, and we'll go on next morning to B." I was in favour of doing whatever was simplest and agreed. Actually this S.G. was an odd chap; clearly a successful business man, also very hospitable. He only charged me 1000 francs for the whole journey, and fed us all continually on venison and guinea fowl that he had shot (stopping the lorry every now and then to shoot some more). He had an extremely charming wife and home in Kolokumi, and another much less charming wife and home at Kati; and pointed out that he really needed a 3rd wife and home at Nema, since this would round off his weekly run nicely. So we stopped at Kati, while the lorry went on to Bamako, and I had an excellent civilised meal of soup————[150]

---

149 Mohammad Abdullahi Ould Hassan, interpreter from Nema.
150 Later pages of this letter are missing.

22 November 1952
Telegram from Bamako 22 timed 0805 delivered Oxford, received
10.20 TSF deliver after 1 pm = LT= Hodgkin Somerville College
Oxford Angleterre Just returned Bamako resting here few days all
well journey successful how are your cold love Thomas

To DMCH
22 November [1952]

Hospital Bamako Saturday.
I feel a bit ashamed to confess that at the moment I'm in this
extremely comfortable hospital. Lest this should worry you at all let
me say that after less than 2 days I feel entirely restored – temperature normal – reading Mary Kingsley – and anxious to start eating
again. I suspect that it was common-or-garden malaria (or as they
say here 'Paludisme' – which sounds like an early Christian heresy),
in spite of the really religious way in which I have taken my one
mepacrine a day. But they haven't actually said yet. Anyway I
arrived by this lorry from Nema on Thursday morning feeling a bit
battered, and suspecting it was a little fever of some kind – found
the nice hotel hadn't actually got a room for that night, but would
have next day, and meanwhile they'd put me in a bed with screens
round it in the passage that leads to the bedrooms – so after beg-
ging a newspaper (having seen none for almost 3 weeks), some
aspirin and a thermometer and drunk several goes of delicious
orange juice, I retired – took 2 aspirin – and tried my temperature,
which I found to my surprise was 40: I did a little quick arithmetic
and found that 40° C = 104° F. It really was a surprise since I'd
been walking about, a bit battered, as I said, but perfectly capable,
and wondering what I wanted for lunch and suchlike. Anyway,
having as you know this tendency always to take such illnesses as
may crop up over-seriously, I decided I wouldn't stay in this passage if I could help it – and called out 'Hi' to the first chap I saw
passing thro' the passage to his room. By a great stroke of luck he
turned out to be the doctor from Nema, whom I had met at dinner
with Saint-Gratien, the Commandant, a very nice young man, who
got me shifted up here that same afternoon – where I have been,
am being, looked after admirably – and now feel perfectly well, if
a trifle weak – not surprising since they believe in injections like

anything in this place – injections of penicillin, of quinine, of something else to pep you up, and something else to make you sleep (that only the 1st night – when I was quite glad of it). Also they believe in taking lots of samples of your blood: otherwise it's quite free and easy. You can smoke, have visitors when you like and suchlike. I sent yesterday a little message down to Sheila Ogilvie[151] saying it would be nice to see her and could she bring me something to read. She sweetly brought me all the English reading she had (including Q. Durward[152] wh. I suppose I might face in desperation!) – but the best of her lot for me is Mary Kingsley's 'Travels in West Africa' – which I didn't know, and much enjoy and there's a lot of it. It's also a very nice hospital from the point of view of situation – on the top of a hill – looking out over hills. As I lie here – with doors wide open I see the garden close by and wooded hills stretching into the distance.

O and I should have said in my wire, thank you for the watch – I haven't actually collected it yet from the P.O. since I haven't had a chance, but I have a note requesting me to call for it. It's lovely of you to have taken all that trouble – and it will be enormously helpful to me.

To DMCH (Diary letter)
30 November [1952]

Page 1. (2nd series). *Timbuktu [French Sudan]. Nov. 30th.*
This is a fantastic kind of world, and can only be described in the language of fantasy. I arrived here last night from Goundam – having travelled by aeroplane from Segou to Goundam – without any clear idea as to the next stage, from Goundam to Timbuktu –

---

151 Sheila Ann Ogilvie, born 1909 and educated at St George's School for Girls, Edinburgh, and Edinburgh and Munich Universities was inspector of labour in Palestine in 1942 and assistant labour adviser to the Colonial Office from 1947. She was seconded as Director of the Inter-Africa Labour Institute at Bamako.
152 Walter Scott's *Quentin Durward* published in 1823 and set in 15th century France. The reading of Scott novels had been a holiday task of Thomas's preparatory schooldays and he was not a Scott enthusiast.

apart from knowing that it was about 90 kilometres, and that cars sometimes travelled between the two. However the Christian principle "Take no thought for the morrow" seems often to work in these circumstances: the commandant of Goundam,[153] whom I had met in hospital at Bamako, was on the same aeroplane, and he passed me on to an admirable French sous-officier (I am becoming very fond of sous-officiers, who are friendly and good company), who had come to Goundam to pick up a camarade who hadn't arrived. So off I set with him in an open Dodge to Timbuktu – not, of course at once, since there were various little odd jobs to do first, including stopping at the campement for a large cognac and water (most acceptable). Also the Dodge was in the common condition of only starting if six men pushed it. When we eventually got going it was getting on for sunset. I sat in the back, and with difficulty managed to avoid having my legs broken by the baggage as we went over the bumps. One had the alternative of looking in front of one and having the breath taken out of one's body with the wind, or of looking behind and having the car's dust in one's eyes. Most of the time I preferred the latter. It was a marvellous sunset. The road was the sandy kind, and once or twice we stopped when we saw gazelles, but the sous-officier wasn't quick enough to get a shot (for which I wasn't altogether sorry). It was all this semi-desert kind of country, with sand and low thorn-bushes, occasional nomad encampments and their animals, but no other signs of humanity. One great eagle sitting on the top of a tree. Then it became dark. The moon (almost full) appeared, and the evening star, and gradually the other stars. It got jolly cold, and after bearing the almost freezing wind for a while, I wrapped myself up in one of the two Soudanese rugs I now carry around with me. Then we lost our way, and kept, whatever we did, landing up face to face with a great lake. The Dodge anyway travelled like a tank, leaving the main track whenever the driver thought fit and traversing the open country, through thorn bushes, and anything else of medium size that stood in our way. So we had to retrace our steps, and

---

153 Jean-Marc-Albert Genevière, born 17 April 1918 at Poitiers (Vienne), France, studied law and at Ecole Nationale de la France d'Outre-Mer, colonial cadet from August 1940, promoted administrateur adjoint des colonies August 1941; from 1952 Commandant du Cercle at Goundam.

eventually found our way back to a parting of the roads, where we had taken the wrong road (wrong at any rate for this time of year, when there is a lot of flood water about). But it was a nice way in which to arrive at Timbuktu, in the moonlight, to the sound of tom-toms: (apparently it was the prophet's birthday last night, so the Imams read the Koran at night and nobody went to bed).

Goundam [French Sudan]. December 6th. At this point my good intentions were interrupted by the arrival of the friendly sous-officier, sergeant-chef Verollet,[154] and a bearded French commercial to take me out to lunch in the Sous-officiers' popote (mess). This lunch began at 11.30 a.m. and went on until midnight, when, in spite of protests (an argument was then going on which, I was told next day, didn't finish until 4 a.m.) I managed to extricate myself. Since then I haven't had a chance to go on with this – partly, I admit, because I thought I had better write my Timbuktu article for David[155] while the place was still fresh in my mind; partly because once it was dark at Timbuktu, in the very primitive campement, it *was* dark – with only one lamp shared among half-a-dozen people, all the others having better claims to it than I.

As I began to say, when I arrived in Timbuktu, I found myself at once in a fantastic world. A nice fat man rolled over in bed, talked a little English, and, when I said I was hungry, procured me a sausage sandwich and a glass of red wine – very welcome after that extremely cold drive. Later I found that he was a middle-aged French civil engineer from Douala (French Cameroons) on his way back to Nice for his leave. He had suddenly decided to visit Timbuktu on his way home, believing it to be an exciting town (as indeed, in its own way, it is); left the boat and his wife in Abidjan; had a miserable few days travelling by camion across country to Segou, where he picked up the Niger boat for Kabara (the port of Timbuktu); found himself stranded in Timbuktu for eight days till the next boat, decided at once that Timbuktu was a hopeless and miserable town (in comparison with Nice, or even Douala), with nothing to see or do. "Not worth spending five minutes on, and I have been here for eight days." Most of the time he seemed to spend in sleep, dreaming of Nice, refrigerators and cold beer. For all that he was a kind and friendly soul, who took me to see the

---

154 Sergent Chef Jean Verollet, from Meylan, Isère, France.
155 David Williams; see notes to letter of 27 February 1951.

commandant[156] and Rene Caillie's[157] house, and was willing to be bored for two hours while we visited the mosque of Sankaré.[158] Eventually he caught the boat for Gao, and I hope is now on his way back to Nice by the trans-Saharan bus.

The other inhabitants of the campement were:- an enormous lion-huntress (French) in her late sixties; her plump amiable daughter – developing the same way (from the point of view both of bulk and occupation); an elderly French painter, badly wounded in the first World War (painting with his left hand, since his right was unuseable), and his young wife. Perhaps it is not entirely accurate to call the lady a lion-huntress, since, though she told me when we first met that she caught the lions by putting salt on their tails, she admitted afterwards that this was a fairy story. She was really a lion-middlewoman, buying from the local inhabitants not merely lions but leopards, panthers, ostriches, and indeed anything in the way of wild animals that she could lay hands on, and selling them again for a substantial profit to a German zoo. The market rate for ostriches in Timbuktu, I learned, was £3, but a lion would fetch as much as £100. (I thought of investing in an ostrich, as relatively cheap, but decided that it would be too difficult to take around with me. Sorry.) Actually, while I was there, the only animal that turned up was a young gazelle, that hung around the campement, rather miserably: this was a disappointment. But this huntress had enormous professional enthusiasm. When I told her that I might have to return to Goundam by camel (in the end I hitch-hiked on a military lorry), she at once said there were enormous tortoises on this route, and would I collect some for her. At the same time she traded with the inhabitants of Timbuktu in European fancy goods, smart combs and artificial flowers, and suchlike. A remarkable and enterprising woman.

---

156 Commandant du Cercle de Tombouctou Joseph-Léon-Roger Vezy, born 14 January 1911 at Sète (Hérault), France, on military service from 21 October 1935 to 4 October 1936, qualified at Ecole Nationale de la France d'Outre-Mer, colonial cadet from November 1936, promoted administrateur adjoint des colonies December 1937, administrateur en chef 1 January 1952.

157 René Caillié (1799–1838), French explorer, first European to reach Timbuktu and return alive, in 1828.

158 Sankaré Mosque in the centre of Timbuktu dates from the 14th century and forms part of the oldest university in sub-Saharan Africa.

The painter was a quieter character, very nice. Unfortunately his wife had malaria the last day I was there, with a temperature of 105 – I hope she's now got over it. The women cooked together, in the intervals of trade, under conditions of extreme squalor, while the painter painted handsome young men, Arabs and Tuaregs, who wouldn't stand still. It was an interesting kind of Bohemian society – very friendly – which gave one the impression that the Quartier Latin had been transported to Timbuktu.

I had almost all my meals with the Popote of the sous-officiers (except for dinner one night with the local doctor and his young wife, who travelled about the desert together). Casse-croute at 8 a.m., dejeuner at 12 and dinner at 7.30. I was therefore enormously well fed, and wined: I have never come across such a kind and hospitable collection of people. I was reminded of a poem (in the Spirit of Man – I have forgotten who by) – 'I remember a house where all were kind / to me, God knows, deserving no such thing.' They would take no money in return, and only asked to become abonnés to *West Africa*. They were an interesting collection of people too. In addition to my original friend Verollet (full of excitement since he was about to return to France on leave, after serving his 33 months at Timbuktu), there was adjutant-chef Benquet, a charming middle-aged man who had had about 25 years service. He had been in Syria during the last War (accidentally on the wrong side) and had been taken prisoner by the British after a vigorous defence of Palmyra, against a much larger British force. He had (I am glad to say) been well treated by the British, who took him to Latrun, fed him well (though he didn't think much of the beer) and gave him free cigarettes and cinema-passes. He was fond of singing, and every now and then would break into song (usually amorous). He had interesting ideas about the country – not very sympathetic to the idea of political advance, with a poor opinion of the capacity of Africans to undertake any kind of responsibility, except under strict supervision (not an uncommon view). He thought that France's policy since the war had been the consequence of loss of 'face' during the war. I argued that there had been comparable developments in the British West African territories, but he said that only showed that the British had lost face too. There was also a young radio N.C.O. who had spent 6 years in a catholic seminary (?intending to become a priest). He loved theological and political argument, and after drink tended to shout everyone else down. We had a long dispute about whether Protestants were heretics from a Catholic point of view: he denied that they were. He thought little of Maritain as a philosopher, and preferred (curiously) Voltaire and Jean-Jacques Rousseau. There was also another very nice chap, concerned with radio, who looked after the mess (and me), quiet and intelligent. Almost all of the local sous-officiers had local 'wives'. These cost, on an average, 2000 to 3000 francs (CFA), i.e. about £4 to £6, and two or three new 'boubous' (cotton gowns). This became quite expensive if one changed often, as many of them did. Sergeant-chef Verollet, for example, had had seven during the past 9 months. The general opinion was that the 'wives' of Timbuktu compared unfavourably with those that they had had in Indo-China – being disinclined to do any work in the home. This helped to account for the relatively high turn-over. (They most of them had served in Indo-China, and were fond of the country, though they had some pretty grim stories to tell of the campaigns there.) The rest of the sous-officiers stick in my memory less clearly, though all were extremely friendly and good company. The last night a fresh party arrived from Taodeni (the centre of the salt-mines in the Sahara, several hundred kilometres to the North). The French privates had a separate mess, where I once had lunch; among them was a charming good-looking Breton from Saint-Brieuc. His father, mother and all his elder brothers had been sent to concentration camps, or forced labour in Germany, by the Nazis, since a local informer had let them know that the family had a store of grenades, hidden in the house. He had exciting stories to tell of how the Breton fisher boats used to evade the Nazi coastguards and aeroplanes, and meet British submarines out at sea. One of his brothers had been killed in Germany by allied bombers. But the rest of the family was still living.

The popote insisted that I should write an article about them in *West Africa*, saying what good chaps they were – so I must try to do this. They have also asked for a French edition of the paper.

One consequence, of course, of the amount of time spent over meals and drinks in the popote was that I had less time for Timbuktu than I had hoped to have. Also in the end I only stayed there four days, since I thought I had better take advantage of an army car, taking the colonel and his aviators back to Goundam at 3.30 a.m. on Thursday morning. This meant another perishingly cold drive, but it at least ensured that I got to Goundam safely to catch the Saturday afternoon aeroplane to Gao. I won't say much

here about historic Timbuktu, since I have already put most of
what I want to say into my article for W.A. It is, in many ways, a
beautiful town – particularly at this time of year when it is surrounded by little pools and lakes where women wash themselves
and their clothes, children bathe and camels drink. It lies, of course,
at the edge of the boundless desert – or rather of this semi-desert
of baked sand and thorn bushes that stretches for miles on both
sides of the Niger. At one end of the town are 'the usual offices' –
commandant's house and office, campement, military camp, dispensary and small hospital (a bigger one is in process of building),
Europeans' houses and such like. These are only about a quarter of
a mile from the centre of the town, where there is an ugly modern
stone-built market, full of the usual gaiety and life – sugar and
matches, bright leather shoes and stuffs, fly-ridden meat, red pep-
pers, tobacco, dates and suchlike – a lot of business going on all the
time. This lies in a square, on all sides of which are shops – two
European stores, one Syrian, the rest African – all seeming to sell
much the same thing. In the square sit many men with sewing
machines, working away making boubous. In the central streets
leading to the square are the grander houses where the merchants
and men of substance live. These are beautiful – built in what one
imagines is the traditional Timbuktu style: four engaged columns,
two on either side of a central door; the door itself of wood, covered with iron knockers and bosses, elegantly carved – in the better
houses; in what are called the houses of deuxieme qualité hammered on ornamented bits of petrol tins take the place of iron, and
the bosses are smaller and fewer, with less design. The door-posts
are decorated with a kind of vine pattern, usually two rows of it,
painted red, blue or yellow. These houses are of two storeys – with
elegantly carved wooden casements (floral pattern) on the second
storey, reminding one of a set for Romeo and Juliet, or Beshir
Balith's house at Aleppo.[159] Like traditional Arab houses too they

---

159 This is a reference to the Balith family and their modest house in
     Aleppo where Thomas stayed for a few days in August 1936. He had
     resigned from his post in the Palestine administration and was trav-
     elling in Syria and Lebanon before returning to Britain to try his
     hand at school teaching. The reference could have been obscure to
     Dorothy since Thomas's travelling companion in Aleppo was Lady
     Prudence Pelham (1910–52) who had studied under Eric Gill in
     Jerusalem. See notes to letter of 21 June 1954 below.

are built around a central court – usually not very large, with a verandah, cloister-like, running round the second storey. All the older houses are built of banco, but there is a tendency now for the better-to-do to build in stone, under European influence, with not very happy results. (I was shown round one morning by a local builder, rather a bore, very proud of the modern style.)

In this area are the houses of the great men who visited Timbuktu: Gordon Laing[160], who was killed here in ?1825; Rene Caillie who spent a fortnight here in ?1827 and got safely away to North Africa across the desert, representing himself as an Egyptian Moslem; and Barth,[161] the German explorer, who visited the town in the 1850's. (The fact that there are large signposts pointing to all these houses, together with the odd collection of people who turn up in Timbuktu, myself included, gives the whole place the appearance of being a tourist centre – a sort of small-scale Venice. While I was there a couple of American Protestant pastors, extremely young and clean-limbed, turned up, looking for a house for the younger of them, intending to start a mission. The sous-officiers showed a proper scepticism about the intentions of this mission, and took for granted that it was more a matter of getting information about the country than winning souls for Protestantism – Baptism to be exact. The citizens of Timbuktu are, one gathers, not easy to convert – the White fathers having been there for some time, without, apparently, having won a single soul.)

Further from the centre of the town are the three mosques – Djinguéréber, Sankaré and Sidi Yahia. The first two according to tradition (likely to be accurate) belong to the 14th Century, and the third to the 15th. Mauny thinks though that none of the existing buildings is earlier than the end of the 16th. century. Of the three Djinguereber is much the most impressive, as well as the largest. It was originally built on the orders of Mansa Musa,[162] King of Mali, on his return from his state visit to Mecca. The main present

---

160 Major Gordon Laing (1794–1826), British explorer, reached Timbuktu but was killed by his Berabish escort on his return journey.
161 Heinrich Barth (1821–65), German explorer and scholar, travelled widely through the West African Sahel and spent eight months in Timbuktu in 1853 and 1854.
162 Mansa Musa reigned as King of Mali from 1312 to 1337; his pilgrimage to Mecca, through Egypt, in 1324 left a deep impression on Egypt of the wealth of Mali in gold.

building consists of two parallel basilicas – one longer and one shorter (22 columns as compared with 10) each containing four rows of columns, which gives you, in the wider part, nine parallel aisles. Outside is a double haram – two surrounding walls. The whole building looks very uneven, being propped up with buttresses all over the place, and having been so often rebuilt – but beautiful none the less. Sankare was the great university centre. It and Sidi Yahia are also both built on a basilica plan, but less grand and elaborate. Sidi Yahia was shockingly restored in 1939 by a commandant with a passion for improvement.

On the outskirts of the town, away from the European quarter, are the suburbs of the poor – round huts of straw in the main, with occasionally a mat worked in to make a door, set, often three or four together, in a compound surrounded by a mud-brick or thorn fence – with some cooking going on, or millet grinding, and a few hens running around. This is where the Bela – traditionally the servile classes (serfs rather than slaves, since there is the duty of protection in return for service), now citizens of the French Union like anyone else, but still (I was told) regarded as servile. The headmaster of the Medersa (primary school), a very intelligent Algerian, told me that among the Tuareg (the nomads of this area, many of whom in fact become settled) one finds five social classes: the 'guerriers' (ahil el mudafi'a); the marabouts (holy men); the 'forgerons' (which he said was a French mistranslation of the Arabic mu'allimin – i.e. the men who know a craft – which may be iron or leather work or cultivation); the griots (who sing songs – an even more low-grade occupation); and the serfs. This wants more looking into, but it seems a rough approximation to the traditional social system. What would be interesting to investigate is – how far has this been upset by the new forces at work – the son of the griot or the serf who goes to school and gets a Govt. job? But apparently among the Tuareg one finds individual tribes which are traditionally tribes of guerriers, or marabouts, or forgerons, or griots.

When I was there the outskirts of the town were full of camels, which had come across the desert from Taodeni laden with bars of salt. These bars are about a metre long, by 40 cm. across by 3 cm. thick, and sell, I was told for about 550 francs each (i.e. about 23 shillings). Each camel can carry four. The salt producer gets the value of one bar and the camel-owner and transporter the value of three. In return they buy tea, sugar, millet, stuffs and suchlike.

These camel trains come in twice a year. It seems one of the few surviving traces of Timbuktu's ancient commercial relations with the north. Though the salt is taken to other centres (I saw some bars and camels at Gao too), Timbuktu still seems to be the main market and distributing centre for the Soudan, and further afield.

What else about Timbuktu? I talked to the Imams of the three mosques, but didn't make a lot of headway with them. Maybe it was language difficulties, but I don't think they were anyway learned men. There is apparently an elderly learned man in Timbuktu, whose name I was given but failed to see. He is writing the lives of the great scholars and teachers of the Tekrur of the past (like Ahmed Baba)[163]. There are also eight or ten (private) Koranic schools in T.

It was pleasant too to sit in the shop of Khalil Baba, friend and political supporter of Haidara Mahaman (he has Haidara's photograph on the wall of his shop). He himself is not very talkative, but there was a young man who worked with him who expressed what I guess is a fairly representative point of view of the younger men, particularly the educated young. He actually was 40, and had lived for 9 years a roaming life, working in various places in AOF. He had even walked with a drove of cattle from Timbuktu to Ashanti (in the Gold Coast) where he could get a better price, and then gone on to Lomé in French Togoland to change his pounds into francs. It is a risky business, he said, since if you don't sell your cattle at once they die. It is interesting the way these chaps get about. I wish one could get more information about population movements. One is continually meeting people who have brothers in Kano, and have spent time there, or have come to the Soudan from French Togoland, or have been to school in the Gambia, and suchlike. While on the subject of travel the question of the Hajj is interesting. Even in as Moslem a town as Timbuktu it seems that not many make the hajj. If you do it the official way, as organised by the administration, it is of course damnably expensive. You go via Casablanca, Port Said, etc., and need a lot of documents as well as cash. There is also an air service for those who can afford it. I was told that about four from Timbuktu and the area made the hajj

---

163 Ahmed Baba, died 1626/7, great Timbuktu scholar carried into exile in Morocco after the Moroccan invasion of 1591, returned to Timbuktu 1607/8.

last year in these ways. But occasionally an enterprising Moslem will go the traditional way, by camel across the desert, and not bother about visas. One man I was told had recently gone all the way on foot, with his luggage on a camel (which is a holier way of doing it), and had taken three years over the journey.

To return to this young man. What Timbuktu needed, he said was 'modernisation' – above all better communications. At present it is entirely cut off from the outside world for part of the year, since it has no airfield of its own; the road to Goundam is unusable in the rainy season, and the Niger boats only run for part of the year. Commercial development, he said, depended above all on an all-the-year transport service. He also wanted a better water supply – more wells; a better health service (there is a small hospital, which is being enlarged, particularly for maternity cases); more technical education – 'artisanat', so as to produce more and better-quality goods in Timbuktu – building, weaving, leather-work and suchlike. (But the French, some of them, argue that the Soudanese won't use wide looms even if you encourage them). From this chap I gathered too that there is some competition between African firms and French and Syrians – the latter tending to monopolise the external trade, and sell European goods to the African trader. This perhaps is general in West Africa. It is another topic that wants more investigation.

It was interesting to visit the Medersa and talk to this Algerian headmaster (whose name I should have written down but haven't) Originally these medersa (or mudaris?) were designed as schools for the sons of chiefs and notables. But now, the headmaster said, they are tending to follow the current of the age and become 'democratised'. He takes as far as possible any child whose parents want him to come – sons of griots and forgerons included, both nomad children and local boys. (In this respect his school is different both from the école régionale across the road, which caters only for Timbuktu children, and from the école nomadique, which – as its name implies – is only for the children of nomads). There is, apparently a good deal of resistance on the part of nomads to having their children educated at all. Some, he told me, are willing to pay as much as 10,000 francs to get out of it. The goumiers scour the country and collect children from unwilling parents, it seems. But as the nice intelligent French headmaster at Goundam said, it isn't always all that different in England or France. Anyway, according to the Headmaster, there is a general preference for his school, since you learn Arabic there, and this carries with it some social prestige. French still remains the basic language. He would like to do more Arabic, but the difficulty is to find teachers who can teach it properly. We talked a bit about architecture too, and the special characteristics of the Timbuktu house. He also has a theory (over which he disagrees with Mauny) that arches are in the Soudanese or Timbuktu tradition. Certainly you find them in the mosque of Sankare.

Bamako. 8/2/52. Back here again, having got up at 5 this morning to catch the aeroplane from Gao, which gets in at midday. Met at the airport by Haidara Mahaman, which was extremely nice of him. Very nice too to receive a batch of letters which had gone to Timbuktu and been forwarded to him here, owing to my foolishness in not warning him in time about this. Nice to be in this friendly French family hotel again, with duck and potatoes cooked in olives for lunch, and orangeade (orange pressé, that is). All the boys here very friendly and welcoming too, including the waiter from Timbuktu, who makes me sit at one of his tables. Nice when queuing in the post office for a quarter of an hour, while a very tired clerk deals slowly with telegrams, to meet the editor of 'Essor' (the RDA paper here) and a young Moor who had travelled back from Nema with me. I am concentrating on finishing this instalment – which is pleasant and restful – for the rest of today, leaving tomorrow for serious work. Back to Dakar by train the day after.

From Timbuktu I went back to Goundam for a couple of days. I can't pretend I did much that was useful there, but found Goundam a very pleasant and friendly town – with an intelligent and kind commandant (the commandant at Timbuktu reminded me a little of Geoffrey Hickson,[164] polite, but obviously finding life a tiring business.) The small French community at Goundam all know one another very well, live round a kind of campus, and everyone is continually entertaining everyone else. I had an excellent dinner with the commandant, and next day with the headmaster, and the large director of public works drove me over

164 Geoffrey Fletcher Hickson (1900–78), educated at Uppingham and Clare College, Cambridge, was Secretary of the Board of Extra-Mural Studies at Cambridge from 1928 to 1967.

to Diré (the Niger port for Goundam) in his Dodge one morning. A lot of sheer kindness. Also I met in the campement the fat chap with whom I had travelled on the boat from Koulikoro, collector of crocodile skins and gallant with the American girls from Liberia, another kindly soul.

The headmaster is a Bergsonian, who put the Bergsonian theory about intuition and all that very well, I thought (I confessing myself somewhat anti-Bergsonian). He also played us Petrouchka on his gramophone until late into the night. It was the feast of the baptism of the Prophet, and one went out from Petrouchka to hear the Tom-toms in the moonlight. I didn't actually go and join in, but it was pleasant to hear, and everyone else danced and ate until late. The headmaster, M. Demolliens[165], showed me his school. One class was learning the geography of the Sudan; another was doing general science (the elephant); another was singing French songs, and put on the one they knew best for our benefit; the little ones were learning to write (French, of course). More interesting in a way was the school for nomad girls, run by Mme Demolliens. It is the only one of its kind in the Soudan. The girls range in age from 10 to 15, and apparently hate coming to school. One is married. They are all boarders, and spend nine months of the year at school. They sleep in beds and have douches, to which they are not accustomed. A bit pathetic in a way was the fact that in the sandy courtyard of the school they had built little model tents, like doll's houses, suggesting that that was still the way in which they really wanted to live. They were all what is called in these parts 'beidan' (i.e. white): that is to say their skins are brown, and they have great mops of wild straightish or wavy hair. They looked a bit like captive animals, and very charming too. The Demolliens' little boy sat in the front row of the class (since there is nowhere else to put him), drawing pictures and distracting the girls. (There is quite an interesting difference in practice between this school, where the girls have beds and modern conveniences, and the Timbuktu medersa, where the boys just camp around the place, and live in their own style.)

I had an interesting dinner with the Demolliens (and also drinks next morning). There was [a] French engineer there who was

---

165 Armand Demolliens, headmaster of Ecole de Goundam.

putting the 'colonial' point of view: that Africans were either unintelligent and lazy, or good workers and 'political'. It had been better in the past before they had been encouraged to become uppish by all this new-fangled legislation. In theory he had nothing against white men working under black ones, but in practice they just weren't qualified to undertake responsibility. This was obviously not Demolliens' view, who was arguing that Africans had essentially the same intellectual equipment as Europeans, and were therefore capable of reaching the same intellectual and technical levels. The engineer was also much against 'literary' education, which he thought produced people who thought themselves superior and were useless as workmen. 80% of those who went to French Universities he thought came back anti-French. "They organise these things better in the Belgian Congo".

At the same time Demolliens was sceptical about the possibility of *knowing* anything about Africa. "After one year here I thought I knew all the answers. After two years I still thought I knew, but with more hesitation. After three years I began to realise my judgments were mistaken. After five years, if anybody asks me, all I can say is 'j'aime l'Afrique'". Teaching, he thinks, is entirely a matter of joie de vivre, and not of pedagogy or techniques. A nice and intelligent man, even when one disagrees with him. One of those who lead devoted lives and don't (I should guess) care about promotion and advancement.

I also spent some time reading a history of Goundam, written by a former French headmaster – of a Herodotean kind – mainly good stories which he had collected from the people of the place.[166] Goundam was founded, traditionally, in the fourteenth century by a daughter of Mansa Musa, king of Mali, who (like Cinderella) didn't get on with her sisters. The main impression which one got from reading it (and perhaps was intended to get) was of the fearful anarchy of the 18th and 19th century, when Goundam, like other towns in the area was ravaged in turn by the Moroccans, Tuaregs, Fulani, Kounta Arabs, famine and epidemics. True enough, I think.

Goundam is beautifully situated, among long low hills, reddish

---

166 This was an unpublished typescript entitled '*Histoire de Goundam depuis sa fondation*' prepared by geographer Roger Rubon in 1941 for use in the school.

in colour, with pools running up either side of it. It also has some good houses, different in style from Timbuktu – symmetrical around the axis of a central door, two-storied, with engaged columns running up the face, ending in points. These columns may be as many as 12 in the wealthiest houses. Instead of windows they tend to have triangular niches.

The journey to Diré turned out rather pleasantly. It is an unexciting little port, except for canoes drawn up along the banks or being paddled along the river. I wandered around the town a bit, and the gay but rather mean market (Public Works is building a new one, of stone.) I had meant to go on and visit the school, but was hailed in Arabic by a chap in a beautiful clean white boubou. He turned out to be a merchant whom I had met on the boat from Koulikoro to Segou, another of Haidara's friends. With him I went into the shop of his friend (whom I'd also met on the boat) Ishaga Bâ, and spent the morning pleasantly there, chatting and drinking tea. (It was the first sweet green tea that I had had for a week, and was very welcome.) As you might expect, the world passed through the shop while I was there. Not that anyone seems to buy anything much, and not that Ishaga Bâ seemed in the least interested whether anyone bought anything or not. He sat on a mat with me and other favoured visitors, quietly making tea, and if anyone looked as though they were for business rather than for company it was a large handsome woman who had to deal with them. Ishaga Bâ really belongs to Timbuktu (another example of migration from old to new centres of commerce.) A young man, the postmaster from Goundam, was there spending his 3 months leave. Various elderly Arabic-speaking cronies dropped in. Also some Tuaregs with their turbans, swords in elegant leather sheaths, and collection of leather pouches (for keeping gri-gris,[167] or money, in) hanging over their chests. Also some Hausa traders from Niger province, young lads. I used to wonder why Africans don't have cafés, but of course shops fulfil the same social function – to meet one's friends and pass the time away.

From Goundam I went by air to Gao on Saturday afternoon. I won't say much about Gao, as I was (unfortunately) only there for Sunday, and this instalment is anyway by now long enough. I

---

167 Gri-gri is an amulet (holding verses of the Koran, or holy charms and tables bound in leather).

made the mistake there of not calling on the commandant[168] (thinking that he wouldn't want to be bothered on a Sunday). Eventually I met him by chance in the hotel at 7 p.m., and he turned out to be a very friendly chap, interested in archaeology, who would have taken me in the afternoon out to see some tombs, had I seen him in time. 'une bêtise' I said – 'pas une bêtise – trop de discretion' he replied. Anyway he did very kindly take me off and show me some more of these extremely beautiful 12th Century tombs of the Songhai royal family. The inscriptions are all in Arabic, and they give the actual Hejira date of the death of the king, queen, prince or princess concerned. The most beautiful are in Qufic characters, some of them with elegant floral designs, or other patterns, round the borders. These are believed to be of Spanish workmanship. The rest are in ordinary Arabic characters, with a much less masterly standard of craftsmanship – presumably locally done. Three of these stones (they are marble, the better ones) are embedded in the wall of the mosque, with a nice French plaque below one of them, reminding the Songhai people of the greatness of their past, and explaining that if they only work hard they can do the same again. The commandant, M. Raynaud, told me that the whole area is full of tombs, simply waiting to be excavated. Old Gao, he thinks, from the superficial remains, must have been a very large city, at least 12 square kilometres. And there are traces of habitation to be found all along the valley that leads to Kidal and Es-suq. It made my mouth water to go there, as I had originally intended, but money (in the form of ready cash) has almost run out, and so has time – if I am to get my visa renewed before it expires in a week's time, and put in this visit to Portuguese Guinea before Christmas. Perhaps we can take it on the way home – since it lies directly, or almost directly, on the trans-Saharan bus route to Colombe-Béchar, and this seems as good and interesting a way home as any other? M. Raynaud told me also that there are still citizens in Gao who have 'tarikhs' (i.e. Arabic histories of the country) in their possession, which can be copied. He showed me too the rubbing of exciting

168 Jean-Marius Raynaud, born 20 August 1912, at Alby-sur-Chéran (Haute-Savoie), France, on military service from 19 October 1936 to 1 October 1937, qualified at Ecole Nationale de la France d'Outre-Mer, colonial cadet from December 1937, promoted administrateur adjoint des colonies December 1938; in 1952 Commandant du Cercle at Gao.

gold coin, with an Arabic inscription, which he had recently come across – also he thinks of the 12th. Century. But he believes that excavation would enable one to find out a good deal about the pre-Islamic period.

Early on Sunday morning I went to see the minaret and mosque of Mohammed Askia – Askia the great – late 16th Century, but like all buildings in banco, presumably frequently rebuilt since. One can't pretend this is a very impressive building architecturally: less good than the Timbuktu mosques, but interesting because of its associations. I picked up the usual man on a bicycle and couple of small boys to show me round. With their help I then found my way to an area where there are still traces of the old Gao, in particular a mosque, with its mirhab, built of brick (or rather foundations of the mosque). This must, I think be 14th century, the mosque built by orders of Mansa Musa. Some good brick tombs in this area too. Indeed over a very large area one finds innumerable tombs, large and small, and a mass of sherds. I went back to the Askia mosque in the afternoon, photographed it a bit, and walked round the old Songhai village (all that was left of Gao by the time Barth visited it in the 1850's) – a poverty-stricken collection of huts, made of matting, just beside the Niger. I seemed here to pick up a crowd of small, mainly naked small boys, who asked for cadeaux, but meanly I refused to give any except to two who had tried to help me (one carrying my shoes round the mosque, to prevent them from being pinched). The modern town of Gao is unexciting. It lacks style, being entirely a product of the period of French administration. Houses compare very unfavourably with Timbuktu, or even Goundam.

I arrived back at the hotel a little before sunset. Everything looking very beautiful – the canoes, the Niger, the green marshes beyond and beyond that a line of pink hills. Then there was the noise of tom-toms and a large crowd appeared, with two smallish boys playing the tom-toms and a somewhat Bacchanal griot dancing and singing, mainly in English, I think, though the only words that I could detect were 'master, kind master'. He took cigarettes out of people's hands and turned them into 5-franc notes, and then proceeded with awful gurglings to produce enormous quantities of pins out of his mouth, and apparently out of his stomach: later he proceeded to turn a bundle of pins into a bottle of cheap scent, which he insisted on dabbing onto all of us. I asked one of the 'boys' where he came from – he was clearly not a local – and he said 'Angleterre'. I thought this improbable. In fact it seemed that he came from Togo or Dahomey. This was only a foretaste. We were told there was going to be a big show in the cinema that night. So there was. The whole of Gao, particularly its women, in all their best, seemed to be there. I came late and didn't stay long – finding his wisecracks more or less unintelligible. His dancing was much more fun. I also, later in the evening, visited a nice Abbé, who was also a palaeontologist, at the Catholic mission. I had been told that he was an archaeologist, but his interest was in fact in ancient bones. However he was a nice friendly soul, who spoke English and knew Le Gros Clark.[169] Lavocat[170] is his name. He speaks moderate English. So we passed an hour pleasantly together, and he is one of the hundred or so whom I have already invited to come and stay with us at Powder Hill.

And so to Bamako. Crossing and recrossing the Niger. First a line of fantastic jagged hills to the south, then a chain of lakes. Then the Niger flood area, and many little villages, cut off from the land, looking as though they were floating in the floods. Then the bare thorn country changing to cultivated patches, till you get to the trees and hills around Bamako

To DFH
6 December [1952]

Gao [French Sudan]
It seems now a long time since I last wrote to you – and my diary letter seems to have got a bit stuck owing to the amount of other things that happen (+ 4 weeks' separation from typewriter). So here is at any rate an interim letter. I arrived here (v. comfortable hotel – for a change – douche in room and suchlike unaccustomed luxuries) by air this evening. I've come because Gao was the capital of the Songhai Empire in the 15th/16th Centuries (and earlier), and there is a mosque of the period, or the remains of it + tomb of Askia the Great. I've got so behind schedule that I've only left

---

169 Sir Wilfred Le Gros Clark (1895–1971), Professor of Anatomy in Oxford from 1934 to 1962, author of *Early Forerunners of Man*, 1934 and other books.
170 Abbé R.J.M. Lavocat, palaeontologist who published many articles on fossils in learned journals in the 1950s.

myself tomorrow – Sunday – to learn about this city – returning to
Bamako by air at 6 a.m. I don't like this rushed way of doing
things – and I'd meant to go on to Tadmekka – 500 km to the NE
in the desert – but don't well see how that can be fitted in now.

Continuing at breakfast Sunday – brioche and cafe-au-lait: excellent. Had supper last night with a gay young Italian journalist who
had tried to cross the Sahara on his 'scooter' – i.e. motor bicycle –
but it had broken down: also two Spanish chauffeurs who could
speak little but Spanish. It was very beautiful yesterday evening
cross the 'boucle du Niger' – beginning with the flooded lands in
the area around Dire and Timbuktu, where the Niger becomes dis-
sipated into channels and marshes – with villages standing out
here and there as islands surrounded by floodlands. Then the
desert, or semi-desert, nothing but sand and thorn-bushes – with
lakes to the south and a line of hills to the North (Goundam itself
from which we started is particularly beautiful – being almost surrounded both by water and hills), no villages here – but occasionally
a road, or track, running N. To S, across the desert (from the
Niger) – and here and there some eruptions of hills. Then the sun
began to set. It had already set by the time we reached the Niger
again and Gao – tho' there was still orange light in the sky to the
West – which the Niger reflected as we passed over it – and as one
got near the Niger one began to get signs of humanity – the burning of the bush – great arches of flame down below. Now I must
walk 2 or 3 kilometres to the mosque and tombs of the Askias.

All goes well – apart from the fact that one is much slower and
does less than one had hoped. But I remember Daddy's phrase 'It's
no use knocking yourself up'.

To DMCH
13 December 1952

Dakar [Senegal]
I forgot in my last letter to send you love and blessings for our
wedding day.[171] This may be a little late, I'm afraid. But I'm

---

171 Thomas and Dorothy were married in Geldeston, Norfolk, on 16
   December 1937.

hoping to talk to you on the telephone this morning – if all goes well. A 15-year anniversary seems a special kind of anniversary – and it's lovely to have been married to you for 15 years. I would like to send you a special kind of present – but that will have to wait till I come back. But I wish I was with you for it. I've been thinking a lot since I got back about whether it would be a good idea just to hop back for Christmas and see how you are. I hate to think of your being ill, and me not there to care for you. But above all this letter is just to say how much I love you – and how good it is to think of 15 years ago – and all the time in between.

Waiting for a bus to take me in from this Airport resthouse where I'm staying to Dakar. It seems strange that it's still dark now at almost 7 a.m. – and quite cool during the day. Dakar has a real winter. I'm trying before doing anything else to knock these ancient cities articles into shape and check them over with Mauny of IFAN to make sure they're factually correct. Transport to Bissau seems a bit of a problem – no air service till next Friday (a bit late) and other means of transport uncertain. Damn – this pen (bought in Timbuktu) seems to be giving out.

To DMCH
15 December 1952

Dakar
I have had great luck. I told Mauny, the very nice IFAN archaeologist, yesterday, that I was trying to get to Bissau (Bissã) – I have a notion one calls it, if one is writing correct Portuguese – Luke will know!). He said at once – Come and see the Portuguese Consul, who lives just opposite. I said 'Fine – if you think he won't mind' – and he, the Consul, has arranged with a kind of Portuguese agronomist, here for a Soil Science conference, that I should travel in the back of his camionette to Bissau tomorrow. That is the way things happen. The agronomist says we leave at 7 a.m. tomorrow – which means that I have today, and to-night, clear to finish these articles on the ancient cities of the Western Sudan, and leave them for Mauny to check.

So I am spending today (Sunday) quietly typing at IFAN – fortunately the back door seems to remain open. I must say I think these articles are pretty good – but we'll see.

To DMCH
16 December 1952

Govt. Rest House – Bathurst [Gambia]
It was lovely to find I could send you a 'social telegram' for six-and-eight. Everything here seems half or a third the price of things in Dakar. Remarkable suddenly to find oneself in this terribly cheap world – when matches are a penny a box, cigarettes three-and-six for 50, and you can live in comfort (with 4 large meals) for £1 a day. Remarkable too to find oneself in this fantastically *English* world – with a substantial tea at 4.30 p.m. – eggs and bacon for breakfast – cold beef and steam pudding for lunch. Where you meet a group of half-a-dozen (African) little boys who say 'Would you like us to sing you some carols?' – and then they give you 'While Shepherds Watched' all the way through, very sweetly, followed by 'O come all ye faithful'! Where everyone knows everyone else in the shops and the bank and the post office – just like Beccles (about the same sized town, I guess): and everyone is friendly and chats when they meet – about their babies and lumbago and the school concert and the boy scouts' outing. I hadn't really meant to come here at all, but you have to pass through, going by road from Dakar to Bissau. I very luckily – with the help of Mauny of IFAN and the Portuguese Consul – managed to pick up a lift from some kind Portuguese, on their way back to Bissau from a conference. Unfortunately the one who owns the car in which we travel (small lorry rather) found he had malaria or 'flu or both when he arrived, and has been in bed ever since. So we are stuck for the moment. He's being very well looked after by an extremely friendly English doctor (who came over and treated him at 10 p.m. last night). So I hope we won't be stuck for long. I go on with my articles on the Ancient Cities, and talk with the other Portuguese, a middle-aged District Commissioner – a nice man. Also I met the African acting Portuguese consul[172] who is at the

---

172 Ibrahima Muhammadu Garba-Jahumpa, born 1912 and educated at Koranic school and St Augustine's Secondary School, became a pupil teacher and then a reception clerk for an airline at Fajara airport. He attended Teacher Training College at Georgetown and was a teacher until 1949. He was nominated to the Bathurst Town Council in 1942 and elected in 1947. He had also been secretary of the Gambia Labour Union from 1939 to 1945 and attended the Pan-African

same time a J.P., member of the Town Council, Secretary of the Gambia Labour Union, and his friend Mr. Small OBE[173], who edits a newspaper, and is President of the Union, a kindly elder statesman. But a good deal of time is spent as a go-between between the Portuguese party and the English – no, that's an exaggeration, but they haven't much English, so one can be of some use – in return for the lift!

To DMCH
19 December 1952

Ziguinchor [Senegal]
I am extremely homesick, having been reading Trollope during dinner and listening to a Strauss waltz. I am also angry and frustrated (somewhat) having been ejected at the frontier of Portuguese Guinea – which I regard as treatment to which no Englishman should be exposed, at the hands of our oldest Ally. I have sent a strong telegram to David Williams, asking him to get in touch with Wigg and Daryll Forde,[174] and raise the matter at the highest diplomatic levels. What damnable cheek! I'm sending you a copy of my letter to David W., so as not to try to tell the depressing story again. I shall also draft a strong letter to the Times, which they can send to Edward if they think fit, I can't think of anything else to do at the moment, except send a telegram to Eden[175] which I can't afford! I

Congress in Manchester in 1945. He was elected to the Legislative Council in 1945 and again in 1951. He was a founder member of the Muslim Congress Party later merged with wider political groupings. In the period from 1954 to 1977 he was variously Minister of Agriculture, Health and Finance.
173 Edward Small (c.1891–1957) founded the *Gambia Outlook* in 1922 and the Gambia Labour Union in 1929. He was on the executive committee of the ICFTU from 1945 to 1957. In 1951 he had been defeated in elections to the Legislative Council.
174 Daryll Forde (1902–73), anthropologist and Director of the International African Institute of which Thomas was a member. Thomas had discussed the Portuguese journey with Forde in London in August 1952, and Forde promised to write letters of support to leading Portuguese researchers and government officials.
175 Anthony Eden (1897–1977), was educated at Eton and Christ Church, Oxford. He was British Foreign Secretary in the 1930s and resigned

mind having wasted about £25 and a week in attempting to visit this miserable colony – Portuguese Guinea – but I mind more the rebuff. In the 19th Century the Foreign Secretary would have sent a battleship – or at least a cruiser – to Bissau for less but, alas, this is not the 19th Century! Nor can I understand why they should suddenly have behaved in this unexpected and ridiculous way.

I am also very fed up to think that there will probably be letters for me at Bissau, which I have tried to recover in various ways, and which I hope I will get back quickly. There is anyway a lovely young moon to-night – and was last night, which is encouraging. Also I've dropped again into a good friendly hotel – with good cooking – and a nice patron, who was in the British navy during the war. Most of the day I've spent typewriting my article on Gao for *West Africa*. I think that this series is very good, myself. I hope I'm right!

Also the photographs (12 rolls of them!) have come out pretty well, which has cheered me a good deal.

Somehow too it's nice to be back on French soil. There is a kind of inhumanity about these Portuguese (apart from Teixeira)[176] that I don't like. Whereas here one feels oneself in the company of civilised people. But I still mean somehow to get to Portuguese Guinea.

Money is beginning to get low. AOF, of course, is shockingly expensive: as one realises when one spends a day in Gambia – where everything seems to cost a half to a third the price. So that I expect – apart from natural desire to be with you and the children – will send me home in March at any rate.

What a gloomy letter. Don't take it too seriously. But the sensation of not being admitted to a country is a curious one – it's like being a prisoner in a way. I'm afraid it's a common enough experience these days – but it's never happened to me before.

---

in 1938, gaining a world-wide reputation as an opponent of appeasement with Nazi Germany. He was Foreign Secretary again in the Second World War years and in the Conservative government from 1951 to 1955, receiving a knighthood in 1954. His brief period as Prime Minister from 1955 to 1957 ended soon after his controversial handling of the Suez Crisis in 1956.
176 Avelino Teixeira da Mota, died 1982, published many works on the history of the Guinea Coast. Thomas never did reach Portuguese Guinea.

However I've had a good dinner, and drunk half a bottle of red wine, and feel better. The patron has proposed that I go out and see the town with him – which seems a good idea. Having worked at this article all day – when I wasn't sending telegrams (which took a vast amount of time) and calling the Administrators – some relaxation will be very welcome.

Dec. 20th. – Luke's birthday: feel much better today. Back in Dakar. Air rest house where I stay full of British BOAC types – aeroplane goes through to London tomorrow – wish I was going too. I'll try to find someone who will take this letter and post it in England. That will save quite a bit of time. And I'll send a little letter to Luke too. Cheery to get a telegram at lunchtime today in Ziguinchor (incredibly quick) from David Williams, saying that he was acting on my telegram. Somehow to be in quick communication with the outside world is always cheering. Also I've finished the 5th of my articles on the ancient cities – and have only one more to do. Dakar looked in a way very beautiful with Cape Verde sticking out into a sea – and waves beating on the rocks – as we landed to-night.

To DMCH
25 December 1952

Resthouse – Dakar [Senegal]
I pledge myself to do everything in my power to avoid spending Christmas away from you again: and Dakar of all places: if one was on a camel in the middle of the Sahara it wouldn't be quite so bad. However there is an excellent, though shockingly expensive, restaurant in this place, and I treated myself to what was intended to be a good though economical lunch. (It was good, though I'm not so sure about the economical). Tomatoes in vinegar (the way you do them); bacon and eggs (two); bread and a whole cream cheese; a small carafe of vin rosé; and a glass of Cointreau and coffee to finish. Not bad – though not quite traditional Christmas fare. I have been reading 'Bantu Prophets in South Africa',[177]

---

177 Bengt Gustaf Malcolm Sundkler, born 1909, was the author *of Bantu Prophets in South Africa*, 1948. He was a Swedish Bishop and

which is interesting stuff: the African waiter at lunch had a look at it, saw a photograph of the Zulu Bishop of a separatist Church in full canonicals, and said 'bon' – clearly thinking it a sound idea that Africans should be bishops. When I have changed I am going into Dakar, or rather Medina (the African quarter) by the car which runs from here (free, which is a mercy), in the hope of attending a Socialist tom-tom, which the Secretary of the party said would be happening to-night. But one can never be quite sure about these things. The trouble is that there isn't a car back here until half past midnight, so it means staying around in this great metropolis for longer than I'd choose. However, this being France, one can always find a cafe open. Otherwise, I am spending this week working, largely at IFAN, trying to fill in the many large gaps in my information, seeing people (so far largely IFAN people, very helpful). I've also had lunch with Monod, head of IFAN, a nice chap, the most learned man in West Africa; and on Saturday have lunch with Mauny the learned archaeologist. So I am not neglected, though I long to be with all of you, and I shall be thankful to be out of Dakar. Three more days – if the aeroplane to Accra leaves on time.

To DMCH
10 January 1953

Kumasi [Gold Coast]
Time goes on slipping away. Another week has gone – and I seem to have left a longer gap in writing than I'd meant – bother – but I've been dreaming of you all a lot these last nights – and of coming home – which has been nice. I expect that's the result of staying with Dennis, Margaret and Stephen.[178] Dennis and Margaret have a nice new house at the edge of the jungle and at least if you look in one direction it's sheer jungle – but in the other

---

Professor and at a meeting in Hamburg in November 1966 of specialists in the study of missions pressed for the foundation of what over the next few years became the International Association for Mission Studies, formally inaugurated in 1972.

178 Margaret was the wife of Dennis Austin, and Stephen was their son; see notes to letter of 10 January 1950 above.

direction, there are one or two more similar bungalows – so one doesn't look in that direction. Dennis (or Margaret?) has got a nice garden organised – with some pawpaws – and flowers of various kinds – but, like Powder Hill, there's a general air of wildness still – and a patch of cassava growing at one end. It's very pleasant to be here – with beautiful meals (cooked by M.) and hot baths (my first, as far as I can remember since October 24th): pleasant to relax a bit after 10 days fairly hard teaching – though in many ways, of course, the teaching was relaxation too.

I've been able to write out in rough the last of these articles on the Ancient Cities – which I must get off to David W. as soon as possible (I've left the whole batch to post from here – since the post is so much cheaper than from AOF). The idea is that Dennis and I go down to Accra on Monday (the day after tomorrow – and then on to Dahomey (God willing!) in D's car for a week or so – returning to Accra. There's the first meeting of the Gold Coast Historical Association (of which I am a corresponding member!) today or tomorrow – which I expect I ought to attend – though it doesn't look a terrifically exciting programme. It's nice too seeing old friends – like John and Nancy Tsiboe and William Boatin. We had lunch and spent the aftn. with John and Nancy – then went on with a young woman from Jamaica, a journalist, to visit a CPP meeting – celebrating the declaration of Positive Action[179] 3 years ago and quite a moving kind of a meeting – mainly in Twi – with bits in English – particularly the hymns and prayers. It was held out of doors in a hollow with all the people – a thousand or so – sitting along the face of the hillside. We sang 'Lead kindly Light' and Mrs Hanna Kojo,[180] an admirable large woman, Asst. Propaganda Secretary of CPP, whom I saw quite a bit of at the New Year School, recited the CPP version of the creed – beginning 'I believe in Kwame Nkrumah'. We were honoured by being fetched down from the side of the hill, and sat on chairs beside the platform.

---

179 On Positive Action see notes to letter of 12 January 1950 above.
180 Hannah Esi Badu Dadson (1918–86) became prominent under her married name Kudjoe, She was the first woman member of UGCC but became one of Nkrumah's first supporters in the CPP and campaigned throughout the Gold Coast to win women's support to his cause.

To DMCH
18 January 1953

Achimota [Gold Coast]
I am writing this from David Kimble's – waiting for a meal –
David having gone off to a party of some kind. A man called
Ward[181] has just come in who is working here on the effect of
Radio-active materials on monkeys – Lalage is collecting monkeys
for him. I thought I would go off to Liberia today, but having
turned up at the airport found that the aircraft wasn't going off till
tomorrow noon. I've been having a mixed sort of day – breakfast
with Dowuona, and his very nice wife and children – full of life –
and liking to ride on one's knees and do 'This is the way the
ladies ride': then round to Helen's to meet Douglas Pirie who is
on his way through the Gold Coast. Lalage turned up there also –
and Kofi Antubam,[182] the painter, and we chatted for a while.
Then a nice lunch of liver and onions and fruit salad with Hugh
Blaney,[183] the Professor of Mathematics, with whom I'm staying,
a very friendly character. The afternoon I spent largely at the airport, partly sleeping, partly discussing Theory of Numbers with
Blaney. Having discovered that the aeroplane wasn't going till
Monday 1 p.m. (I refused to be sure of this until I had actually
got it from the pilot himself) we went back home – worked a bit,
Blaney at Mathematics and I at an article on Timbuktu for the
Observer.

Jan 20th. I didn't – as I'd meant – post this before leaving the Gold
Coast. Now I'm in Monrovia, in the Bank, trying to collect some
money. We arrived yesterday at about 5.30 – a nice party – 13 of
us – I the only European – one of the occasions when I would feel
more comfortable if I also were African – but everyone was
extremely friendly – we had on board 4 leading women from the
CPP, including my friend Hannah Kodjoe who was at The New
Year School (and who, when asked by one of the other CPP

---

181 Allan Ward, then lecturer in physics at UCGC.
182 Kofi Antubam, art master at Achimota, well-known painter and
    author of books on Ghana's art and culture; part-time extra-mural
    tutor in art.
183 Hugh Blaney, Professor of Mathematics at UCGC.

women who I was replied 'my husband'!). Like Hannah, all these CPP front-rank women are fairly large and matronly – but the salt of the earth, and very good at organising, I would guess. On the way in the plane they sang CPP songs, in Twi. The journey took about four and a half hours. We arrived to find a marvellous reception – a large crowd lining the airport – a good many of them, I suspect, Gold Coasters resident in Liberia. Drumming and shouting; one particularly nice little band of drummers and dancers – looking a bit demonic, with feathers on their heads.

Now it is nearly lunchtime. I've been having a useful morning, collecting American dollars (it's entirely U.S. currency here) and sending off cables to you and to Dahomey (to explain to the Govt. there that I won't be turning up there yet). I've also met some of the educational people here – nice American woman concerned with Literacy work – and an Indian (scientist I think) called Dr. Reddi[184] in charge of the UNESCO mission. I've fixed up some visits – but quite how I spend my time, as between seeing the things and people that I'd anyway meant to see and covering Kwame Nkrumah's visit, I don't quite know. It's certainly very interesting to see the relations between Liberians and Gold Coast people – with the quite large Gold Coast community here in Monrovia as intermediaries. Paid a very pleasant visit last night to the Assistant PMG and his family – entertained with beer and ginger ale. The last hour I've spent with Mr. Hollbrook,[185] Editor of the Accra Evening News, leading CPP paper, and some of the Gold Coast people in Monrovia – members of the local CPP branch, discussing racial relations – and the changes which have gone on in the G.C. over the last few years – the gradual disappearance of old colonial system, and the gradual recognition on the part of Europeans that they could no longer claim special privileges. A rather nice concert of classical music is going on somewhere near – Beethoven, I should guess – a familiar tune anyway.

---

184 Dr S. Reddi was head of the UNESCO mission in Liberia from 1952 to 1954.
185 Charles Clifford-Holdbrook, who was business manager rather than editor of the *Accra Evening News*. He, like Thomas, was in the official party accompanying Nkrumah's visit to Liberia in January 1953.

To DMCH
21 January 1953

Monrovia [Liberia]
This is being an interesting time, and I'm jolly glad I came. The
only trouble is that I find myself a bit lazy, and do a good deal less
in a day than I mean to. But that's largely because it's a bit hot, and
I get given too much beer. I'm writing this at about 10 p.m. –
having started to type an article for David about Nkrumah's visit –
but Mr. Hollbrook, the Manager of the CPP daily paper, the Accra
Evening News, one of our party, has borrowed my typewriter, so
that gives me a good excuse for writing to you instead. Kwame
Nkrumah arrived this morning on the Presidential Yacht. We all
got up before daybreak to greet him. After a period of worry about
whether our car would arrive two turned up, and we went down to
the harbour. A large crowd there – all the personalities (I should
guess) of Monrovia + pretty well all the large Gold Coast community here – carrying the green white and red Ghana colours, flags,
caps, blouses, ties, etc. The girls in their Ghana blouses and caps
looked particularly attractive. A lot of singing of CPP songs too.
Then the yacht appeared, round the breakwater. Great excitement – guns fired. Even more excitement when the yacht
eventually berthed beside the quay – Kwame Nkrumah on the
bridgehead. After quite a bit of delay Kwame was escorted off the
yacht by a large General with lots of gold-braid, the President's
ADC – and Liberian and British National Anthems were played.
Then Kwame inspected the guard of honour, the Liberian Frontier
Force, which marched up and down a bit, with a glorious band,
and drum-major twirling his silver staff. After that he went and
greeted the Gold Coast contingent – great excitement – more
singing of CPP songs – waving of CPP flags – eventually he drove
off – and I had a chance to meet some friends among his
entourage – Welbeck, Bankole Timothy[186] (editor of the G.C.

186 Emmanuel Bankole Timothy (1923–1994) was a Sierra Leonean jour-
    nalist working in Britain, Gold Coast and Ghana. He went to Accra
    in 1951 after some seven years in British journalism to become assis-
    tant editor of the *Daily Graphic*. He published *Kwame Nkrumah, his
    Rise to Power* in 1955, but was deported from Ghana in 1958 after
    criticising Nkrumah's personality cult. After the death of Nkrumah
    he published *Kwame Nkrumah, from Cradle to Grave*, 1981. Timothy

Graphic, etc.). Off we then went to Duker Hall, where Kwame and his party are staying. I then slipped off to the Ministry of Public Instruction, where I should have gone at 9 a.m. – by then an hour late. However it didn't seem to matter too much – I was in time to go up to the Hospital and visit the Literacy classes there. Met a very nice Doctor, a German called Meyer, who runs the TB hospital, very well I should guess – they find learning English is good from a therapeutic point of view. Saw some patients at work – taught by a young lad from Sierra Leone. Then back to Duker Hall – where there was a lot of dancing going on – Gold Coast men – with drum and cymbals (I've forgotten the right name for these iron instruments you hit together). One man with a large Liberian flag which he waved round his body – others crouching and jumping up again with guns. Inside Duker Hall I met Krobo Edusei,[187] Under-Secretary for Finance and Chief Govt. Whip (Gold Coast), whom I last saw in Oxford the summer before last. Nothing much seemed to be happening there – except a delegation of CPP ladies from Monrovia bringing a food offering to Mrs. Hannah Kojo and the other CPP ladies of our party. This was interesting – there was a short address, and an exchange of the CPP watchword 'Freedom' – and the Party salute. From there I went to the State Dept., to pay my respects: saw a nice friendly Asst. Secretary there, called Padmore.[188] And so back home to lunch. In the afternoon we went down to the ceremony of Kwame Nkrumah's reception by the President. At least I got in for the beginning, but got separated from the rest of the party, and so failed to get in for the end (drinks and talk in the Executive

---

spent his later career in public relations in the diamond industry and the latter years of his life in London.

187 See notes to letter of 30 March 1951 above.

188 This is not the Trinidadian socialist and Panafricanist who was close to Nkrumah, but the Liberian George Arthur Padmore, born in Monrovia in 1915 with a paternal grandfather Arthur Barclay, President of Liberia from 1904 to 1912, and maternal grandfather George Stanley Padmore, who was one among 346 immigrants sent to Liberia from the West Indies by the Barbados Colonisation Society. Padmore was educated at Liberia College and became a brother-in-law to President William Vacanarat Shadrach Tubman (1895–1971). Tubman appointed Padmore as Assistant Secretary of State in 1951 to institute a foreign service training programme for Liberia. In 1961 he represented Liberia on the UN Security Council.

Mansion) – which was a bit of a pity. Kwame and his fellow ministers and the rest of this party all gathered together in Duker Hall – we then proceeded in a fleet of cars to the Mansion – a large handsome white building – and Kwame again took the salute from the Frontier Force – dozens of photographers – large and enthusiastic crowd. After this I went off to Dr. Reddie – a charming Indian – head of Unesco mission here – ex-St. John's (senior to me a good deal). Had an extremely interesting conversation with him about his work and problems. He has an equally charming daughter – 18 or so I would guess – who appeared half way through, elegant in a sari, having just been working at her stamps. I gave her some Gambia ones, and she gave me in return a lot of nice Indian ones – which I'll send on to the family. She is interested in Greek history and wants to go to Greece. It was very pleasant to find oneself in this kind of family. Dr. Reddie was about to go to the Presidential dinner, and kindly took me home in his car (he lives about 2 miles out – quite a warm walk – but good for one – since otherwise these ample regular meals, I fear, will make me fat again – I was pleased to find when I weighed myself lately I was quite a bit lighter than when I left!).

Now my typewriter's back. Better try to finish this article and then go to bed.

To DMCH
26 January 1953

Monrovia
I spent yesterday pleasantly enough – talking to Unesco people all morning. Today I am, I think, going out into the country, a place called Klay, with an Englishman working with Unesco – ex-Nigeria – called Clarke.[189] Klay is where the Fundamental Education project has started. It will be good to see something of

---

189 John Digby Clarke, born 1901 and educated at St Michael's College, Tenbury, and Cambridge University, was superintendent of Education in Nigeria from 1926. He was author of *Omu: an African Experiment in Education*, 1937. He was appointed senior education officer in 1942, and in charge of fundamental education for UNESCO in Liberia from November 1952 to August 1953.

the country, after nearly a week in Monrovia I am being a bit slow in doing what I mean to do here – and doubt if in another week I can complete what I've planned. But I had better leave in a week's time, I think. Spent Saturday visiting the President's farm – a very elegant building – where we had breakfast of ham and scones and beer at 11 a.m. – very welcome. Then on to the Agricultural Experimental Station – more food, more drink: all this with the P.M.'s party. It has some advantages this way of travelling, since one picks up quite a lot of free trips! But one learns less than the other way.

To DMCH
3 February 1953

Monrovia
I am writing this in Dr Schnitze's[190] surgery – or rather waiting-room – where I have just gone to have my piles or pile attended to. It's not at all serious and seems to be getting better. Dr Schnitze's surgery – like James's[191] – is the kind of place where one had better be prepared to settle down. It is also quite expensive. However, in return for my 8 dollars I have had 2 goes of treatment + 40 minutes extremely interesting conversation with Dr S., a many-sided man, with definite views about world politics, representative of Liberia on WHO, has been here for the last 15 years, originally from Germany – or central Europe. Says that the trouble with the British and French colonies is that they in practice exclude *specialists* (like himself) who aren't British or French, whereas Liberia accepts them. I am now delayed here a bit: I was told on Saturday that there was likely to be a truck going through to Nzerekore (French Guinea) this evening. Called this morning, and was a bit disappointed to find that there had been a truck *yesterday* evening, and might be another tomorrow morning. So I am stuck here for to-night anyway. However I did some more seeing of life this morning, and finished drafting another article on Liberia and Nkrumah's visit this afternoon. So I can employ myself usefully. Only one has a desire to be moving – since one has the feeling that

190 Assistant Public Health and Sanitation Director.
191 James Gillett was the Hodgkin family doctor in Oxford.

the further one moves the nearer home one gets – perhaps illusory. Also I don't think that there is much more work that I can now put in on Liberia – plenty still to be found out, but it would need a new beginning really.

About the watch – I'm very fed up about that. I fear it must be still at Nara. It never got forwarded to Dakar as I asked. It will, I'm sure turn up eventually but I could get no news of it before I left French West Africa. I'll send some letters to Bamako and Nara when I get back to French territory and hoped they may produce some result. But I think I had better tell them to send it home now rather than let it chase after me during this last part of the journey. It's sickening after all the trouble you took.

In spare moments I read Nicholas Nickleby – the only novel I have with me now. It fits these surroundings, and my way of living, quite well. This wandering character, without much cash. However I lack his nobility of spirit. I am very pleased to have moved out of this rather awful (German) Studen Hotel, where the hotel-keepers were usually cross, and shouting at some one, into the French Hotel, kept by a charming woman from the Cote d'Azur (who knows La Croix)[192] – with excellent French food, and a nice little veranda, overlooking what would be the road if it was made yet! It's true that it's a bit more primitive – the lavatory is also a passage – and the water's cut off during the day – and the mosquitoes come in and bite one during the night. But it's a much friendlier and more pleasant atmosphere. Quite interesting company too. A man from Los Angeles who's sold his business in order to come here and collect chimpanzees, leopards, baby elephants and hippos. Two nice young Dutchmen working in a shipping firm – one came over in a yacht, with many adventures, and all of them decided to stay and work here, having run out of cash. This West Indian architect who runs various businesses (mainly bus and taxi) on the side. So it's quite a lively world.

Wednesday. At the office of the Franco-Liberian Trucking Corporation. It seems that the truck will leave some time today – which is good. I am waiting here to find out when. I shan't be sorry to leave Monrovia. It's not a beautiful town – in that state of semi-

---

192 In the Var in France where Thomas and Dorothy spent their honey-
    moon in December 1937.

chaos which all towns that are growing rapidly tend to be. With handsome paved streets which suddenly go down in the world and become mountain paths: half-finished houses with a lot of families living in them and showing no sign that they are ever likely to be finished; elegant whitewashed concrete mansions side by side with half-derelict wooden shacks. The town being largely built on the side of hills many of the houses are lifted off the ground with stilts. But there are some lovely views around – the beach, the sea, and the mouth of the Mesurado River.

To DMCH
8 February 1953

Gagnoa [Ivory Coast] Sunday
I write this inside a lorry beneath which many men work. (This type of fountain pen is not really well suited to hot climates, since one sweats on the page and everything runs. Biros are not to be found in Monrovia.) We have a broken spring. We have stopped to mend it twice. This is a third go – I hope more successful than the others. Meanwhile my deadline for reaching Abidjan – midnight to-night – becomes more and more remote. I have tried to bribe the driver – a nice handsome young man – with a Nephertiti kind of profile – to get there to-night – but bribes are not of much effect when confronted with broken springs, and we are still a good 300 km. from Abidjan. Frankly I am not too keen on spending another night in the open – having spent 4 in this way already – one at Monrovia, waiting for transport, one on the frontier at Ganta, one beneath a beautiful mountain at a place called Nzo, and last night at Daloa. So my present feeling is – Forward to Abidjan, whatever the consequences. I have been trying to inspire the boys with the same idea – I don't know how successfully. (I've now been turned out of the lorry to make room for operations, and am sitting on the step). I don't regret having come this way.

Of course, it's fantastically slow and all that. (I could have reached Abidjan in 2 hours by air on Thursday, but one does see the country and meet people in a way air-travellers never do.) One is at once on the same social level as everyone else. I've just been to a low Restaurant called 'Ici Holal' with the boys and had rice and meat cooked before your eyes – actually the sight of the meat uncooked as it lay on the table there was such that I concentrated entirely on rice: helped down with some rum, provided by a friendly police corporal, who is generally keeping an eye on me.

I better, I expect, in a more or less coherent way, try to explain how I got here – so far as my remembrance, what's left of it after this journey, will let me – and so far as one can think to the tune of these constant hammerings. I meant to leave Monrovia at 2 p.m. on Wednesday – having been told by Soto, the boss, or a boss of the Franco-Liberian Trucking Corporation, to turn up then. I turned up half an hour early and was told that the trucks for Nzerekore had left at 12. This made me cross – especially as I had been had once this way already – and I nearly gave up the idea of the Nzerekore journey altogether, and decided to go by air after all. But the FLTC seemed genuinely anxious to help and Soto, a friendly but silent red-faced chap (Frenchman) said he would be starting at 3.15 a.m. next morning, and I could come with him. Well I turned up in that bloody yard at about 2.50 a.m. – having not gone to bed for fear I should oversleep – and, after I'd decided several times that I must have been betrayed again, he eventually turned up at about 4.15 a.m. Off we went to Firestone, where he had some jobs to do, including buying a 2nd-hand car for 200 dollars, and there we were stuck from 6.30 a.m. to 5 p.m., kicking our heels among the rubber trees. However once we got going, I admit we went well, and with a stop for a meal at a kind of restaurant-cum-brothel kept (I was told) by the President's wife (one can say such things now!) where one paid half a dollar for a plate of rice, we reached the frontier at Ganta, by, I suppose, about midnight.

There being nowhere else to sleep I slept on the ground, wrapped in a blanket, borrowed from Soto, and stupidly caught a heavy cold in consequence, which is now gradually wearing off.

The lorry, I must say, travelled very well. I slept most of the way, and woke up at intervals, to find each time we were a bit nearer Abidjan – the driver, this nice handsome young lad, did extremely well. I distributed largesse and we parted warmly. We actually arrived here well before dawn. It always seems odd to change the proletarian kind of life one leads in a lorry for the upper-class kind of life one leads in this sort of a grand hotel – exchanging at the same time an African kind of life for a European. Immediately, of course, it was jolly nice to have a good breakfast of brandy and soda, coffee, bread and butter, 2 eggs and ham (total cost almost £1, I fear!) followed by a shave, wash and shower. (The gramophone is playing a very familiar bit of music – nice – piano – I ought to know who it's by, but don't).

Great achievement – by ordering a lunch of omelette, yoghourt and coffee (which was what I really wanted) I got the price down to 15 shillings! I'll continue the story of this journey. We got up in the grey moist misty dawn at Ganta and waited for the Customs to open – ate some bread and drank some tea to pass the time. Eventually the Liberian flag was hoisted and an official turned up. Usual process of bag-searching, etc. I have tended to become nervous about possible frontier incidents – however none occurred this time. We were allowed to proceed to the French side – across a series of barriers which had to be removed: one was padlocked at the entrance to a bridge across a beautiful river – so we had to wait for the man to come and unlock it. Quite a pleasant wait – with women leaning up against the bridge – ? on their way to market. We next stopped at the French Guinea frontier post – a pleasant spot – a little group of round thatched houses with an office beside them – the Customs officer a friendly Senegalese, with an extremely beautiful daughter of about 5, whom I tried to photograph in various attitudes – also other nice little boys. We passed through this without difficulty and then set off for Nzerekore – only about 100 k.m. away, but along an appalling road which meant that the journey took about 4 hours. Very hilly too – all forest covered – few villages – streams here and there. So it was getting on for 1 p.m. when we arrived at Nzerekore. Had a refreshing beer and ordered a room at the resthouse, and was about to settle down to lunch when a dark-looking chap came and talked to me – he turned out to be a Corsican merchant – heard me saying that I was trying to get to Abidjan. Said he was leaving in an hour and going in that direction – offered me a lift. After weighing advantages and disadvantages it seemed on balance best to go with him – since transport seemed uncertain – though it meant postponing a bed and a wash, and (worse) missing talking to Jean Colle[193], whom I was anxious to see, and to whom I had a letter of

193 Jean Colle was the representative at Nzerékoré for the Franco-Liberian Trucking Corporation.

introduction, from Malrieu,[194] who was at Oxford in the summer –
a Frenchman who runs this Franco-Liberian Trucking Corporation
and knows Liberia well: a bore this, since he would have been
interesting, and I think with a bit more bargaining I could have
squeezed in a visit to him. Stupid of me in retrospect.

Indeed I fear I've got to a stage of making unnecessary mistakes.
I am in rather a mess at the moment since I've tied myself up to
wait here till Ouezzin Coulibaly,[195] whom I met in Paris, chooses to
ring up, or turn up, thereby losing time which I might otherwise
have spent in seeing other chaps, and in drinking drinks that I
don't really need. Whereas what I should have done was making
some definite plan with the chap. The fact is that one's capacity for
intelligent planning and use of time seems gradually to run down.
However, no doubt it'll work out somehow. Only I don't see how
I can well do the various jobs that I want to do in the remaining
day which I've proposed to spend here.

Continuing the story – I set off with the Corsican and his wife
at about 3.30 p.m., having said 'hullo' and no more to M. Colle. I
didn't find him an altogether engaging character, though his wife
was a nice quiet middle-aged thing. He had a way of cursing
Africans for charging too much and suchlike which I found dis-
agreeable. So, I thought, did his wife – at times. But we passed
through marvellous country – great mountains suddenly appearing
in front of us – trees part way up, but bare at the top – sharp out-
lines – unlike anything I've seen before in these parts. Also good
villages of round houses – with conical thatches, like one of those
French engravers – I've forgotten which.

Combined effect very good – I can't draw them though.
Unfortunately, when we got to a place called Szo, the car broke

194 Pierre H. Malrieu, who held a post in Dakar as Directeur de l'Office
    des Changes de l'AOF and was visiting Oxford in August 1952,
    wrote letters of introduction for Thomas presenting him as a former
    Oxford University teacher making a study of political ideas among
    Africans.
195 Daniel Ouezzin Coulibaly (1909–58), from Upper Volta, formed the
    first teachers' trade union in Francophone Africa. He was a founding
    member of the RDA in 1946 and its first political secretary. Coulibaly
    worked in the whole of AOF, he only turned his attention to Upper
    Volta in 1956 and became Prime Minister of Upper Volta from 1957
    to 1958.

down – I stopped to take a photograph, and when we tried to start again it seemed that the car was *en panne*, as the French say. The dynamo wasn't doing whatever dynamos should do. The Corsican wrestled with it – meanwhile it got dark. The lamp had no paraffin, and the boy got cursed in consequence. Eventually we gave it up as a bad job, and decided we'd have to stay the night there. I was passed on to a friendly middle-aged African who had taken an interest in the proceedings and turned out to be an *Infirmier* in the Trypanosomiasis Service.

Unfortunately I didn't make the best of my chances of conversation with him – as, after 10 minutes conversation with him, in the course of which he told me that he didn't think much of RDA, I fell asleep, and continued to sleep with moments of waking till about 9.30, when he, not unnaturally, decided to go to bed. I, feeling thirsty and slightly hungry, decided I'd better find out what had happened to the Corsican and wife, and discovered that they'd been expecting me to return to them. I apologised and spent an hour in the back of their camionette, being fed with beer, bread, and pate de porc, of which I didn't need very much, while the Corsican told stories of his experiences in England when he was with the 8th Army, and the friendly way in which he was treated by a Manchester businessman, which had led him to look with a kindly eye on all Englishmen, myself included. Eventually I pulled myself away, went back to the Infirmier's round house, and slept on his spare bed. In the middle of the night, it seemed, I was woken by tremendous hootings of a motor horn, which continued, intermittently, for a long time. It turned out by degrees that this was a car – a lorry, leaving for *Man*, and eventually (no exact information when) for Abidjan. I could go on this – at a price which I thought exorbitant. However it seemed again best to choose the bird in the hand, and I whispered my goodbyes to the Corsican and his wife, sleeping in the camionette (it was still quite dark) and climbed aboard, with baggage. Next stage begun. We had not gone a league, a league, a league but barely twa', or, to be more exact, about 100 yards, when the lorry refused at the first hill heading out of the village. All the passengers (except me, who as '1st class', i.e. travelling in front, seemed exempt) had to climb down and walk up the hill. With this lightening of the load we succeeded in getting going again – very painfully. In this way – with frequent spilling of the passengers, and frequent stops to try and mend the engine, we proceeded. But it was a very slow process – and I thought, as dawn broke, that the Corsican and his camionette might overtake us. But he didn't. A long time was spent on this next stage of the journey, through the western parts of the Ivory Coast. It wasn't till about midday that we got to Donane – where we had to go through an Ivory Coast Douane, and have all our baggage unloaded and examined, to see if we were smuggling fire-arms, or textiles or Lucky Strike cigarettes from Liberia. Here we could get coffee – of a kind – which was a comfort. When we got started again we had a block in the road, on account of a lorry which had gone overboard and collapsed and was being towed back to the road again – then an enormous long halt for engine trouble in a village in which a nice fishing ceremony was taking place – men and boys marching down the village street with their fishing nets. Two nice things about this journey: one was a long halt when we had to go across a river by ferry – and unpack a lot of our load of palm-nuts before we could get on board, and even then we broke the planks that led onto the ferry. But it was a beautiful river and one could drink red wine in a hut by the bank. The other was the effect that in many villages in this part the whitewashed houses were painted with all kinds of designs in red – lizards, humans, flowers, patterns and so forth – natural colours – ochre? Bless you beloved. I must go to sleep now. Ouezzin Coulibaly did turn up in the end, I'm glad to say

To return – by late afternoon this lorry was approaching Man – when it saw another lorry, bound for Abidjan. So we stopped, and a taciturn police corporal and I were trans-shipped. This seemed an excellent idea. And away we started again. It wasn't very comfortable, as the Proprietor insisted on travelling in front along with the corporal, the driver and myself. He wasn't very wide, but four abreast is too many – and we spent a good deal of the time kicking one another. This vehicle seemed to go better than the other – it didn't have to shed its passengers going up hills – an advantage – though of course we had the usual sorts of stops – to pick up fresh passengers, to make departing passengers pay before they could abscond, to fill up with water, to tinker with the engine, and suchlike. After dark fell we reached Douekoue, where we enquired for cold beer, and were directed by a friendly woman across the way, where we found an elderly Syrian, a Catholic priest, a frig., and a lot of bottles. We drank our cold beer and talked about the Cote d'Ivoire. 'Do they eat people here much still?' I asked. '*Rarement, très rarement*' said the Priest. After sitting around a bit we moved back to the friendly woman's cafe and ate some bread and sardines. After a lapse of time the driver reappeared and we started off again. We drove till we reached another river (I think, the Sassandra) and waited an enormous long time for the ferry to come over and fetch us. It was quite pleasant though, under the stars, beside this quite broad river, with the forest all round. Some lads eventually offered to take me across in a canoe. This seemed a little dangerous as the canoe they fetched was full of water. However they bailed it out and we crossed – just as the ferry got going from the other side. After some stumbling we found our way to a restaurant which was still open, though it was 11 p.m. They gave us beer and rice with a bit of fish – all they had. Quite welcome. The Corporal, the driver, and various extras (the corporal's wife and child, I think, among them, who were made to ride behind while the corporal rode in front with me) got through all the available food – and we started off again. I hoped we were going to travel all night – but when we got to the next town – Daloa the driver pulled up beside the house of the cousin of the proprietor's son, and there we anchored for the night. I wasn't very pleased at having to sleep another night this way, and insisted that I should have a chance to wash and shave next morning. This was agreed. So I settled down to sleep in the front seat. This wasn't so bad while I had it all to myself, but unfortunately towards morning the corporal reappeared from somewhere, and sat himself down where my legs were. And from that time on I had little joy. When morning came we got up, and the cousin of the proprietor's son appeared, a very nice friendly large man, who let me wash, and shave, and change in his room. After which I felt much better. He was a merchant, an RDA man, and we chatted pleasantly over a bowl of coffee. He refused to take any money. At about 8 a.m. we got moving again – but this was not real movement, since we spent a long time hanging about in the market square, picking up more passengers, and then a long time looking for the corporal, who had mysteriously disappeared, and then a long time driving round and round the town on various errands, and then back to the market square again. It must have been about 10 a.m. before we finally moved off – and the rest of the day's progress was equally slow – so that we had only reached

Gagnoa (where I began this letter) by evening. A good deal of the delay was due to the fact that we had broken a spring which kept having to be hammered back into place by two lads lying on their backs underneath the lorry. During these intervals we usually managed to find some beer to drink, and on one occasion I mixed this with more bread and sardines and two slightly sweet, extremely dry, biscuits. And then, as I said, when we did eventually leave Gagnoa we pushed on marvellously, with no more spring or other trouble and reached Abidjan while it was still night. And that is really the end of this very minor Odyssey.

I write this at the gates of the Treichville *Ecole Regionale*, waiting for this Social Worker who has gone inside on some job that seems to be lasting a very long time. Still it's nice to have had a chance to finish this. The place is thick with children who tell me that they are off school because they are sick and have had to see the school doctor. But they seem fairly full of beans. Treichville is like Medina at Dakar, but rather less horrible.

To DMCH
13 February 1953

Achimota
I've changed my plans now again a bit, and am staying here till Sunday morning – then going on by air to Brazzaville. Hugh Blaney (with whom I'm again staying – long-suffering chap – he will, I hope, put in a long visit to us when he comes to England in the summer – he'd enjoy meeting Henry Whitehead[196] and suchlike) was prepared to drive me to Lome yesterday to catch the boat, for Pointe Noire, but I'm afraid I just felt too feeble, this cold having developed the way yours sometimes do (though more mildly), pains over the head and eyes and general congestion. So Hugh, saintly character, took me to the doctor, who gave me various drugs, including Ephedrine drops, and I cancelled the boat, and

196 John Henry Constantine Whitehead (1905–60) was educated at Eton and at Balliol College from 1923 to 1929, with a break as a stockbroker from 1926 to 1928. He became a Balliol Tutorial Fellow in mathematics. He was elected Waynflete Professor of Pure Mathematics in 1947 and held the chair until his death.

bought an air passage to Brazzaville, and then another up North from Brazzaville to Fort Lamy, from which it's only a step or two to Kano. So I feel well provided for. It's a bit more expensive, but I thought it worth paying a bit more to have 3 quiet days here. I'm feeling better already – after a very good night's sleep. Will take it easy today – going in to the Legislative Assembly (which I've never visited) this morning, with Helen Kimble, and Hugh – but doing little else today. Quite glad – indeed very glad – to think that this is going to be the last lap. Nice to be among friendly people again here. 'Ali, Hugh's Moslem servant from the Northern Territories, treats me very well – has washed all the dirty clothes I left behind, and taken off some more for washing today. When I asked him if he would kindly do some handkerchiefs he said at once, with a smile "I know, I know, I know – I see, I see, I see". Actually, oddly enough, I had some difficulty in getting into this country yesterday morning. Arriving at about 9 a.m. by air from Abidjan I was asked for my return ticket. I explained that I had none, as I wasn't returning. Followed a lot of palaver, including several telephone conversations with a Police Officer called Price[197] (British) who said that unless I could produce either a return ticket or a deposit of £100 I would be sent back on the 'plane to Abidjan. I said this was fantastic – since I'd come in one and a half months ago in precisely the same way and no-one had bothered. Anyway I couldn't buy my ticket on to Brazzaville until I had met friends raised money and so forth. And how could I do all this if I wasn't allowed to leave the airport? Anyway I was ill and needed to see a doctor. This might have gone on for some time had the very nice Frenchman in charge of *Air France* not suggested that I should buy a ticket on to Lome for £5. This, it seemed, would satisfy the authorities. So, somewhat grudgingly, I was given a permit to stay 5 days in the country. Actually I only want to stay 3, so that is more than adequate. But it seemed an awful lot of fuss.

Later. I visited the Leg. Assembly this morning. Heard a speech from Kwame Nkrumah – on the Budget – followed by a debate on Lunatic Asylums and another on the reform of Municipal Councils. Quite interesting. But I found this headache came on again, so I didn't stay awful long. Had a nice chat with the Asst. Clerk to the

---

197 Possibly Assistant Superintendent of Police K.A. Price seconded to the Gold Coast.

Assembly[198] – a friend of Asa Briggs,[199] from whom I picked up
some documents, though not the one I wanted most. Then came
back here to lunch and sleep. It seems a bit lazy – to neglect
opportunities of seeing people and all that – but I hope will turn
out to be justified. David Kimble is away in South Africa – lecturing! – it seems possible I may meet him at Leopoldville at the
end of the month. I've seen a little of Helen though, and her nice
children.

To DMCH
16 February 1953

Pointe Noire [Moyen Congo]
The trouble with this damned cold and sinus trouble has been that
it has interfered with work. I did far less than I'd meant in Abidjan,
and almost nothing in those 3 days in the G.C. One gets to a stage
at which one says 'To hell with everything – I'm just going to sleep
as much as possible'. However I did get hold of Boateng,[200] a nice
Oxford geographer at Achimota, who remembers you, to arrange
for a map to illustrate these Ancient Cities articles – and got photographs sent off to David Williams. Otherwise the time (what
wasn't used on sleeping) got taken up in odd ways – being driven
out in the car by Hugh Blaney on Saturday afternoon to Aburri –
the hills about 15 miles away – and back home by a country lane,
where all the children waved. Lunch with Helen Kimble – and a
bit of playing with her nice children (David being in S. Africa for

198 The Assistant Clerk was J.E.Y. Bosompen. He published a booklet
    'The Legislative Assembly of the Gold Coast', Accra, 1955.
199 Asa Briggs, born 1921 and educated at Keighley Grammar School
    and Sidney Sussex College, Cambridge, historian, fellow of
    Worcester College, Oxford, from 1950 to 1955 and Provost from
    1976 to 1991, and Chancellor of the Open University from 1978 to
    1994. He was one of many distinguished scholars who came to the
    Gold Coast and Ghana to lecture at New Year Schools.
200 Ernest Amano Boateng, born 1920 and educated at St Peter's Hall,
    Oxford, where he graduated in 1949, and went on to a thesis on
    human settlement in the eastern province of the Gold Coast. He was
    a geography professor and later Principal of the University College of
    Cape Coast from 1969 to 1971 and Vice-Chancellor from 1971 to
    1973.

a School). Dropped in on Lerner[201] – Literature Lecturer – to
borrow a laxative – and found him and 3 others starting reading the
Life of Benvenuto Cellini aloud – to improve their Italian – so
stayed for this.

Brazzaville [Moyen Congo] – Tuesday 17/2/53. Continuing on
this half-sheet so as to be sure that this letter (with Liz's and
Toby's bits) isn't overweight. Got through formalities yesterday
with minimum of trouble. Landed up at frantically expensive. and
inconveniently situated Air hotel, where I only stay till I can find
something better. This damned sinusitis doesn't seem cured so first
job was to seek a doctor. Called at British Council and was pleased
to find Consul-General was a nice man called Mason[202] who knew
Teddy in Baghdad. Very friendly. After a bit of chat he drives me
up to the doctor, who passes me on to Ear-nose-throat specialist
who prescribes treatment calculated to cure this complaint in minimum time. Consists of various things – sulphonamide tablets –
ointment – 'Optalidon' (whatever that means), and AEROSOL
treatment at the hospital twice a day. This sounds formidable, and
I don't yet know what in practice it means. But it seems to include
Penicillin and Antistine – ? injections, if I know the French.
Anyway he seems a nice chap who knows his job, and I am prepared to submit to anything in order to get cured as rapidly as
possible. For one really can't work or be effective till it's out of the
way. Which is a nuisance, since this seems an interesting place –
and there are lots of people whom I want to see. Anyway I expect
with this intensive attack it will clear up pretty soon. Meanwhile I'll
post this, and hope it doesn't sound a gloomy account. You know
how I tend to take any ailments over-seriously. Anyway I've now
reached, I think, the furthest point of this journey and when I start

---

201 Laurence Lerner, poet, of South African origin, was later Professor of
   Literature at the University of Sussex and author of *The frontiers of
   literature*, 1988.
202 Robert Whyte Mason (1905–84), educated at Glasgow Academy and
   Morrison's Academy, Crieff, was attached to the Ministry of
   Information as Director of Policy for the Middle East Services in
   1943 and was at the British Embassy in Baghdad in 1945. He was
   consul-general in Brazzaville and later Director of Research at the
   Foreign Office from 1960 to 1965. He wrote a dozen books including
   several thrillers.

to travel (apart from a brief call at Leopoldville, across the river) I shall be travelling home. Hurray.

To DMCH
19 February 1953

Hotel Relais Brazzaville
I am fed up to hear of your being ill – and having this temperature. It seems to me that everything points to the desirability of my getting home as quick as possible. Indeed I well could come more or less any time now. I have collected already enough information about AEF to produce something in the way of articles. And tho' another 3 weeks out here would be quite useful it isn't by any means essential. Also the cost of living here is so incredible that I expect I shall pretty soon be broke. It's not only this wildly extravagant hotel (I managed to keep my dinner last night under £1 by having only thick soup, scrambled eggs and black coffee – a triumph). But transport costs the earth. At least in Dakar everywhere is near everywhere else, but here distances are fantastic and (apart from an irregular bus service and one's somewhat feeble legs) the only means of transport are taxis – at a minimum of 8 shillings a time. The Centre d'Etudes Centrafricains (which corresponds to IFAN) is particularly inaccessible. In spite of all this I am quite fond of the place. The people are helpful. Today I've been seeing Herbert Pepper[203] – the authority on African music (of English ancestry as his name suggests), a very nice Director of Information, called Pairault,[204] who has given me a vast amount of material – I staggered away under the weight of it – and Gervase's friend, the Bishop and Apostolic Delegate, Biéché[205] (not a Breton, as I think

---

203 Herbert Pepper, musicologist, collected and worked on Fang epic song.
204 Probably Pierre-Henri Gabirault, born 11 September 1907 at Chauvigny (Vienne), France, on military service from 22 October 1931 to 6 October 1932, colonial cadet 1933, *administrateur* first class January 1942, second class January 1948, reclassified as an *administrateur* of overseas France 1951, *administrateur en chef* 1952.
205 Paul Biéchy, of the French missionary order Prêtres du Saint Esprit et du Coeur Immaculé de Marie founded in Paris in May 1703, served in Nigeria and became Roman Catholic titular bishop of

Gervase said, but an Alsatian). He showed me his new rather beautiful cathedral – built in the style of a forest of palm-trees, pale purple stone and thin red brick: very effective. I am looking too for an African priest of his the Abbé Fulbert[206] (good mediaeval name) who is said to know the African quarter, Poto-Poto, better than anyone else. So I am anyway fit for work again though still feeling somewhat feeble. Indeed I don't see how anyone could have pumped into him the quantity of penicillin, antistine, sulphonamide, cocaine, cascara and whatnot that has been pumped into me without feeling like a walking drug-store. But it does work. The sinusitis seems a lot better. I no longer have these crashing headaches. Just a certain residual feebleness and an unwillingness to work after 4 in the afternoon. But I've neither the time, nor the money, nor the energy, to do any serious work on the Belgian Congo this time: I'll go across the river and have a look at Leopoldville for a couple of days, I think, but nothing more serious than that.

Must start meeting some Africans tomorrow. All contacts so far with Frenchmen – nice ones, but it's not what I've primarily come for.

What I like about the French is their general casualness, and lack of fuss about regulations and suchlike – in contrast with most other nations.

To DMCH
23 February 1953

Grand Hotel, Brazzaville
A little line to you before I go to sleep. I don't know though whether I shall have a chance to post it tomorrow, as I'm going out

---

Thelepte. He was in 1936 appointed Vicar Apostolic at Brazzaville and took up his post in January 1937.
206 Abbé Fulbert Youlou (1917–72), founded the Union Démocratique pour la Défense des Intérêts Africains (UDDIA). He was elected Mayor of Brazzaville in 1956 and was President of Congo (Brazzaville) from 1960 to 1963. Conservative and corrupt, he was overturned after a three-day strike but spirited away by supporters and lived in exile in Madrid.

into the country for the day, with Sautter,[207] the very nice geographer at the Centre d'Etudes Centrafricains.

The more I think of plans the more I tend to telescope my journey – what's left of it – unless you do come out. This is partly sheer eagerness to be home, and partly the financial situation – due to the frantic cost of living here. The fact is that I'm now reduced to £60 in French money – which at the present rate can't last more than about a fortnight – living simply. In addition I've about £20 in West African pounds – and that won't get me far. Of course if Mallam Abba Gana[208] turns up in Maiduguri with transport I shan't need much Nigerian money – but this is not certain. Also I want some money for presents for everyone, since most of the things I bought in the Sudan I presented to the Gold Coast Museum. It seemed a pity in some ways, but Lawrence[209] wanted them (and paid me in francs for them – which I needed at the time!) So I think I had better get Barclay's to send me £50 to Maiduguri to cover contingencies. I probably won't want it all – but it's as well to be on the safe side. I'll write – or wire – to them, and ask them to do this – but you might, if it's not a bore, jog them to make sure they've done it. I suppose it had better be Poste Restante, Maiduguri. The chap I hope to meet there is an extramural tutor called *Reed*[210] (don't know his first name) – but I'm not sure that that's a safe address. I suppose one *can* send money to Maiduguri! It's not exactly a centre of finance as far as I know. If that's impossible they'd probably better send to Kano – but Maiduguri would be better.

Sorry for all this! Quite a nice day today. Spent 4 hours going round Poto-Poto with Apollinaire Ippet, the nice intelligent young interpreter from the Centre d'Etudes Centrafricaines. Met an enormous quantity of his relatives and had some useful talks. Now I must sleep,

207 Professor Gilles Sautter, born 1920, researched in human geography at the Institut des Etudes Centrafricaines at Brazzaville. He provided source material for some of Thomas's own later writings.
208 Mallam Abba Gana was an extra-mural tutor in Nigeria.
209 Arnold Walter Lawrence, born 1900, was author *of Trade Castles and Forts of West Africa*, 1963, and major works on Greek architecture. He edited *T.E. Lawrence by his friends*, 1937, about his brother Thomas Edward Lawrence (1888–1935).
210 Donald Reid, Resident Tutor in Maiduguri for the University College of Ibadan Extra-Mural Department.

Tuesday. Continuing. Yesterday was an interesting but extremely exhausting day. Not exhausting in that I had anything much to do – beyond tramping around the fields with Sautter – while he asked a great number of detailed questions about methods of cultivating ground-nuts and manioc. But it was my first day of full activity for a while – we left at 7 a.m. and got back at 10 p.m.

To DMCH
26 February 1953

Leopoldville [Belgian Congo]
Quite why I am in Leo'ville I don't know – except that it seemed silly not to cross the Congo and see what it was like the other side. But I've given up the idea of trying to do any work on the B. Congo – as beyond my present powers and means. So I'm not really trying to see any of the people to whom I have introductions. Indeed doing nothing but have a look at the town (and only the European quarter at that) – and eat a substantial lunch – and probably buy a few stamps for the children

To DMCH
[28 February 1953]

Bangui [Oubangui-Chari]
Here I am in a cafe beside the river Oubangui – wide and beautiful – with a great hill the other side. And would you believe it? The gramophone or whatnot has just been playing Toby's tune – 'Put another copper in to old Charlie's treacle tin' – which never fails to make me cry. It is a beautiful river, with little sandy beaches – and a line of rocks across it. – and fishermen wading in and casting their nets and pulling them in again full of fish – and little canoes scattered about the water – and the flush of the sunset, across the river, and in front, beyond the rocks, up the river, the great white full moon rising with little clouds around it. One couldn't really. ask for more by way of scenery and surroundings, with this pleasant background of sentimental music. It's a nice simple family hotel in the French style. I was very lucky to land up here – picked up by a couple of friendly compassionate Englishmen at the airport,

who drive a private aeroplane for a sisal planter – they kindly drove me here – (I not having a ghost of an idea where I was going to stay – or how to get there. I think too that it is relatively *cheap* – which is very important for me at this stage of the journey and when my main concern is to keep enough money to get on to Maiduguri. Gosh, the moon is beautiful making a line of moonlight across the river.

. . .

This being the week-end it may be a bit difficult to do any work here till Monday. I have introductions to the Govt. and I am also very anxious to meet M. Boganda[211] (Claude Gérard's friend – the ex-Abbé and deputé), but don't know whether he is here. (A canoe is just passing across the path of the moon in the background – with a black rock behind it.)

To DMCH
3 March 1953

Bangui
I really am having a nice time at Bangui. In a way unexpectedly so. It is largely due to two facts: first, this sympathetic relatively cheap family hotel – looking over the river – with a little court – and friendly management; and, even more important the kindest, most intelligent and helpful French administrator that I have yet come across, M. Goreau[212] – head of the *Services Politiques*. He has fathered me admirably – done far more than one could reasonably ask. Yesterday he took me to see the President of the *Assemblée Territoriale*[213] and the head of a large cotton company *Cotonafric*,[214]

---

211 Barthélémy Boganda (1910–59), ex-priest, elected first African member for Oubangui-Chari to the French Assembly in 1946. He founded Mouvement d'Evolution Sociale en Afrique Noire (MESAN) in 1949. He wanted to preserve the unity of AEF but had to accept separation and became Prime Minister of the Central African Republic in December 1958. He was killed in an air crash in March 1959 that may have been caused by sabotage.

212 Probably a reference is intended to J. Grivaux, who was responsible for Affaires Politiques in Bangui in the mid-1950s with the grade of administrateur of France d'Outre-Mer.

213 Henri Mabilie, a teacher in Bangui, representing a minor party of Oubangien Independents.

who said I was the first journalist whom I had met in his 21 years experience in AEF! He then took me home for drinks – with another friend of his, passing through – to meet his wife, and little boy, aged 5, called (not surprisingly!) Jean Pierre. This morning he took me round the town – to see the nursery school, and the sewing and knitting class for married women, and the houses they are building for Africans and suchlike. This afternoon he arranged for me to meet 2 Trade Unionists, two Catholic Youth, and a Vice-President of the *Assemblée Territoriale* – and one of the leaders of Boganda's party – M.E.S.A.N. (Mouvement d'Evolution Sociale en Afrique Noire).[215] We met in the hall of the *Mairie* for 2 hours this afternoon. He told me just now that he was rung up and asked 'What the hell's happening here?' and explained that he'd arranged it. Of course the idea was that I should see these chaps individually. But, as one might expect, each group stayed and overlapped with the next – and we ended with a general conversation – dealing with matters (as far as possible) which concerned Trade Unions, Youth, and MESAN. Tomorrow he has arranged for me to have a car to go out into the bush – to see a new textile factory and a waterfall – which is an excellent idea – and has also invited me to dinner in the evening. So altogether I am profoundly grateful to him. In the aeroplane I was wondering whether it was really a good idea to spend 4 to 5 days in Bangui – but it has clearly justified itself – largely thanks to Goreau. Bless him.

Now it's dark again – in this cafe overlooking the river Oubangui. It remains a most beautiful spot even when one has lived here for 3 days. The noise of the croaking of frogs (when the sentimental music doesn't drown it) and these little lizards coming after the innumerable flies. A kind of swallow (with more colour to

214 Cotton was grown under compulsory cultivation in the colonial system and in the early 1950s the production in Oubangui and Chad accounted for more than half of the revenue for the AEF. Four cotton companies held purchasing monopoly privileges over large areas; one was entirely French and three were affiliates of cotton companies in the Belgian Congo. Among the latter was Société Française des Cotons Africains (Cotonaf) based on another textile company established in Oubangui in 1928. Thomas would probably have been meeting M and Mme Baudot, the local director and his wife.

215 The MESAN vice-president was probably a private school teacher Etienne Kabylo, born 1918 and a member of the AEF Grand Council in the 1950s.

it than ours) flies around in the day time – and there are always people washing themselves and their clothes and canoeing. (They're astonishingly quick these lizards – the way they make a sudden dart at a fly, almost when it's on the wing, and swallow it). There was a gorgeous moth too in the lavatory – staying so still that it might almost have been artificial.

In spite of my fondness for this place I shall be glad to move on the day after tomorrow. The fact is that, though now properly healthy, I haven't the energy to do a great deal – and am absorbed with the idea of getting back to you. Not surprising! It's bad when one reads what the explorers of two generations back went through (I am reading a life of Brazza at the moment, a rather sympathetic character, having finished everything else). It's an interesting country this. Much less advanced than any I've yet visited (Liberia excepted) – with this fantastically small population 4 million – for an enormous territory. One finds a good deal of difference between the attitude of the administration, relatively liberal, and that of the businessmen, who tend to say that everything is moving too quick – and so forth. Actually I've had rather more chance of meeting representatives of the French business community here than in A.O.F., and this has been interesting. From the point of view of meeting Africans it's been rather less good – but that's been partly because I started with less in the way of introductions – and partly because there are many fewer leading Africans to meet (though plenty of nice intelligent rank-and-file people, and I've seen a fair amount of them, one way and another).

To DFH
15 March [1953]

Kano [Nigeria]
It seems too long a time since I've written – and it won't anyway be long now till I'm back. Now it's a Sunday afternoon – I've been to sleep after a fairly hard-working morning – and am expecting Dorothy early tomorrow. The idea is then to go on next day, Tuesday, to Maiduguri, where I hope we will find Mallam Abba Gana, who stayed with us in Oxford, and some transport, and to travel with him, fairly gradually, down to Jos, where it's hilly (and therefore cooler): then back to Zaria, and eventually Kano, and

home. I'd like to take Dorothy to Katsina too – but am not sure whether we'll be able to find the transport (or the time for that matter) for that. It's warm – but not I think oppressive – with quite a bit of wind. I got here on Friday from Maiduguri – by aeroplane I'm afraid (other forms of transport seeming a bit difficult to organise) – since when I've been relatively idle – seeing some officials,[216] including a very nice and informative Resident,[217] but not doing much else (apart from typing out an article, which I'm sending in to the Observer) – partly for lack of transport. This Air hotel where I am staying, though convenient for the airports, is extremely inconvenient for everywhere else – and Kano is a town which has several quarters – all miles apart.

Monday 16th. Lovely. Dorothy turned up – very punctually – at about 7.20 a.m. this morning (6.20 your time).Our plans are to go by 'plane back to Maiduguri tomorrow, where I hope we shall find Mallam Abba Gana, a friendly Nigerian who works for the Extramural Dept. of the University College, with a car, or truck. He will, I hope, then drive us gradually down via *Yola* to *Jos*; then we'll go back via *Zaria* and possibly *Kaduna* to Kano: arriving here, I hope, by the morning of the 28th – and leaving for England on the afternoon of March 29th: back on the morning of the 30th.

I hope that all goes well. It's lovely to thing of being home, and seeing you soon. We had a nice morning visiting the old city – climbing the minaret of the mosque and looking down from it over this great walled town – with its still mainly mud houses – with little pinnacles, painted various colours, reddish-brown, white and green, some of them, and visiting the market – which I'd never seen before – full of lovely things – pottery, basket work, woven cloths, charms, spices, antimony (for make-up), vegetables and such like.

---

216 Administrative nomenclature was changing in the early 1950s from the usage for half a century of the designation 'Resident' that arose from the preferences of Frederick John Dealtry Lugard (later the first Baron Lugard).

217 Bryan Evers Sharwood-Smith (1899–1983) was educated at Aldenham School and awarded a scholarship to Emmanuel College, Cambridge, in 1916 but chose to go into the army in 1917. He was a colonial cadet from 1920 and was Resident in Kano from 1942. He was Lieutenant-Governor and Governor (another change of nomenclature in 1954) in the north from 1952 to 1957, receiving a knighthood in 1955.

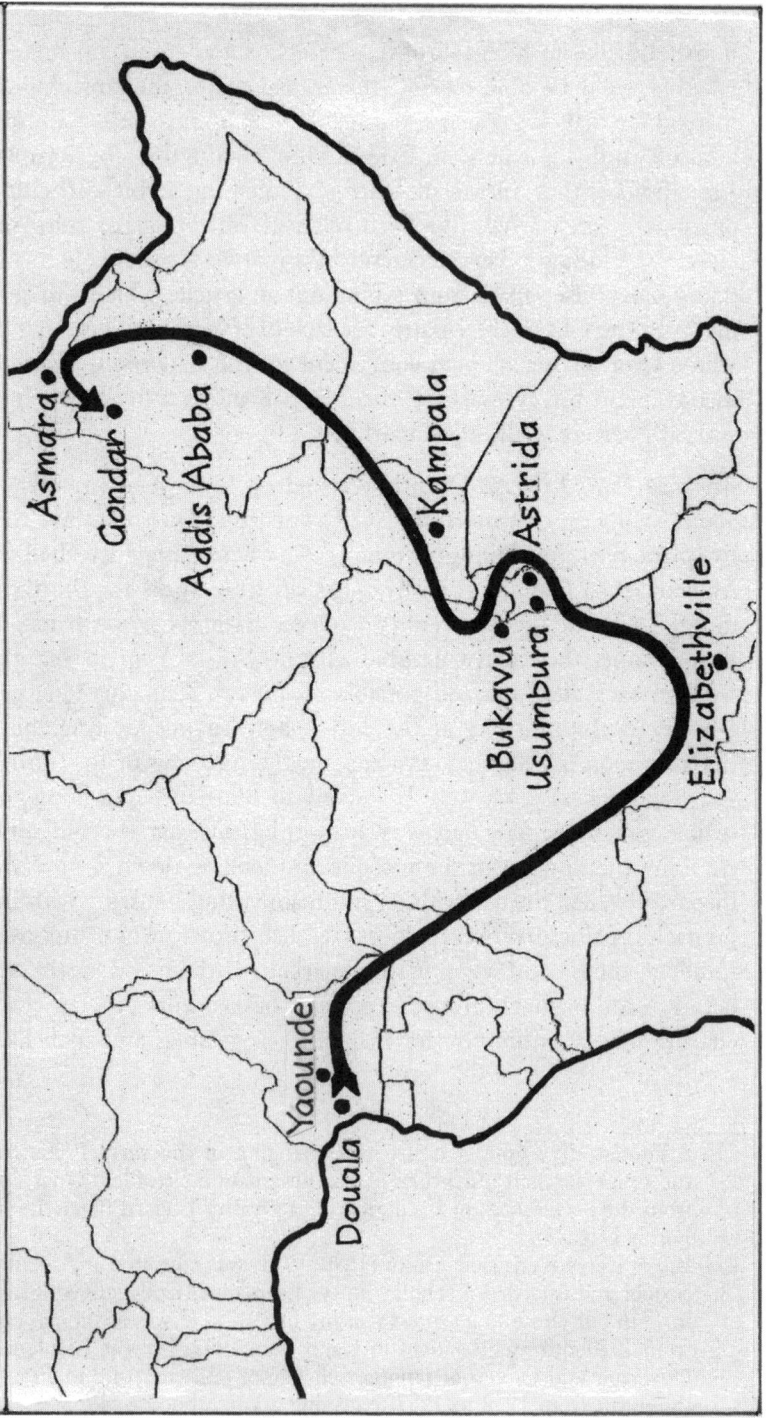

sixth African journey

Sixth African journey:
to West and East Africa
May 1954–July 1954

Thomas in the mid–1950s had no full-time post but continued to teach (philosophy to adult education classes) and to lecture. He was in demand to speak on Africa and the modern world, and on nationalism about which almost nothing had been published in book form. He had a commission by 1954 from a publisher for the book on nationalism that he had been contemplating in 1952. Through personal contacts and observation he was making himself into an authority on the differing impact in Africa of the main colonial powers – Britain, France and Belgium – and on the neglected area of pre-colonial history.

The wide-ranging sixth African journey in the summer of 1954 was supported by his journalism as in previous years. It was for a shorter span than the previous long journey but still ambitious and complex and with the groundwork even more carefully prepared. To avoid visa or police problems Thomas made sure that all the colonial authorities on his line of travel had advance notice of his itinerary and interests, and he was particularly careful to arrange how he might cross sensitive frontiers.

Since the Belgian Congo was at the heart of this travel he made a preparatory visit to Brussels in May 1954 to identify officials and institutions that would be helpful in the Belgian colonial and mandated territories. He went briefly to Paris and could now point to the articles that had appeared on French West Africa to reassure the authorities that he could safely be allowed to write on other areas of French influence.

Thomas included North-East and East Africa in the itinerary. This took him beyond the prime interests of the magazine *West Africa*, but his *Spectator* contacts encouraged the *Manchester Guardian* to take Thomas's contributions. He was in part filling in some of the gaps in his earlier travels, including Togo, Cameroon, the Belgian Congo, Ruanda-Urundi, Uganda, Kenya and Ethiopia, returning via Sudan. He had hoped to return to Mauritania, but went instead to the Gold Coast and delayed the start of the journey by two weeks as he was concerned that Dorothy was temporarily in poor health.

Thomas collected further material for his study of African nationalism. He contributed topical articles to the *Spectator* as he travelled and found himself in the predicament familiar to journalists of writing a thoughtful piece on one country while distracted by the sounds and sights of another. This took up much time and Thomas felt in retrospect that he had over-committed himself to the journalism and was trying to cover the ground too quickly for in-depth study of political movements he needed for the book. A series on 'The French Cameroons' was published in *West Africa* in the period from 20 November to 18 December 1954.

Thomas had earlier embarked on an historical enquiry into modern organisations in Africa. He was seeking the origins of the modern organisations, such as political parties, trade unions, churches, youth and women's organisations, and of modern forms of leadership. He distilled these themes – historical and modern – in his book *Nationalism in Colonial Africa*, that was ground-breaking when published in 1956 and has since become a classic.

To DMCH
30 May 1954

Lomé [Togo: postcard of Pieter Brueghel La Chute des Anges rebelles *from Bruxelles, Musee d'Art Ancien]*
Beloved – Sorry to send you such a grim picture – all I have left (except the massacre of the Innocents – by young Brueghel – I've just been eating an enormous lunch – which I don't really need – at 10.30 a.m. There is a change here – and I have to pick up a different aeroplane to take me to Douala – but Avocado pear, tomatoes, cold meats, mushroom omelette, mutton and saute, salad, gruyere, banana and orange + red wine at this hour of the day is a bit overwhelming. Still it passes the time. I must really get some Gold Coast articles written now – aiming at the issues of June 12th and 19th (which will be just after the elections). Supper with Polly

Hill[218] and her husband (great luxury) last night. We talked about
A.V.[219] and you and homes where both partners work and suchlike.
Kimble family saw me off – early, sweetly.

To DMCH
30 May [1954]

Approaching Douala [Cameroon]
We've been flying over creeks and am now flying over the sea.
There've been occasional villages – islands in the green – with
straight roads radiating out from them – the sky full of little clouds.
Time seems to have gone quickly in a way – and the fact that it's
only 7 weeks and a bit till we meet makes it seem much better than
last time. I'm a bit behind schedule already of course, but couldn't
have stayed much less time in the G.C. and as it was I didn't see
Kwame – and didn't do a few other things I'd hoped to do. Partly
my own stupidity – I could have made a bigger effort the first
evening and found him probably. The lesson one's always learning – that it never pays to put anything off. Less serious – I
missed Anthony Smith[220] at the *Drum* office – he'd gone off to
Lagos. But I had very interesting and useful talks with Rameshirean

---

218 Mary Eglantyne Hill (Polly), born 1914 and educated at Newnham
     College, Cambridge, was a civil servant from 1940 to 1951 and on
     the editorial staff of the magazine *West Africa* from 1951 to 1953.
     She married in 1953 Kenneth Humphreys, Registrar of the West
     African Examinations Council from 1952 to 1960. The marriage
     was dissolved in 1961. Polly Hill published numerous studies of
     Ghana and rural Hausa. including *The Gold Coast Cocoa Farmer. A
     preliminary survey*, 1956 *and The Migrant Cocoa Farmers of Southern
     Ghana*, 1963.
219 Polly Hill's father, Archibald Vivian Hill (1886–1977) was a physiol-
     ogist who had jointly won the Nobel Prize for 1922 and was married
     to Margaret Neville Keynes (1885–1970), sister of John Maynard
     Keynes (1883–1946), one of the most famous economists of the twen-
     tieth century.
220 Anthony John Francis Smith, born 1926 and educated at Blundell's
     School and Balliol College, was a journalist with the African magazine
     Drum from 1954 to 1955. He was Thomas's first cousin as the second
     son of the marriage of Thomas's maternal uncle Hubert John Forster
     Smith (1899–1984).to Diana Watkin.

Rao (the Indian Commissioner),[221] Danquah,[222] Yaw Adu (in charge of Africanisation), Peter Canham – and would have had an interesting talk with that very nice man Kofi Kanwah[223] – if I hadn't been half asleep most of the time (he's now father of 10 – eldest 22, youngest in arms – terrific!). David and Helen were very kind and hospitable – and their extremely nice children (3 and 2) – Jane and Judy – Jane particularly gay and friendly. (Now we're approaching land again, with what might be the Cameroon mountain in the background, wreathed in clouds.)

I'm feeling at the moment this is too rushed a journey – probably. Trying to get a quart into a pint pot – not the result of starting late, because if I hadn't I would have tried to fit in Mauritania too and that would have probably turned out madder still. It doesn't really suit my temperament to try to move quickly. Still one must make best of the present opportunities – and if Ethiopia gets a bit crowded out this time – that just can't be helped. Anyway I'll get to Paris somehow by that week-end July 24/25 – if not before.[224]

(Now one can see Douala – a big spread-out sort of town. Mountains in the background.) This is (as I know from past experience) a fiendishly expensive country – and I suspect this comfortable room in the Hotel Akwa-Palace – where I landed up –

---

221 J. Rameshwar Rao, born 1923 and educated at Nizam's College, Hyderabad, was First Secretary at the Indian Commission in Nairobi from 1950 to 1952 and acted as Commissioner for the Government of India in West Africa from 1950 to 1951. He was Commissioner for the Government of India in the Gold Coast and Nigeria from 1953 to 1956. He was a member of the Indian parliament Lok Sabha from 1957 to 1980.

222 Joseph Kwame Kyeretwi Boakye Danquah (1895–1965), founded the UGCC in 1947 and invited Nkrumah back to the Gold Coast. He became the leader of the opposition to Nkrumah in the early 1950s, among the founders of the GCP, defeated in the 1954 elections. He was detained in 1961 and again in 1964, dying in detention.

223 Kofi Konuah; see notes to letter of 12 January 1950 above.

224 Thomas was hoping to join Dorothy in Paris where she was speaking at the Sorbonne on the progress her Oxford research team was making on the structural elucidation of Vitamin B12 that culminated in a formal announcement in 1956. This work was the basis for Dorothy's winning of the Nobel Prize for Chemistry in October 1964. As letters below from Thomas in June and July 1954 make clear he was not able to keep to the Paris plan.

is beyond my means. Still it will do for the night – and I have at
least made good use of it to type an article (my first) for Taplin.[225]
And I've had a week of free excellent meals, which I feel I have
stored up in my hump somewhere.

Had a good breakfast. Nice chaps (Trade Union) – working, in
this hotel – going to bank, post, and government offices now.

To DMCH
2 June 1954

Douala
Writing this before setting out to see (I hope) M. Soppo Priso,[226]
Cameroonian politician, A rather patch morning: doing some useful
reading in IFAN Library (kind half-African girl in charge) and not
meeting people I'd meant to meet. It's a country which it is difficult to get much of a grasp of in a week – but some most exciting
peoples – Bamileke – Bamum and so on – the latter (like the Vai in
Liberia) invented their own script – but ideograms – not a syl-
labary – in 1897

To DMCH
4 June [1954]

Yaounde [Cameroon] Thursday night
I'll just begin this letter to you – though, as it's after midnight I'll
not try to finish it till tomorrow. I have accidentally struck very
lucky – and am staying in extreme comfort, luxury indeed, with a
nice man and his nice French wife, working for John Holts here.[227]

---

225 Walter Taplin, editor of *The Spectator* from 1953 to 1954, commis-
   sioned articles from Thomas.
226 Paul Soppo Priso, born 1913 and elected to the French Assembly in
   1946. As President of the Cameroon Assembly he sought reconciliation in 1955 with the nationalist Union des Populations du Cameroun
   (UPC) and was one of the leaders of the Courante d'Union Nationale.
   In 1960 he virtually abandoned politics to continue building a substantial fortune as a businessman.
227 John Holt was a Liverpool trading company prominent in trade with
   West Africa for more than a century.

This all arose out of the English consul in Douala[228] telephoning to him that I was coming – and he nobly met me at the airport (damnably late aeroplane, I'm afraid) and then invited me to stay. An excellent thing from every point of view (including economy), It's a rather beautiful place this – a bit like the British Cameroons – 2,000 feet up and more – rocky rather than mountainous (a bit like Jos too). Hills covered with woods. I've been able to type out my second *Spectator* article, which I'll post with this tomorrow. Now I find myself growing increasingly sleepy – it's said to be a sleepy place.

Friday. Making some calls. Spent the last one and a half hours at the Education Dept talking to Pauvert,[229] a sociologist, concerned with mass education – a big and interesting scheme it seems. But I learned less from him than I'd hoped. Maybe he was just shy – or doesn't like journalists much – or I didn't probe sufficiently. From him I went on to Klein[230] – the fat cheerful anti-clerical Director of education – and got a lot of information from him in a short time. Now I'm waiting for the bearded intelligent young Directeur des Affaires Politiques[231] to appear. I have a date with him to learn about the Communes Rurales, but he hasn't appeared yet – in conference I'm told. I had 2 hours yesterday – very useful ones – with M. Becquay[232] – who handles UN, foreign relations, and all that. Tomorrow – if I can get a place in a plane – I go back

228 Brian Surtees Phillpotts was appointed vice-consul in Douala in June 1952 and consul in January 1953. He entertained Thomas to supper on 2 June 1954 and gave him introductions for Yaoundé.

229 Jean-Claude Pauvert, born 1923 and educated at the University of Paris, was a sociologist and research officer for the Office de la Recherche Scientifique et Technique Outre-Mer (ORSTOM). He worked on Togo, Gabon, Cameroon and adult education in Francophone Africa. He was head of the base education service in Cameroon from 1952 to 1954.

230 Pierre Klein, from Paris and Bordeaux, France, was *licencié du cadre commun supérieur* and served in Yaoundé in the early 1950s as Directeur de l'Enseignement au Cameroun.

231 Possibly Joseph-Edouard-Georges-Marie Rigal, born 30 April 1908 at Saint-Eugène, Algeria, on military service 27 November 1928 to 15 October 1929, qualified at Ecole Nationale de la France d'Outre-Mer, colonial cadet from January 1934, promoted administrateur adjoint des colonies January 1935, posted to AOF June 1940; *administrateur en chef.*

232 M Becquay was in Service des Rélations Exterieures at Yaoundé and recommended by Phillpotts.

to Douala – on to Brazzaville and Leopoldville (God willing) on Sunday. I must try to get away from these towns in the Congo a bit. One has too much of them. The best chances would seem to be in the Bakuba country – between Leo'ville and Elis'ville – and in Ruanda-Urundi. But there's always a risk of being trapped in towns – just because they're the places where it's easiest to be.

Now about news. The 3 days in Douala were reasonably profitable. The people at IFAN (all Africans) were nice and helpful – and I used to drop in there when I had nowhere else to go. The British Consul was an extremely good egg. I called on him first because I was stuck over cashing my travellers' cheques. The French bank didn't like the way they were endorsed – and I found myself in a penniless state. However he rang up the Bank of British West Africa and fixed things. He also provided me with an excellent guide – called M. Ekwalla – who works in John Holts – of a Douala chiefly family – who took me out for the evening. After various bad shots we succeeded in meeting the chief of the Dido,[233] his uncle, and some of their friends – including an old man who spoke German, and a very intelligent young man, who gave me his views on Cameroonian affairs at great length. We spent a pleasant evening together – getting through a bottle of brandy and a bottle of soda and 4 bottles of beer – quite expensive, but the kind of expenditure that one feels justified. The consul also had me to dinner – on Wednesday – and I ate and drank and (I'm afraid) talked a lot – and it's always nice to be able to break into English for a change. His wife's expecting a baby – and there was a cheerful young Englishman from Nigeria there. I learned quite a bit too from some Catholics – a Frenchman with a wooden leg and two of African CFTC (Catholic Trade Union) friends – a useful kind of source. We drank beer together out of bottles and discussed Trade Unionism (CGT[234] is the strong

---

233 The Cameroon coast was historically under the rule of a king known as Bele, but often spelt as Bell, and later by a ruling Douala dynasty that broke away. They included Akwa, Priso, and Ebele – the latter based at Bonabela and known as Dido.
234 Confédération Générale du Travail (CGT) one of the French trade union bodies within whose framework trade unions were organised in Francophone Africa. Thomas observed that the relations between unions in France and French Africa were closer than those between the independent trade union organisations in Britain and the British Trades Union Congress.

organisation here – I've called at their office and made a date for tomorrow), I've tried – unsuccessfully so far, to see Um Nyobe[235] mal vu, leader of a party which demands the unification of the Cameroons – found some of his friends but not him so far. An interesting character is M. Soppo Priso – very rich contractor (De Cargonet[236] spoke of him), living an extremely elegant palace with a French amante and private secretary – member of the Socialist party in France, conseiller à l'Assemblée de l'Union Francaise, said to lean both directions at once here. Highly intelligent – we had half an hour's conversation and arranged to meet again tomorrow. I've never met an African who combined wealth and intelligence in quite his way.

Later. At this point my bearded friend turned up – and I had a useful one and a quarter hours with him – learning a bit about the organisation of Local Govt. Back here at midday – a large and beautiful lunch – conversation particularly about mixed marriages – and now it's 2.30 and I should be at work again. I have my host's 2nd car – a magnificent white object, put at my disposal – which makes everything easy. I'll post this, and my article to the *Spectator* at the same time. Try to get a seat on the 'plane tomorrow – and try to see some more chaps. But I'm having an extraordinarily easy time here really.

To PEH
8 Jun 1954

Postcard of Mokolo (Cameroun) Cases Kirdi-Matakam –
Leopoldville [Belgian Congo]
Another round of architectural postcards for you. I think these are rather nice – like a kind of fungus, I'm afraid I didn't get to see them though. In fact the trouble with this journey so far is that I

---

235 Ruben Um Nyobe, Secretary General of the UPC militant nationalist party banned in 1955. Ruben Um Nyobe then took to the *maquis* and was killed in September 1958.
236 Thomas is referring to a meeting in Europe with De Cargonet who suggested contacts in Africa and had particular knowledge of Cameroon.

get stuck too much in TOWNS – which, to be honest, I detest (big modern ones, I mean), though I can see that they are necessary and all that.

. . .

To DMCH
21 June 1954

Train to Elis'ville [Belgian Congo]. Monday
I seem to be having this carriage all to myself – which suits me on the whole, since one can usually pick up people to talk to in the corridor. I had a long talk this morning with the Belgian chef du train – I'd thought him a bit stiff, but he unbent entirely and we discussed the religion and marriage customs of the English and the Congo a bit. He was bothered because he'd heard that there were objections to Q. Eliz. visiting the Pope – yet we were supposed to be such a tolerant nation. At intervals I've been reading Turgenev's *House of Gentlefolk* – but I don't think it's one of his best – too inevitable, though there are beautiful episodes. And T.'s gentle melancholy isn't anyway the best kind of reading for one like me who am anyway feeling nostalgic, and anxious to be back with you, and this increases the nostalgia. We are rattling along – so that the beer bottle finds it difficult to remain upright – through country that is different from yesterday – less beautiful – dryer, more level, more wind and dust, fewer trees. More like northern Nigeria really. Here and there trees with purple flowers, like lilac, and plenty of green bracken still. I suppose we are in the Province of Katanga by now. Red, sandy earth. I've finished the article for the Sp. It will have to do, though I am not altogether pleased with it. Should do at least one for David Williams now. Also letters.

I still feel in a way full of Mishengue,[237] though it is difficult to pull it together in any intelligible way. And I spent too little time there, and talked too little to Africans, to make an article of it. But I had an extremely interesting conversation with M. Schillings,[238]

---

237 Officially spelled Mushenge, and usually pronounced as Nsheng.
238 René Schillings was a territorial officer in the Kasai from 1920 and in

the administrator from Mweka, who kindly drove all the way up to Mihengue (with a Forestry Officer who had an English mother) to fetch me back on Saturday evening. He is really the first official whom I've met who had an entirely independent nonconformist point of view, based on his own experience as an administrator. It was like talking to Kitz,[239] or Austen Harrison,[240] or the Essikardihene,[241] or someone one knows intimately. He clearly had a great affection and respect for the Bakuba (he'd been Administrator at Mishengue himself till quite recently). They had, he said, a beautifully balanced society, with this great emphasis on crafts, and design, and peace, and morals. Their chief, c. 1700, Shamba Bolongongo (whose statue is, I think, in the British museum) was reverenced as a man of peace (he forbade the use of all weapons apart from the common knife), a patron of the arts (he introduced the system whereby the various crafts were represented at the royal court) and a philosopher. In theory the king was absolute and divine, but in practice his power was limited by a whole range of councils, in some of which he was not allowed to participate.

Now the Missions were teaching the young to despise the old ways. But they had nothing of equivalent value to offer. The

the mid-1950s was administrator resident at the Kuba court. His fore-name was Flemish from the French, but he appears in some sources as Charles Schillings.

239 Probably an Oxford friend, William Edward van Heyningen, born 1911, a microbiologist.

240 Austen St Barbe Harrison was the Palestine Government architect when Thomas went to serve in the administration in 1934. It was Harrison who invited the sculptor and calligrapher Arthur Eric Rownton Gill (1882–1940) to Palestine to carve panels for the walls of the Rockefeller Museum. Harrison became a lifelong friend. He was also close to Dorothy's parents and frequently exchanged hospi-tality with them in Palestine and in England. Harrison in architectural partnership with R. Pearce S. Hubbard, another of Thomas's friends in Palestine, went on to work on a plan for the Region of Valletta in Malta.

241 This would have been a reference to Nana Kobina Nketsia; see notes to letter of 18 January 1950 above. When the University of Ghana was set up by statute of 1 October 1961, Nkrumah became the first Chancellor of the University, with Nana Kobina Nketsia as interim Vice-Chancellor for a year. He held an Oxford BLitt and DPhil and his traditional title was Omanhene of Essikado.

Bakuba had an entirely reasonable attitude to authority. The king represented God on earth, but you could criticise and even mock him publicly for all that. But White authority was represented as being above criticism. The Missions had burnt the fetishes – but fetishes were no different from images – a symbol through which men approached the divine power. It was said that the Bakuba worshipped the moon; they didn't *worship* the moon; they just took the moon seriously. And why not? Could anyone deny that the moon had profound influence on human life – through the periodicity of women and suchlike – which we didn't entirely understand? Conversion to Christianity was now being carried on as a kind of vast commercial enterprise – 100,000 a year, it was claimed. But this sort of mass conversion was fantastic. Christianity as a religion no doubt had certain excellences, but the process of movement from the one religion to the other should be slow, and a matter of personal conviction if it was to have any meaning for people. As it was the main meaning it had was a desire to imitate the White – to *be White* – like straightening your hair and wearing spectacles. Thus it could only lead to disillusionment – since the African could never *be* White, nor ever be completely accepted in the White world. Besides, while Bakuba religion was part of the stuff of life, Christian religion was distinct from life. The African who became a Christian quickly found that the bulk of Europeans were not themselves practising Christians. He learned that it was wrong to eat meat on Fridays, and then went to work in a restaurant full of White men being served with meat on Fridays. And nothing happened. They didn't drop down dead. They weren't expelled from the Church or publicly condemned. Similarly he found them breaking the rules of Christian marriage – and neither God nor the Church seemed able to make them suffer for it. So the African thinks 'this is a funny kind of religion – it's clearly a religion specially designed to meet the needs of White men – not me'. This is one reason, of course, for the development of breakaway Churches – the leaders of which are usually good Catholics and Protestants who have been disillusioned. For Africans are deeply religious – far more so than Europeans, and they cannot exist in isolation. But our policy is to deprive them of their religion and break up their traditional communities – the Missions do the one, and the business interests do the other. In its place we offer essentially individualist values and aims – getting on, making money, accumulating bits of property. But the African doesn't really respect our religion or our values – even when he conforms. What he does respect is our vital force – our capacity to push ahead, and get things done, shape the course of events; this is the quality which he knows he lacks, and wants to acquire. But for the rest of our philosophy of living – except when he is passing through the stage of imitation – he knows his own is superior.

In a way, of course, there is nothing new in all this. It is very like what I remember of parts of Gluckman's[242] thesis – and has been said elsewhere. But it was deeply interesting to find this view stated with such conviction in this new context – particularly since the official theory is that, provided everyone goes on getting richer (and more Christian) political problems can largely be left to look after themselves.

Usumbura [Ruanda–Urundi]. 27/6/54 Let me try and stick down, before I lose them, some impressions of Elis'ville. In a way it was a pity having only three days there – since it meant leaving much undone. It seemed, certainly, a much more genial atmosphere – the admirable Strebelle family – than Leo'ville. For one thing the division between the European town and the *ville indigène* is much less rigid – is much less rigid – physically and humanly – than in Leo. For another, there is this kind of regional, anti-Leo, nonconformist (in a non-religious sense, of course) atmosphere reflected in the local paper *Essor du Congo*, run by a man with the cheerful name of M. Sepulcre,[243] who is the brains behind it (and whom I meant to see but didn't), and edited by a man with the equally symbolic name of Lamorale (and which I wrote as L'Amorale – but I gather it might equally well be thought of as 'La Morale'). It's true that the paper expresses a moderate pro-*Colon* point of view, but at least it has a point of view, and attacks the Government when it wants to. Lamorale himself spoke strongly about what he regarded as the flabbiness and unwillingness to take decisions of senior officials –

---

242 Max Gluckman (1911–75), Professor of Anthropology, University of Manchester. His first and last works were on the judiciary among the baRotse of Zambia.

243 Jean Sepulchre (1894–1969) went to Elisabethville in 1927 and founded the newspaper the following year. He continued publication until 31 December 1960 when it became an African newspaper *Essor du Katanga*.

Governors, etc. Well, in a way, I suppose this is a normal *colon* attitude. I had quite a bit of conversation with a young Pole on the
staff of the paper, who had been temporarily at Magdalen in 1943,
and who was much moved by the fact that I lived at Oxford, and
kept asking after Tizard[244] and Lionel Curtis[245] and suchlike. We
ended up with beer and a somewhat undergraduate conversation
about Sartre and the Native Question, etc. But a nice chap.

Another thing that makes Elis'ville interesting is CEPSI – *Centre
d'Etudes des Problemes Sociaux Indigenes*. I had a long talk about this,
and other things, with M. Toussaint,[246] a very interesting and able
man, aged 63, Director of Social Services for Union Miniere.
There is a tendency to say that CEPSI is Union Miniere, which is
no doubt true insofar as everything is Union Minière – like Hegel's
Absolute. But it's also true, I think that CEPSI has influenced the
policy of Union Minière – in the way that the thoughts and actions
of finite individuals affect the character of the Absolute. The
Fabian parallel seemed a reasonable one, and Toussaint was willing – even pleased – to accept this: a group of intellectuals –
Administrators, U.M. and Big Business functionaries, lawyers and
priests (and doctors) – interested in social reform, and occupying
the kind of key positions in which they could influence policy,
achieve particular reformist ends. But what makes CEPSI important from my point of view is its willingness to co-operate with and
encourage the African *elite* of Elis'ville, all, of course, on a basis of
acceptance of the accepted religio-political assumptions, but liber-
ally interpreted. I was given a remarkable 250-page CEPSI Bulletin,
written entirely by a group of young Congolese, members of the
Cercle d'Etudes of St Benoit, on family and social problems,

244 Sir Henry Tizard (1885–1959), scientist in the Ministry of Defence,
President of Magdalen College Oxford from 1942 to 1947.
245 Lionel Curtis (1872–55), one of the founders of the idea of the
Commonwealth as a union of free democratic countries. He was a
research fellow at All Souls College Oxford from 1921.
246 E. Toussaint had been director of the mining company's department
dealing with indigenous manpower for the mines and was also the
Africa adviser for the company on indigenous matters – in the ter-
minology of the time. However he was also active in the CEPSI
branch at Elisabethville, an outpost of the headquarters in Brussels,
and this brought him into contact with a range of international institutions and scholars.

extremely well done, and pretty outspoken. First-class source material.

Astrida [Ruanda–Urundi]. 1/7/54 Have just been having an extremely interesting conversation with Van Sina,[247] anthropologist who is working among the Bakuba. I promised not to publish anything that falls within the field of his own work, since he has a book and articles on the Bakuba in preparation. A great deal of Torday and Joyce's[248] work on the Bakuba is inaccurate – for obvious reasons.

To ECH
26 June 1954

Usumbura [Ruanda–Urundi]
Dearest Edward

This is really rather an exciting place – on the north shore of Lake Tanganyika – surrounded by mountains. I set out this evening for a walk meaning to climb the nearest ones – but they were further off than I thought – which is the way with mountains – so I didn't get further than the neighbouring fields. But they are a splendid sight. Too bare to make one think of Alps – more like a Balkan mountain lake – Jannina or Ochrida. And marvellous to see the sun drop behind the mountains on the West shore – leaving a kind of radiance behind, even when it was getting quite dark.

It's a profoundly interesting country – Congo Belge – much too

247 Jan Vansina, a leading Belgian Africanist, published on the basis of secondary sources *Les tribus Bakuba et les peuplades apparentées*, 1954. After extensive fieldwork in Africa he published *De la tradition orale*, 1961, that became widely known in an English version *Oral Tradition: a study in historical methodology*, 1961. He wrote several Kuba books including *The Children of Woot: A History of the Kuba Peoples*, 1978. He reworked the themes in *Oral Tradition as History*, 1985. The letter continues with a long description of Vansina's ideas.

248 Emil Torday and T.A. Joyce *Notes ethnographiques sur les peuples communément appelés Bakuba, ainsi que sur les peuplades apparentées; les Bushongo*, 1910. Emil Torday (1875–1931) wrote prolifically on travels in Africa and on ethnography and anthropology. Thomas Athol Joyce (1878–1942) was an ethnographer on the staff of the British Museum.

large and complicated to find out much about in a month, of course. Still it's being a thoroughly useful time – and I've been lucky, I think, in having the chance of meeting a good assortment of people with very varied points of view. It's a disadvantage, of course, that as compared with W. Africa, one meets relatively few Africans – and, those one does tend to be fearfully polite. I tend to find myself quite a lot among the Missions (Catholic – of course) and, though one can't always accept their assumptions, the Fathers know a lot, of course, and are ready to talk in an unofficial and friendly kind of way.

I got here at about 11 a.m. today – coming by air from Elisabethville – flying bumpily over mountains – and finally over this great lake. Had 3 pretty strenuous days in E'ville (as we say) – and a much friendlier pleasanter place than Leo (as we also say), I thought – and would have stayed longer – only there isn't another aeroplane till Wednesday. And I am, I'm afraid, by now seriously behindhand – with no chance of catching up on myself. It looks as though I shall probably have to pick up a lorry to get me across to Kampala, since the bus service has been cancelled. It sounds as though Uganda was being quite interesting at the moment. In which case I expect I shall want to stay there a few days – and that will mean not getting to Addis Ababa till July 12th – and therefore not really trying to see anything much of Ethiopia – a pity. But I want to be back by hook or crook by July 24th – when I've promised to meet Dorothy in Paris – 4 weeks today that is. Still if one spends a week travelling North from A.A. to Kassala one will probably see a little of the country (Ethiopia I mean). I've now finished Margery Perham on Ethiopia – a curiously bad book – she's such a schoolmistress – and never tries, I think, to see what's going on from inside – but applies a sort of Lugardian metaphysic to everything.[249]

The fact is I'm damnably sleepy which is why this letter is tailing off into snippets. I am being extremely well treated here – met at the

---

249 Dame Margery Freda Perham (1895–1982) was a devoted admirer of Frederick Lugard and the doctrine of indirect rule. Lugard expounded his theory in *The Dual Mandate in British Tropical Africa*, 1922. Dame Margery, and with Mary Bull for later volumes, edited Lugard's diaries and was herself a prolific writer on colonial administration.

Airport (having remembered for once to send a telegram to the Governor[250] saying when I was arriving) by a nice young official. A Govt car has been organised to take me to Astrida on Tuesday – all very unlike what one's accustomed to. Of course this kind of journey involves a lot too much town – and I miss camels and chaps and the open air. But it was obviously going to be like that.

It was lovely to have your letter in E'ville. Nice too about the *Spectator* – I've done 3 articles for them so far – and should be able to fit in another couple before I get back. There's a lot to be said for writing as one goes – even though it's bound to be a bit rough about the edges. I see the Gold Coast Elections turned out fairly expectedly. (It would have been distressing if they hadn't).

To DMCH
29 June 1954

Astrida

Today spent mainly driving through these marvellous mountains – not surprising that they're marvellous since one crosses the watershed of the Congo and the Nile. Now I'm on the Nile side. The mountains are hard to describe – sometimes they make one think of Scotland – the ranges of steep misty hills one behind another in all directions. But in other ways very different – the terrific density of population – up to 500 per square mile – for one thing, meaning that all the hills are covered with signs of cultivation – terraces in the steepest places – banana groves, etc. And no villages – just quantities of individual huts – round and square – one hut and then a little way on another hut – and every now and then a small herd of those famous cattle with their small bodies and great lyre-shaped horns. One wonders how so many people ever got here – coming from the empty Congo – and why they never thought of having villages. One idea seems to be that the Batutsi invaders kept them (the Bahutu) separate so as to have no trouble. But it's a strange country suddenly to find oneself in – the cool mountain air and the half-mist after the heat and sunshine of the plains. I travelled in this swell Govt car – driven by a Congolese soldier from the *Force*

---

250 Alfred Claeys Boüaert was the Belgian colonial governor at Usumbura from 1952 to 1955.

Publique – a quiet sort of chap , who turned up one and a half hours late this morning. Not that that mattered much. I said good-bye to that kind man M. Delcourt[251] – and an extremely intelligent and frank Director of Education, M. Schepmans[252] (from whom I also learned a lot in a conversation yesterday). By about midday we reached Bukeye – where there was a Catholic mission – the road full of crowds of people – men, women and children, most of them carrying little stools – having just come from church. It was a feast-day today – St Pierre and St Paul – the Père told me later they'd had 12,000 to 15,000 on the premises that morning. Since it was a feast they had only a half-day – so I couldn't see the schools functioning – but I saw about 250 girls in the Teachers Training College, aged between 12 and 18, eating their dinners in blue somewhat orphanage-looking uniforms. Actually the fact that it was a feast meant that I did very well since the Fathers asked me to stay to dinner – and we had a magnificent meal – which I hadn't in the least expected – with red wine – and excellent meat (as well as hors d'oeuvres and soup) ending up with delicious coffee-cream gateau and tangerines. The *Père Supérieur* made jokes about the advantages of foreign journalists who travel in luxury motor cars – I tried to explain that this was an unusual experience. There were 3 Burundi fathers there – one at least a highly intelligent, sophisticated character – very like a particular kind of don (? Herbert Hart)[253] in fact – Batutsi I suppose – an Abbé, and member of the *Conseil*

---

251 Léon Delcourt was a district commissioner in the Belgian adminis- tration at Usumbura where he was responsible for the indigenous manpower service. Thomas knew of him through a former Makerere College economics lecturer who was doing research at Nuffield College, Oxford, on labour issues in Uganda. The researcher on Thomas's behalf gathered suggestions for contacts from a Colonial Office official in London who had recently served as labour commis- sioner in Uganda and knew key functionaries in the neighbouring Belgian territories.

252 M Schepmans, Director of Education at Usumbura.

253 Herbert Lionel Adolphus Hart (1907–92), educated at Cheltenham College, Bradford Grammar School and New College, Oxford, was fellow and tutor in philosophy at New College in 1945 and was Professor of Jurisprudence from 1952 to 1968. He was Principal of Brasenose College, Oxford, from 1973 to 1978. He was married to Jenifer Fischer Williams who in 1947 had joined the staff of the Oxford University Delegacy for Extra-Mural Studies to work with Thomas.

Superieur of Urundi – and I was taught never to confuse Urundi (or, more correctly, *B*urundi) with Ruanda – as bad as to confuse England with Scotland, or perhaps rather Ireland, they said. So I promised – in return for my excellent dinner – to try to explain all this to the British public.

Next stop was at Kayanza [Ruanda–Urundi] – 50 Km this side of Astrida – the whole journey from Usumbura to Astrida being 105 miles – about the distance from Oxford to Stoke – but of course up and down mountains and along ridges – with hairpin bends – seeing the road now high above and now far below most of the way. I called on the Administrator and was taken by him to call on Chief Baranianka[254] – a friend of Malengreau's[255] at Louvain – described as a 'Self-made man' – but only in the sense that he had educated himself, and taught himself French (which he preferred not to speak) and become very rich through coffee-growing – 'earns more than the Governor' – he is anyway hereditarily a very important Mututsi chief. His son[256] has just taken his degree – in Political Science – at Louvain, and is shortly coming home to finish his

---

254 Pierre Baranyanka collaborated with German colonisers and was leader of an aristocratic Rundi faction generally allied with the Belgian administration, and at this time regarded as the most important political character after the King. In late 1955 he moved towards party politics through Mouvement Politique Progressiste for the post-independence phase. His wealth was based on coffee and reputedly a levy on illicit gold panners taking their gold to Kayanza market.

255 Professor Guy Malengreau, born 1914, a liberal Catholic scholar was Director of the Africa Institute at Belgium's University of Louvain and author of classic studies of peasant cultivation. He was instrumental in creating the Catholic private University of Lovanium in Belgian Congo in 1954. He was later the Louvain representative in the field. Thomas visited him in Belgium in May 1954 for advice on the forthcoming journey to Belgian Congo and Ruanda-Urundi. Malengreau was regarded in Belgian official circles as a critic of Belgium's colonial policy.

256 The Chief had several sons educated in Europe. Thomas appears to be referring to Prince Joseph Baranyanka-Biroli who was the first African from the area of Belgian colonial influence to go for university training, after an authorisation given for him by the Belgian colonial minister visiting in 1948. Biroli studied at the University of Louvain and went on to further studies elsewhere. His fellow and rival student was Mwami Mambutsa's son, Prince Louis Rwagasore (they stayed in the same student hostel in Belgium). Biroli was a founder in 1959 of the Parti Démocratique Chrétien (PDC) where his

thesis. I was given some of Baranianka's excellent pure Coffee Arabica – of a kind one doesn't apparently normally get in Europe. Conversation was polite rather than exciting – difficult in the circumstances to get onto major topics. What with all this it was after 6 and getting dark when we arrived in Astrida (I stopped to photograph a Murundi – just before we crossed the frontier into Ruanda – and his cattle) – within a couple of minutes about 20 adults and kids had arrived to join the group – almost from nowhere. It was also pouring with rain – unusual as it's the *saison sèche*. We went straight to the house of the Administrator – M. D'Arian,[257] a Russian by origin (used to be called d'Arianoff) with a marvellous collection of lances (but 6 examples are missing, he said). He was suffering from boils, poor chap – otherwise I would have liked to stay longer. A very intelligent man who clearly knows a lot about Ruanda history – and gave me a list of sources – including some of his own works. I then installed myself in a cheap room in this *Hotel Faucon*. Quite pleasant – and decided that I might indulge in another meal – in view of economies in other directions – not only today – but yesterday, when visiting the Usumbura hospital, I met a young Brain Surgeon and Psychiatric Specialist (in Hugh Cairns'[258] field), Belgian, but American-trained, and married to an Englishwoman from Tunbridge Wells – a constant reader of the *Spectator*, oddly enough. I spent an extremely pleasant evening with them – and till 7.30, with Chotteaux[259] (who had been taking me round the town) – then Chotteaux went off, and I stayed (pressed by them) for another 3 hours, having supper and talking about the country – a nice and very interesting couple.

---

leadership was disputed by his brother Jean Ntidendereza. Biroli supported political fusion of Rwanda and Burundi. Rwagasore as a newly-appointed Prime Minister was assassinated by shooting in October 1961. Biroli was one of several accused hanged in 1963 for alleged participation in the assassination plot.

257 Arkady d'Arian (d'Arianoff) had written a paper 'Histoire des Bagesera, souverains du Gisaka' and published in *Mémoires de l'Institut Royal Colonial Belge, Classe des Sciences Morales et Politiques*, volume 24, third fascicule, Brussels, 1952.

258 Balliol Rhodes scholar and neurologist Sir Hugh William Bell Cairns (1896–1952) married to Thomas's maternal aunt Barbara Forster Smith (1896–1987).

259 Guillaume Chotteaux possibly in service at the Faucon.

An eye specialist also dropped in. And now, I suspect, I had better go to bed, so as to try to be sure of getting up in good time to start seeing people tomorrow – IRSAC[260] (the research institution) and the school people in particular

Bukavu (Costermansville) [Belgian Congo] – 2/7/54 Friday
I'll add a note to go on with this before I take it to the post. Days still pretty full. Have just this morning come down from Astrida by the Govt car – 185 Km. of winding mountain road – hairpin bends ever 100 yards – lovely views – beautiful flowers. Now I'm uncertain whether to try to get on an aeroplane to Entebbe tomorrow or to hope to pick up a lorry. I'll have to make up my mind this afternoon, but I'll try to pick up some information and opinions first.

3/7/54 I'm sorry not to have got this off yesterday, but I got caught up in occupations – useful and interesting ones. Governor not here, but talked with his deputy[261] – interested in Hodgkin's Disease and Liberia. He passed me on to the Director of Education[262] – a nice interesting chap, who took me up the hill to see the new Technical School – calling on the Administrateur de la Ville Indigène on the way – a friendly talkative chap – exhausted by a football match (organising not playing) the day before – and admitting in a nice open way that the last thing he wanted to do was to show anyone round – anywhere. But after a bit of chat we agreed amicably that he would pick me up this afternoon (Saturday) at 3.30 p.m. I've decided, I'm afraid, to take the aeroplane to Entebbe tomorrow. It seems a bit feeble in a way – but it seems to me that one might spend almost any amount of time going by road – and I haven't any amount of time now to spend. And perhaps my mental picture of winding in a lorry through the Mountains of the Moon is a bit romanticised. But I always regret being reduced to taking an aeroplane. Anyway I should be in

---

260 The Institut pour la Recherche Scientifique en Afrique Centrale (IRSAC) had its headquarters in Lwiro near Bukavu, and a centre at Astrida. IRSAC was founded in 1947 for interdisciplinary research on aspects of health, environment, society and culture of Central Africa.

261 The Belgian colonial governor in Kivu province in 1954 was J.P.A. Brasseur. Thomas probably met the territorial officer or administrator on his staff Emile Willemart.

262 Probably Mathieu T.L. Moffarts, Directeur Service de l'Enseignement, Bukavu.

Entebbe by 5 p.m. tomorrow. I'll write to John Colman[263] and let him know. Spent yesterday evening with M. De Malingreau – leading *Colon* – the Delamere[264] of the Congo (only a much more attractive person) and his wife – they gave me supper – interesting talk – he's been here farming for 33 years – and, while his views are essentially *Colon's* views, they are a more humane, intelligible form of the theory than one often comes across.

To DMCH
5 July 1954

Bukavu

Still here – my aeroplane which should have gone yesterday midday having got stuck. That's what comes of deciding it's best to be quick and go by aeroplane. I'm now sitting in the early morning sun – beside the airfield – hoping we'll get there this time – feeling somewhat empty inside. They haven't yet put the luggage in the aeroplane – and it may be quite a while before we start. Though a bore having to wait another day – and a Sunday when one couldn't well get hold of people – it wasn't altogether a waste time. I finished an article for WT[265] on Ruanda–Urundi, which at one time I thought was good, but am now more doubtful. And I climbed the hill to *the Ville Indigene* to watch an exciting football match between Kivu Excelsior Football Club and the Old Boys of the Fathers of the Holy Ghost (odd titles they have). KEFC – in yellow jerseys – won 3–0. I was sitting among KEFC fans – so it was just as well. It was a pleasant occasion – I sat between two nice

263 John Colman was an Extra-Mural tutor in West Oxfordshire from 1949 to 1953. His wife Rebecca Violet Hughes was formerly a tutor in Sussex, Buckinghamshire and Oxford. Their son Charles was born in 1951. John Colman was Warden from 1953 to 1956 of Northcote Hall at the then University College of East Africa (later University of East Africa), and from 1956 he was director of Extra-Mural Studies.
264 The well-born settler Baron Charles de Maleingreau is distinct from the academic of a fairly similar name. Hugh Cholmondeley (1870–1931), became 3rd Baron Delamere in 1897. In Kenya he received 100,000 acres of land in Njoro, became leader of the white settlers and strongly opposed the concept that the interests of the Africans were paramount.
265 *Spectator*'s Walter Taplin; see notes to letter of 30 May 1954 above.

young African chaps – one a *commis*[266] in the Town Office whom I had met the day before – the other who seemed highly intelligent – I don't know what job – but connected with the African monthly magazine, *Aurore*. On the way home I fell in with a street row – the Administrator and 10 African police trying to restore order – I didn't stay to watch. It is a marvellous site – Bukavu – on the side of this mountain lake – only somehow one doesn't enjoy these things properly alone. And the feeling that one ought to be getting somewhere else has a bad effect.

Now we're flying above the lake (Kivu) – with these long islands down the middle – wisps of mist lying around. Now unfortunately we're in cloud ourselves – but the mountains of Urundi are visible above the clouds on the left. A bright sun shining in. A cup of coffee – very welcome. Also *Le Soir* of July 2nd and *the New York Times* of June 30th – I'm sorry to see Oppenheimer[267] has lost his appeal by 4 to 1 – also the Americans seem to have won in Guatemala.[268] But I haven't yet discovered how Mendes-France is getting on.[269] – Now we're going down the valley towards Usumbura river[270] winding below. And here we are at Usumbura – or over it rather.

This really is beautiful – flying over Lake Victoria – passing quantities of little islands.

Makerere [Uganda] – 9-ish a.m. – All turned out very easily. Poor

---

266 *Commis* loosely describes an assistant or clerk.

267 J. Robert Oppenheimer (1904–67) was a United States theoretical physician and director of the laboratory in Los Alamos, New Mexico, where scientists working on the Manhattan Project in the mid-1940s developed the atomic bomb. In 1954, during the McCarthy period of anti-Communist hysteria, his military security clearance was withdrawn. The clearance was reinstated by President Lyndon Johnson in 1963.

268 A Guatemalan leader who had expropriated large estates including those of the United Fruit Company fled to Cuba when ousted by a military revolt mounted with secret US help.

269 Pierre Mendès-France (1907–82), a Radical Socialist French politician was Prime Minister in 1954 to 1955 when France declared an armistice with Indochina. He was forced from office because of his liberal policy toward Algeria. Thomas in June 1954 was interested that Mendès-France seemed to be making serious efforts to end the Indochina War.

270 Thomas would have meant the Ruziz river.

John Colman and family had turned up the day before – so weren't there yesterday. However there was a friendly Immigration Officer, and we got on to De Bunsen,[271] and tried to find John Cairns[272] in the Telephone Directory – unsuccessfully. Eventually I was given a lift over here (about 25 miles from Entebbe) by a friendly Indian (Isma'ili – Aga-Khan Community) customs official – who gave me excellent tea (tea and milk boiled up in the pot together) and sweet spiced cakes – with his wife. Very lucky in that I had 2 hours free tutorial on the Indian problem (a subject I promised Taplin to try to find out about). This chap – called simply Mr S. Haji – pretty anti-Nehru and encouragement given to African Nationalism. Lunching today with De Bunsen and Lady Cohen – nee Helen Stevenson – Old Dragon! (junior to me).[273]

Spent a very nice evening last night with John and Vi Colman – drinking magnificent white Chianti – a large quantity – after a good supper – gossiping and learning about their life (quite a tough one – from the job point of view – John is Warden of a hall for 230 African students and in charge of the College Appointments Board – so has not time, unfortunately, for teaching) – and about Ugandan affairs – complicated. I'm sorry I've been vague about dates. But the one definite date in my diary is July 24th –

---

271 Bernard de Bunsen (1907–90), educated at Leighton Park School and Balliol College from 1926 to 1930 (so part contemporary with Thomas). He was Professor of Education at Makerere College in 1948 and Principal from 1950 to 1964, receiving a knighthood in 1962. He was Vice-Chancellor of the University of East Africa from 1963 to 1965 and Principal of the Chester College of Education from 1966 to 1971.

272 Hugh John Forster Cairns, born 1922 and educated at Edinburgh Academy and Balliol College from 1940 to 1944, chemical pathologist. He was Thomas's first cousin, as the son of Hugo and Barbara Cairns. John Cairns was at the Virus Research Institute in Entebbe from 1952 to 1954.

273 Andrew Benjamin Cohen (1909–68) was educated at Malvern and Trinity College, Cambridge. He was appointed to inland revenue in 1932 and transferred to the Colonial Office in 1933. As Assistant Under-Secretary of State for the Colonies from 1943 and later as head of the Africa Division he played a part in drawing up the Gold Coast constitution that led towards the independence of Ghana. He was Governor of Uganda from 1952 to 1956 and awarded a knighthood. His wife Helen had, like Thomas, been at the Dragon School in Oxford.

Saturday – and somehow or other I'll get to Paris on that Day – and find you at the Cité Université – College Neerlandais – or at the Sorbonne. That is lovely to think of.

To DMCH
10 July [1954]

Train Saturday night
I suppose we might be in Kenya now – though there's been no obvious sign of crossing a frontier – perhaps that comes later. It's on the cold side. I have this carriage to myself for the moment, and I suppose might really as well go to bed. Most of the day I've spent retyping an article on Ruanda-Urundi for Walter T. – written a week ago – but I didn't like it in its first form. I miss you – to tell me what needs altering. This train is not nearly so smart as the Congo train – and much dirtier – but meals are relatively cheap – so I have two. And the chiefs of trains, instead of being Belgian, are elderly dignified Sikhs with beards and turbans. The usual gay throngs at stations – both Indian and African. Buganda girls I thought were usually beautiful. Quantities of fruit on sale – bananas, oranges, pawpaws, melons, ? passion fruit (with a lot of seeds). People seem to travel especially with several sticks of green bananas. Black babies passed through windows. Plump Indian dowagers in the compartment next to me. A multi-racial restaurant-car any rate. Lavatories are labelled 'European type' and 'Non-European type' – very discreetly.

But I must try to tell you about Uganda. It was interesting and very pleasant though of course too short to learn much. But staying with the Colmans was almost ideal – since one didn't have to make any efforts and they were extremely good about driving me wherever I needed to be. An admirable couple – and Charles, their son, a charmer – a sort of goblin type – with the strong pro-parental feelings and anxieties that seem to go with being a first-born. And though I was pretty lazy, I somehow succeeded in meeting most of the people I wanted. Tuesday I lunched with De Bunsen, whom I like very much (he has this kind of goodness and simplicity which is unusual), and Helen Cohen – he went off, and I stayed and talked with her. – they clearly both mind very much attacks in the British papers – particularly a recent one in the NS and N[274] (I read it – not very intelligent) – having started very optimistic about the new atmosphere they wanted to create – having lots of Africans and Indians to Dances and parties and so forth. Now it's a time of mourning – and Africans – Baganda anyway – tend to keep away. I liked her as a person. Then I went into Kampala – to the Information Office – met the Director – a cheerful man, ex-journalist, called Horace White,[275] helpful. In his office I picked up a man I wanted to meet, a historian on Makerere staff, called Low[276] – and went off with him.

He was enormously useful – working on pre-1900 Uganda history – but also *Times* correspondent – so knowledgeable about contemporary history too. I must try to stick down what I learnt from him before it evaporates. We mainly discussed the past history of Uganda nationalism – and why it had developed so late. (No national political organisation at all till 1952, when the Congress was started). I stayed there two and a half hours – having an excellent tea – and chatting – forgetting the time almost – with the result that I stupidly missed the Stonehouses[277]: a young couple (he was Labour Candidate for Burton) whom Fenner Brockway[278] had got out to work for the Uganda Farmers' Partnership – a kind of African independent Co-op (Producers') – which seems to have

---

274 *New Statesman and Nation.*
275 Horace White, Director of the Information Office, born 1911, edited *British Ally* in Moscow during the war, had been press attaché in Teheran in 1946 and Information Officer in Cyprus 1948; in Uganda from 1952, edited *A Guide to Uganda.*
276 Donald Anthony Low, born 1927 and educated at Oxford, was at Makerere University College from 1951 to 1958, part author of *Buganda and British Overrule 1900–1955*, and author of other books on Uganda and (later) Asian history. He became Smuts professor of History at Cambridge and later Vice Chancellor of the Australian National University at Canberra.
277 John Thomson Stonehouse (1925–88) was educated at Tauntons School, Southampton, and London School of Economics. He was an MP in Britain from 1957 to 1974. He was married in 1948 to Barbara Joan Smith. He faked death by drowning in an attempt to escape financial difficulties and later married for a second time.
278 Archibald Fenner Brockway (1888–1988) was a member of the Independent Labour Party who became a left Labour MP, and was chairman of the Movement for Colonial Freedom (later Liberation) formed in 1954 to campaign in Britain and abroad for all those struggling to achieve freedom from oppression and exploitation.

existed more on paper than in reality. It's a sad story – most of which I got from Mrs S (a sweet pretty thing – recently down from LSE, with two children), They've been living for a couple of years or so in an African house in the toughest quarter of the town. Everything went wrong: the farmers' Co-op S. thought too disorganised – so left it after a while, to form a Consumers Co-op – which went extremely well for a time – but then was dished by the spontaneous boycott which followed the Kabaka's[279] Deposition. He actually left the country on Wednesday – to go back to England and look for a job – she follows soon. The saddest thing is that he left with a case for embezzlement (clearly absurd) filed by one of his African directors against him. Impossible to know exactly what went wrong. It all sounds rather like the Narodniks who 'went to the peasants' in Tsarist Russia. But tough for them. I suggested they came and stayed a bit with us when she gets back. (No home to go to, etc.) I dined with John in Northcote Hall – interesting talk afterwards with a highly intelligent Kikuyu. Then early bed.

Wednesday – I spent the morning calling on Indians; first Mami,[280] highly intelligent ex-LSE, nominated Mayor of Kampala – Leg. Co., etc. A Liberal. Then Verjee[281] – a very prosperous lawyer – Isma'ili – and some of his nephews. Passionately Anglophil – with a son at Hove College – and extremely conservative – only too anxious to tell a journalist all about the Ismaili community (which is certainly fascinating) and the directives of His Highness the Aga Khan. Verjee is in charge of all the community's educational work in Uganda – 2000 children in 34 schools. They're a bit like Quakers the Ismailis – only more complacent.

Sunday morning – 11/7/54 – Timboroa – 9001 feet – No wonder it's chilly – the next station is called *Equator* – presumably because it's exactly on the Equator. This is totally different country from

---

279 The Kabaka of Buganda was deported to Britain in 1953.
280 Sir Amar Nath Maini (1911–99) was educated at the Government Indian School, Nairobi, and the London School of Economics where he took B.Com. with honours in 1932. He was the first Mayor of Kampala from 1950 to 1955. He became Minister of Corporations and Regional Communications and left Uganda for Britain on retirement in 1969.
281 J. Verjee was administrator of the Ismaeli Education Department for Uganda.

Uganda – a sort of Salisbury plain – wide green open country – with patches of forest-pines – and Scotch mist hanging over everywhere – a lot of wild flowers – lilacs (red and white) and flowering shrubs – we've just passed a notice saying 'Equator' – with one finger pointing North and the other South. Everyone looks fairly cold in this early morning mist. Africans seem to wear Army blankets as a rule – Englishmen wear jackets – one sees why they felt it 'just like home'. Soon, I suppose, we descend into the Rift Valley – other end of the Jordan Valley and the divide between Lebanon and Anti Lebanon. All this area looks fairly thinly populated – occasional European farms. I've just had an excellent 3-shilling breakfast of the usual substantial British kind – here is 'Equator' – wild nasturtiums beside the line – beautiful. Down to 8,716 feet. The station entirely bordered with pines. Indian gramophone music going all the time in one of the carriages. Small wooden round African thatched huts. Looking down towards what I suppose must be the Rift. Down now to 7,600 feet. Sun has come out – but still cloudy – I warmed myself up a bit standing in the sun at the last station.

To go on with the story – I learned a good deal from Mr Verjee about the Ismaili community – and one of his very elegant intelligent (? ex-Cambridge) lawyer nephews[282] took me round to visit one of their schools – housed behind the mosque – with an Englishwoman teaching the little ones – and an Indian teaching Algebraic geometry to the bigger ones. They are moving shortly into grand new premises – with a boarding school – and a full secondary, as well as primary, course (6 years of each) – to be opened by His Highness[283] when he comes to celebrate his platinum jubilee in September. H.H. has given firm instructions that they should assimilate as much as possible – no teaching of Gujerati in schools – but English as their first language, and Luganda (or another African language) as their second. But whether assimilation means becoming more and more British or more and more African seems

---

282 The nephew was almost certainly Bahadurali Kassam Suleman Verjee, barrister-at-law, whose B.Com. degree was taken at the London School of Economics in 1936.

283 Aga Khan III (1877–1957) became leader of the Ismaili Muslim sect from 1885. He was president of the League of Nations General Assembly in 1937.

unclear. To Mr Verjee senior it's clearly the latter[284] – Hove is his Mecca.

I then picked up Martin[285] – in charge of the E. African Statistics Dept (friend of Taplin's) – he drove me over to Entebbe – useful as I was dining with Cohen, and had to get over somehow – we had a quick lunch and a bit of talk together – quite pleasant – but I might have got more out of him with more time. Spent the afternoon at the new Local Govt and Community Development Training Centre. Interesting. Spent an hour listening to a discussion on water supply, food, etc. for a dozen African Labour Inspectors admirably conducted by a nice man called Beeton, who took me home and gave me tea afterwards. Also listened at some length to the Principal – a man called Williams – Ex-Kenya. It's in a lovely position just next to Govt House, looking out over the Lake and the Islands. It's apparently Cohen's ewe-lamb. Then back for a drink with Martin. Dinner with Cohen – 3 hours interesting conversation – partly about the Congo – partly about Uganda. More about the future than the past. Of course he's much more intelligent than most Governors – and sees the inevitability of development on Gold Coast lines. At the same time he's got involved in this trouble – which he clearly hopes Hancock[286] will sort out. My Lukiko[287] friends were a bit difficult to get at – partly because they are tied up, many of them, with Hancock most of the day – in this study-cum-discussion group – at the Bishop's Palace. (Great mountains in the distance – the other side of the Rift presumably – passing through ? millet fields – and hills covered with beautiful woods). Eventually – on Thursday – I found Mr Seka Banja[288] in his office – acting President of the Uganda National Congress (President withdrew to London – next

---

284 Thomas means the former.
285 Cyril John Martin, born 1919 and educated at Wolverhampton and Manchester University, was a statistician who had been on the UK delegation to Paris Conference on reparations in 1945 and director of Statistics in East Africa since 1946.
286 William Keith Hancock (1898–1988), from Australia, director of the Institute of Commonwealth Studies in the University of London from 1949 to 1956 and receiving a knighthood in 1953. He headed the constitutional mission to Uganda in 1954.
287 The Buganda parliament.
288 S.M. Sekabanja, acting president of Uganda National Congress founded in March 1952.

acting President in gaol for seditious publication). A nice man – no inhibitions about talking. UNC is clearly still very young – and only beginning to organise itself. Still – it has a 5-point programme – and a party card – and this boycott which it has been organising seems to have had some success (partly perhaps because there was a spontaneous partial boycott in Buganda anyway). Its main object clearly is to develop national, as opposed to tribal, feelings. Opinions differ about its effectiveness. One would have to travel about the country to see. Then I had lunch with Audrey Richards[289] – whom I'd never met before – Director of the E. Afn. Inst. of Social Research – a vigorous amusing woman, much interested in local politics – a nice mixture of sociology and gossip. Also met a young man called Gutkind,[290] who's doing a local survey and much disapproves of Crossman's[291] NS and N article some months ago. Later in the afternoon – evening rather – John C, drove me out to find Mulira[292] (editor of a successful newspaper) who was on the Lukiko's Delegation. We had some difficulty in finding his house – since no roads have names – and houses and bush (as on Boars Hill)[293] are very much mixed up. After one or two false trails

---

289 Audrey Richards (1899–1984), anthropologist especially of the Bemba people, studied under Malinowski at the London School of Economics. In the 1930s she taught in South Africa where students included leading anthropologists of the next generation. She was founder and director of the East African Institute of Social Research (EAISR) from 1950 to 1956. She later founded the Cambridge University African Studies Centre.

290 Peter C.W. Gutkind was educated at the University of Chicago and was at the EAISR in his early career. He went on to be Professor of Anthropology at McGill University, Montreal, Canada. He was also at the University of Warwick and author and editor of many books. He chose Thomas's paper 'Mahdism, Messianism and Marxism in the African setting' for republication in Peter C.W. Gutkind and Peter Waterman, editors, *African Social Studies: A Radical Reader*, 1977.

291 Richard Howard Stafford Crossman (1907–74) was a senior contemporary of Thomas's at Winchester and a friend at Oxford University. He took WEA classes and schools. He beecame a Labour MP and Minister in the 1960s Labour Government, editor of the *New Statesman* from 1970 to 1972.

292 Eridadi Medadi Kasirye Mulira, born c.1917 and educated at King's College, Budo, and London University was editor of a Luganda language newspaper and elected to the Lukiko in 1953.

293 Some four miles out of Oxford, where the Hodgkin family were living at a house named Powder Hill.

we eventually found him – and I had a very valuable hour with him and his beautiful wife Rebecca, mother of 5 (but doesn't look it) – had recently been on a YWCA-sponsored tour in the USA. Active in the Mothers' Union. Has recently organised the Uganda African Women's League – which sent a protest deputation (with the Bishop) about the Kabaka's deposition to the Governor. Also there in the background, heavily-swathed was one of the Kabaka's sisters. Mulira is a moderate – sympathises with the Congress but doesn't belong to it. I got from him a very interesting account of the events of the last few months. He drove me – a little late – to meet Mr Verjee – who had invited me out to dinner to talk more Ismaili community business.

But first he took me to a 'Sundowner' given by another wealthy Indian – where all the *elite* of Kampala was gathered. I talked to a group of Indian businessmen (Chamber of Commerce), the Chief Secretary, a man called Thornley[294] (his brother a contemporary at Winchester – scholar), the Katakira[295] (how spelt?: Prime Minister anyway) and Chief Justice of the Lukiko[296] (+ 2 of the 8 Regents – the PM has by tradition to be an Anglican – and the Chief Justice a Catholic).

Then dinner with the Verjees – rather hot (food) – and a lot more about the Aga Khan. Home about 10.30.

Friday – the last day – consisted of odd jobs in the town – tickets, etc., then tea in John's office at 10 (luxury) with his domestic bursar[297] and a man who runs the electricity distribution here[298]

---

294 Colin Hardwick Thornley (1907–82) and educated at Uppingham and Brasenose College, Oxford, joined the colonial service in 1930 and was serving in Kenya in 1945 before going to Uganda as Chief Secretary. He was Governor of British Honduras and awarded a knighthood in 1957. He was Director General of Save the Children Fund from 1965 to 1974. The brother who was at school with Thomas was Ronald Howe Thornley, who went from Winchester to Clare College, Cambridge. He was managing director of Ideal Standard radiators from 1952 to 1967.

295 Katikiro – Chief Minister.

296 Chief Justice (Omulumuzi) to the Kabaka's kingdom; it was the highest Baganda position to which a Catholic could aspire. The Omulumuzi in 1954 was Matayo Mugwanya.

297 Mrs Alma Bavin, Domestic Bursar for Northcote and New Halls, had previously been in Corfu and Palestine.

298 Peter Kibblewhite was the local manager of Callenders Cables

(and has the useful function of employing Vi Colman and Mrs Stonehouse part-time). Then the rest of the morning with Sempa,[299] Secretary of the Lukiko – a charming man – who used to be at Achimota. Remembered Uncle Herbert[300] – as a boy. I learnt a lot from him about the Lukiko – as well as about the present state of affairs. Lunch with Margaret Stanier[301] – who seemed cheerful – looks after herself – had made the dinner – enterprising girl – drives herself over to Ruanda–Urundi – all round Uganda – collecting blood samples – and into Kenya – all on her own. She said her research was going well – and she was about to publish a paper. Sent her love – and was sad to hear about the sinusitis. Then called on Kearney[302] (Margaret S. had to go off to a tutorial at 2.30), Catholic chaplain, friend of Gervase's – spent an hour talking with him – then back to John's office to wait for your call to come through. Dropped off for a few minutes. It came through very punctually at 4.15 p.m. (which I suppose was 1.15 for you). Lovely to hear 'I've got Mrs Hodgkin on the line for you'. One of the wonders of modern science of which I wholly approve. It made a lot of difference to be in immediate touch in that way. Back to tea at John and Vi's – where Mrs Stonehouse turned up – of which I was glad. Went off at 6 with Morris[303] –

---

running electricity cables from the Jinja dam at the source of the White Nile.

299 Amos Kalule Sempa had studied at Achimota in the Gold Coast (six Ugandan boys were sent there as an experiment). He became Minister of Finance in the Kabaka's government.

300 Herbert Gresford Jones (1870–1958), educated at Haileybury and Trinity College, Cambridge, was Bishop of Kampala from 1920 to 1923 and Bishop of Warrington from 1927 to 1945. He was the husband of Thomas's paternal aunt Elisabeth (Lily) Hodgkin (1873–1972).

301 Margaret W. Stanier, who had her first degree and doctorate from Oxford University, was lecturing in the Department of Physiology.

302 The Reverend Father George Carney, who was educated at Cambridge and a member of the Mill Hill Mission, joined Makerere College in 1947 as Roman Catholic Chaplain and Lecturer in Geography.

303 Harold Stephen Morris, born 1913 and educated at Edinburgh University, was a senior research fellow of EAISR from 1952 to 1955 and made a sociological study of Asians in Uganda. He published his findings in articles and a book *The Indians in Uganda*, 1968. He became lecturer in social anthropology at the London School of Economics.

sociologist, working on the Indian community – an admirable and very interesting man – I wish I could have had longer with him. But I had to get back (a bit late) for dinner in hall with John: an interesting Nyasalander there – who left early to rehearse *King Lear* (he playing K.L.)[304]. After supper went over to De Bunsen's, and had a long talk with him – partly about John, who – De B. Agreed – ought to be teaching and not so overburdened with administration: partly about College affairs in general – and his problems – and extra-mural work. It was nice of him to take so much trouble – a very kindly man. I had the chance to put in a word for Lalage[305] – who I know would like to do a tutor's job over there. Back about 11. And that's pretty well the end of the Uganda story – a bit condensed, I'm afraid. But I must try to get something written in the course of today (We don't get into Nairobi till 7.30 p.m.). Vi, John and Charles came and saw me off at the station – but Charles didn't like seeing the trains too close. Now we seem to be travelling along in the Rift – a wide plain – with mountains in the distance – occasional very English-looking herds of British Frisians

Lake Nakuru [Kenya]. Extremely beautiful – lying between two ranges of hills – rather like Tiberias. It's incredible country.

To ECH
14 July 1954

Addis Ababa [Ethiopia]
I meant to send this sooner, but got delayed. Hence the swish Norfolk Hotel notepaper – I actually did spend the night in that historic hotel, not through choice, but because my Ethiopian

---

304 David Rubadiri, born 1930 in Nyasaland and educated at King's College, Budo, Uganda, and at Makerere, Bristol and Cambridge Universities. A poet and fiction writer, he served as Malawi's ambassador to the United Nations and later as Senior Lecturer in the Department of Literature at Makerere.
305 See notes to letter of 10 January 1950 above and several earlier references to Lalage Bown. She arrived in Uganda in December 1955 and began her extra-mural tutorial work in East Uganda early in 1956.

Airlines hotel [sic] was delayed a day, and they put me there gratis for the night.

It's nice to be here. I had 4 useful days in Uganda, and learned as much as one can reasonably hope to in that time. But I'd rather be a giraffe than an African in Nairobi. This is a somewhat vague sort of place – but extremely friendly – and one travels in red and yellow imperial buses (made in Italy), with charming Ethiopian women in their flowing braided gowns and black, or coloured, bonnets. Being late, I shan't be able to do a great deal, I'm afraid. But I hope to be able to go to Khartoum *via* Gondar and Asmara – if I can spend 2 or 3 days in Gondar that will be something. It's very wet and English, One sees the purpose of the umbrella symbolism. Met a nice Quaker in the Ministry of Education called Lister;[306] also an ex-Bodley-librarian Amharic expert called Wright,[307] and Mrs Sandford,[308] here for 30 years, runs a school – was at Girton with aunts Rosalind[309] and Barbara; and some (but not yet enough) Ethiopians.

To DMCH
14 July 1954

Hotel Ras – Addis Ababa
This is really only a line, written a bit late at night – with the rain pouring down outside – about plans. I've been discussing travelling plans with BOAC and Aden Airways. It does look as though it won't

306 Douglas Lister, in the Ministry of Education at Addis Ababa.
307 Stephen Graham Wright, Director of the Ethiopian National Library, formerly at the Bodleian Library in Oxford, published *Ethiopian incunabula from the collections in the National Library of Ethiopia and the Haile Sellassie I*, 1967.
308 Christine Lush, who died in 1975, was married to Brigadier Daniel Arthur Sandford (1882–1972) and went to Ethiopia with her husband in 1920. After the liberation of Ethiopia from Italian occupation she started the Sandford Community School in 1943. She was the author of *The Lion of Judah hath Prevailed*, 1955.
309 Thomas's maternal aunt Rosalind Grace Smith (1892–1984), historian, married first in 1915 to historian Murray Wrong from Canada, who died young in 1928 of heart disease, and second in 1951 to Sir Henry Clay (1883–1956), Warden of Nuffield College, Oxford, from 1945 to 1949.

be possible to get to Paris until July 27th – Tuesday-evening – unless I either miss out Gondar altogether, or don't stop even for a moment in the Sudan. I'm a bit torn – but, though longing to be back, feel that I'd perhaps better try the plan that should get me to Paris on the Tuesday – since you say you don't mind too much if I do this – and one doesn't know when one will be back again in these parts.

But, as I say, I'm torn, since it would be lovely to hear you talk about B12 in the Grande Salle of the Sorbonne on July 23rd at 9 p.m. – that's very exciting. And I'm so glad it's come out so beautifully – that's grand – and admirable. No wonder you're all elated. So am I.

To DMCH
18 July 1954

Addis Ababa Airport
Sunday 6.45 a.m. I think there's time to scribble you a line before my aeroplane goes (if it does go) to Gondar. I am almost half asleep – having not tried to sleep much last night. I visited the University College Students' Ball – and only left at 1 a.m. – then slept and packed. However the extremely smart Airport official who has just dealt with my ticket hasn't slept at all – since he was dancing all night. He is an Eritrean who was in the Sudan from 1942 to 1947 – last 2 years at Gordon College – speaks excellent Arabic. I've just been talking to a little – Ethiopian or Eritrean? – boy – talks very good English – on his way home (Asmara) from school – told me I looked like a teacher – and took my address, since he wants to go to Oxford eventually. I've been having a pretty strenuous (but very useful) three days. Lister, the Quaker (ex-F.A.U.)[310]

---

310 The Friends Ambulance Unit (FAU) was an unofficial body with no formal ties to the Society of Friends, and was started at a training camp in 1914 under the leadership of Philip Noel-Baker (1889–1982). It was composed of pacifists, Quaker and non-Quaker, who originally worked in France under the direction of the military, but purely in a non-combatant manner. The work was both with the civilian population behind the lines and with the wounded at the front. The FAU was revived in 1939 to undertake wartime medical work. Its members served in Europe, the Middle East, India, and China.

in the Ministry of Education, has been looking after me marvellously.

To JWC and GMC
22 July 1954

Asmara [Ethiopia]
This seems a rather awful town – the usual kind of European trappings – and too many seemingly semi-employed Italians (though this – the *Albergo Italia* – is a pleasant cheap Italian hotel). But Gondar, where I've just come from is magnificent – and I must tell you a little about it. It was, as you probably know, the effective capital (though crownings still took place at Aksum) of Ethiopia from 1632 till about 1855 (when Theodore moved to Magdala), And it has these marvellous castles – built mainly (I gather) by the Emperor Fasil – an interesting character – who expelled the Jesuits (in 1632) and brought Ethiopia officially back into the Coptic Monophysite fold. They are extremely impressive – several castles – mainly in good preservation – within a 12-gated *enceinte* – great keeps, 5 or 6 storeys – flanked with round towers, somewhat tapering, with conical tops. There's a theory of Portuguese influence – or architects – but Stephen Wright (Amhara scholar – formerly at the Bodleian – now Director of the Ethiopian National Library) says this is rubbish – if they're like anything, they're like Freya Stark's Hadramaut castles.[311] Great battlements along the main rampart – with minor castles within it. Rounded arches mainly – for doors and windows – with Renaissance style capitals – often of a kind of violet stone (tufa?) let into the main building. Other castles on surrounding hills – all with the same round towers. The two best I saw were Debra Berhan, which is really a fortified

---

311 Dame Freya Madeline Stark (1893–1993), traveller and author of many books including *Seen in the Hadhramaut*. She was married in 1947 to Stewart Henry Perowne (1901–89), an orientalist and historian who joined the Palestine Government education service from 1927 and then held other posts in the administration. He was transferred to Malta in 1934. He was in diplomatic service in Baghdad from 1941 to 1944. He was a friend of Thomas and of Edward Hodgkin (ECH).

church, Basilica shape, instead of the usual round form – where
Jesus the Great (Adiam Ighad Iyasu, 1682–1706) is said to have
meant to have himself crowned – but the Church made him get
crowned at Aksum in the traditional way; and Cusquam, castle of
the Queen mother Iteghe Mintiwab, who had about 25 years'
regency in the middle of the 18th Century, friend of the Scotch
traveller, Bruce. A very beautiful ruined hall there. The Debra
Berhan Church has good paintings – Madonna, Trinity (3 men
with beards; all identical), Saints (especially George of course), the
Passion and Crucifixion, and a nice little painting of Mohammad on
a horse (or camel?) being led down to Hell by the Devil. There's
also a beautiful Bath of Fasil – a pool (mainly weeds now – with
bright birds flying about) – surrounded by a wall – and a small fortified house above it. An admirable quiet place to work in. I had tea
with the Governor-General of the Province of Begemder and
Semien (everyone is 'General' – all Doctors are 'Doctors-General,
and Secretaries 'Secretaries-General') – a nice intelligent youngish
man, ex-Oxford, I think – Asrat Kassa – a son of Ras Kassa[312] –
knowing a good deal about Ethiopian history. His Govt House was
the fortress of Ras Mikhail – friend of Bruce's – who established
himself for a time as more or less dictator of Ethiopia.

But, apart from the castles, Gondar is a very pleasant town to
live. A primitive and friendly hotel – where water floods over the
floor (it was raining hard a good deal of the time while I was there),
and one looks out over marvellous mountains. A very kind Director
of Education – called Groom – who took me round, and showed
me castles and schools and a vacation course for teachers.

And everyone stops and talks in the streets. And no one seems
to be in much of a hurry. And the Director-General of Police is a
genial man in an elegant lounge suit who gives the impression of
having all the time in the world. Yemeni Arab shopkeepers – and
priests in white turbans all over the place – and a market full of
women with straw umbrellas. One must really come back – with
more time to spend – this journey to Sennar would be interesting

---

312 *Ras* (Prince) Asrate Kassa (1918–74), trained in the military academy
   (he was a Colonel) and became Governor of various provinces, at that
   time of Gondar. He was killed by the Dergue in 1974. His father, *Ras*
   Kassa, a cousin of Haile Selassie, had fought at Adowa, helped to
   bring Haile Selassie to the throne and gone into exile with him.

and profitable – in the dry season anyway. I hope to get on to Khartoum tomorrow – and Paris (insha'allah) on Tuesday.

They speak warmly of Hussey[313] here. I must see him when I get back.

---

313 Eric Robert James Hussey (1885–1958), educated at Repton and Hertford College, Oxford, was a member of the citizenship sub-committee of the Advisory Committee on Education in the Colonies. He was author of *Tropical Africa 1908–1944. Memoirs of a period* [1959]. He had been director of education in Nigeria and from 1942 to 1944 was educational adviser to the Emperor of Ethiopia.

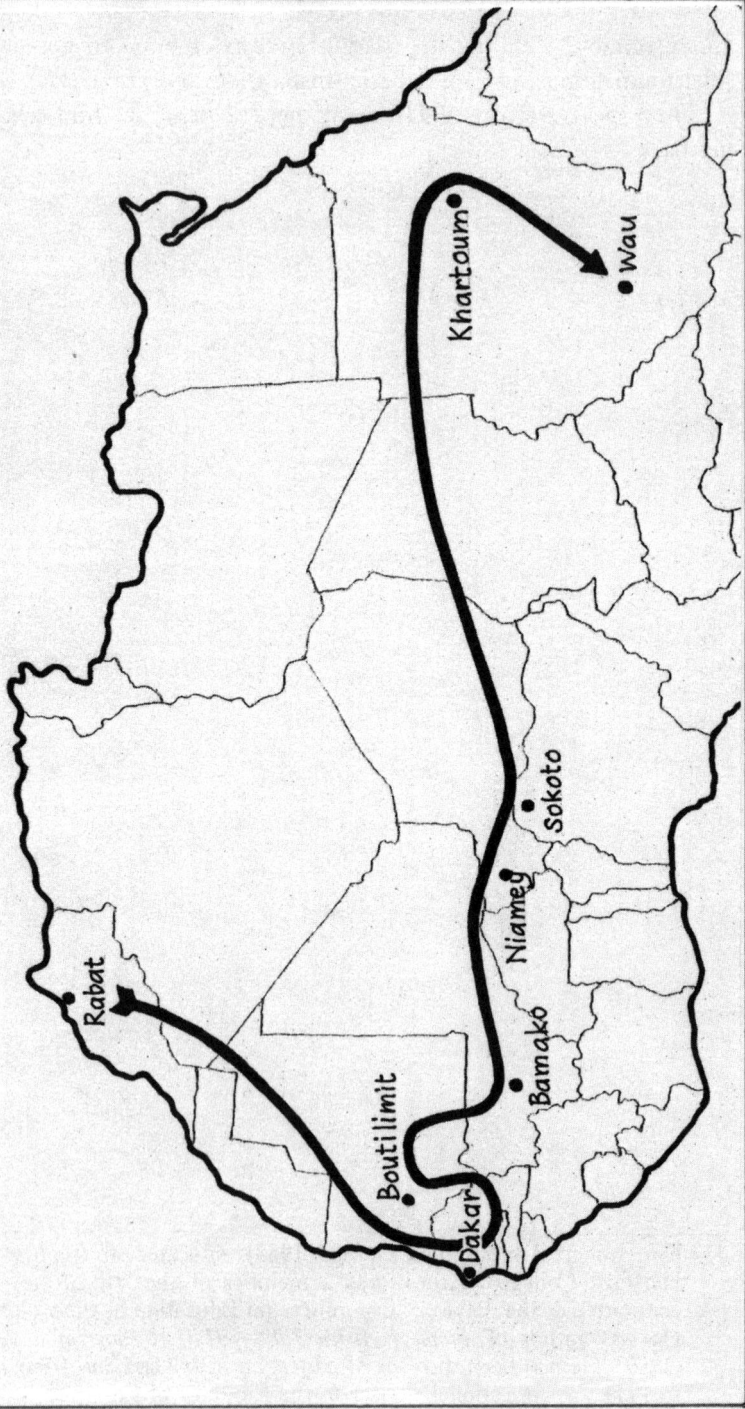

seventh African journey

Seventh African journey: across Islamic Africa
May 1956–July 1956

Thomas's interest in Africa that began in 1947 as an incidental of his university extension work, had soon become his central professional and scholarly concern. He brought an understanding of Arab and Islamic civilisation and culture gained during his work experiences in Palestine in the 1930s as archaeologist and civil servant. He observed the vital role of Islam in African history and in contemporary politics of the 1950s.

The seventh African journey in the summer of 1956 had as its main objective the study of Muslim Africa south of the Sahara. Thomas planned to go to Morocco and cross to the ancient cities of the Sahel and West Africa, then to return from West to the East of Africa and to visit Egypt on the way home. The issues that attracted him were communications across the Sahara, religion and politics in Mauritania, and lateral communications across Muslim Africa including the movement of West Africans to and from the Sudan. He proposed to follow the Hajj route to Sudan, mainly by lorry. In Sudan he would look at the general situation, particularly developments affecting the southern Sudan.

Thomas by now had four or five publications ready to take his contributions, but expected reluctantly to draw on some capital for his travel since the expected return from the articles could not cover costs even on the modest scale of expenditure he would allow himself. Thomas could not do all that he wished on this journey but he could include Morocco, several countries of French West Africa and Sudan. And there were many more journeys to come. A series of articles on 'Islam and politics in West Africa' was published in the magazine *West Africa* from 15 September to 10 November 1956, and related pieces in other publications.

By now the academic world was increasingly aware of the value of Thomas's innovative scholarship. He began to be offered part-time appointments in United States and Canadian universities. European colonial ascendancy in Africa was drawing to an end. The independence of the Gold Coast as Ghana on 6 March 1957 was clear proof of the new dispensation. Ghana was one of the countries where Thomas sustained a distinguished scholarly and academic university career.

To DFH
25 May 1956

Rabat [Morocco]
I'm writing this sitting outside the *Istiqlal* headquarters – a smart new building – signifying that they are no longer a clandestine party being chivvied around, and having their leaders stuck in gaol and exiled intermittently, but the dominant party in the Govt of this new independent Morocco. I've just been having a second, and very useful, talk with Party's Secretary, Ben Barca,[314] an extremely intelligent young man, and a former Professor of Mathematics (in the French sense). Now I want to see M. Abd-el Krim Fullous, who I'm told is responsible for running the popular theatrical companies which seem to have sprung up everywhere, as part of this national renaissance. [Later]. Abd-el Krim turned out to be a nice chap – but we agreed to meet tomorrow morning. I am now involved in doing so many different things tomorrow morning that I don't know quite how I shall fit them in – since I want to go on to Fez in the afternoon.

Oh dear, I've been writing far too small. I'm afraid. I'll try to make it a bit larger. Outside is the familiar, and to me always pleasant, sound of Arab music. There's a big celebration taking place, in honour of King Feisal of Iraq, who has just flown over from Spain for a 2-day visit. Though not (as you know) much in favour of Kings and Queens in general, I can see that this is a big event –

---

314 Mehdi Ben Barka (1920–65), Moroccan nationalist leader, was acting General Secretary of the Istiqlal (Independence) Party but broke away in 1959 and reconstituted his wing in the Union Nationale des Forces Populaires (UNFP). He was assassinated in a plot reputed to be organised with the connivance of Morocco's General Mohammed Oufkir (1920–72), the French *deuxième* bureau and Israeli Mossad.

since it's the first occasion on which another reigning Arab
monarch has visited the Sultan since Morocco became an independent State – (there must, I suppose, have been many such visits in
the old days of Moroccan greatness). I have a feeling that I am
being lazy in not having gone to join in the revels. But somehow by
10 p.m. I find I feel unlike making further efforts – if they involve
walking. One way of both economising and getting my weight
down (I hope) is to refuse to take taxis – but that does mean walking a good many miles a day between offices – these being spread
out over a largish area – so that one is fairly footsore (though not
unpleasantly so) by nightfall. But I hope I'm not missing too much.
The *Tour d'Hassan*, just outside my window, has been illuminated
for the occasion – which is nice, as it's a magnificent tower, standing up among the ruins of this enormous mosque – covered at the
top with a kind of lattice work (in stone), that I suppose is one typical thing about Arab (or Moorish) architecture.

I must say I find myself growing fond of this town. It's partly
the walls, and gates, that appear continually almost wherever one
is – a pleasant reddish-brownish colour – reminding me of
Jerusalem a bit. A large part of the modern French town is within
the walls – and it's well planned – with lots of Bougainvillaea,
orange trees, palms and flowering shrubs around. One must give
Lyautey[315] a good mark for this. I was even more reminded of
Jerusalem going over to Sale (two syllables) this afternoon – it's the
old town on the other bank of the Wadi (or Oued as they say here)
Bou Reg-Reg – the river mouth beside which Rabat is built. (It
apparently changed its course completely as a result of the 1755 –
Lisbon – earthquake, which was equally shattering here.) Over
there one found the same kind of gates, with old men sitting
inside, and chaps selling hot sausages, and playing gramophones,
and boys selling sweets, and veiled women (with veils of all colours)
trailing along behind their ancient husbands. I managed to combine
seeing something of Sale with mingling with the crowd, waiting for
the Sultan and King Feisal to go past – the crowd being, of course,
a good deal more interesting than the royal procession, when (after
an hour or so) it came past. However, I will say that the Sultan had

---

315 Marshal Louis Hubert Gonzalve Lyautey (1854–1934) was resident
general of Morocco from 1912 to 1916 and from 1917 to 1925, holding it against the Germans in the First World War.

the amiability to stop almost opposite us – Enormous cheering – of course, his exile, and later restoration must have increased his prestige enormously. He is this interesting kind of phenomenon – a national, popular monarch – and he looks well, dressed in this monkish grey robe, with a hood (or cowl) attached – middle-aged and intelligent. I was sold one of these medallions with his head on it, and a ribbon with the national colours – red and green. And most of us there seemed to be wearing this decoration.

To DMCH
11 June 1956

Postcard Mirador de Bandama, Tafira, Gran Canaria, Las Palmas
It never rains but it pours. Having bought a ticket to Dakar on a boat that calls tomorrow, and thought myself lucky to find one, I now hear this evening that I have my permit to go to Villa Cisneros. Quandary! I think though that I must go to Dakar – having delayed so long – and feeling the need for some company and intellectual stimulus – not to mention your letters. Perhaps there'll be a change of getting back to the Sahara later – for which in many ways I also pine . . .

To DMCH
16 June 1956

Chez IFAN – Dakar [Senegal] French West Africa
Between us IFAN and I seem to have been more than usually idiotic over letters. I asked the Secretary this morning for them this morning and she said she'd sent everything to Powder Hill. Horror. Stupid of me, of course, not to have written telling them to keep post.

One ought to be more efficient. I forgot what fiends these people are for forwarding (Remember the watch!). Otherwise all well. I'm staying free in an IFAN *case de passage* – which is excellent. Pearson,[316] the very nice Colonial Consul with a nice French wife,

---

316 David Morris Pearson, born 1915, was appointed consul in Dakar in March 1954.

kindly met me on the boat, and took me home to an excellent
dinner last night

To DFH
17 June 56

Chez IFAN – Dakar French West Africa Sunday
I really have been employing myself usefully this last hour, not
writing an article as I'd intended, but washing some of my dirty
clothes, with a packet of Lux and a nail-brush (bought in Agadir –
the latter for the collars and cuffs of white nylon shirts). The kind
French wife of the African Librarian (with two nice brown children) in the next door little house to my 'case de passage' (IFAN
property and situated in this pleasant IFAN garden) said she would
iron what needs ironing – so it was a chance too good to miss. But
really handkerchiefs! – especially if, like me, one's recently been
having a sort of cold (finished now) – they are filthy things – and
extremely difficult to wash in cold water – even with the best
French Lux. I am entirely converted to Kleenex, or whatever the
paper ones are, and swear I will give up inflicting this disgusting
process on poor Alice,[317] or whoever does it normally. My other
main problem was a thin summer (cotton) jacket, which is wash-
able – but I don't know that I've washed it properly, since once I
had it in the suds I had forgotten where the dirty patches were, and
could only rinse and squeeze hopefully. But perhaps it will look
improved in the end (it is all the less attractive at the moment as I
had also forgotten to remove deposits of tobacco shreds from the
pockets before washing).
    I hadn't meant to concentrate on this sordid subject – but it is
uppermost in my mind at the moment. I am very lucky really,
living for nothing in this nice bare hut – at least it has a bed – a
table – a few chairs, a sink, and a douche, + electric light, and one
really needs nothing more. But as Dorothy has probably told you,
my real imbecility has been to fail to give careful instructions about
keeping letters for me here – with the result that they've sent them

---

317 Alice Elliott with Edith Mutters evacuated from East London during
    the Second World War, worked for the Hodgkin household in
    Oxford.

all home. Very sad. A bit absurd – but I hadn't written recently saying when I was coming – so it's more my fault than theirs. Otherwise all is well. This is a bit of a pause – since, being Sunday, I can't really see officials and suchlike till tomorrow. What I want to do is to push off to Mauritania for a few days as soon as possible – returning here for a night before setting off for Bamako, Niamey and Northern Nigeria.

To DMCH
26 and 27 June [1956]

Dakar station – Midnight, June 26/27
I really am an idiot – more than usually so – since I seem to have left a quite nice long (6-page) letter to you + notebook containing useful notes over at the University of Fann this evening – I have left instructions which I hope will lead to it being posted and sent off to you in the course of the next day or two – but I'm fed up with myself for the delay – particularly as you've had nothing for nearly a week – and this letter contains a fair amount of the news of the past week it seems the best plan to post at least a line to you before I leave on this Bamako train to-night – if I do leave. This should be all right. But it's an interesting situation – a 24-hour strike (midnight to midnight) is just coming, rather gradually, to an end. The African personnel (those who haven't already been hanging about here for some time) are returning to their posts, gradually, making clear that they don't mean to be hurried – the station is gradually unlocked – the Europeans – who aren't in the strike, appear out of their offices in the interstices of the station – eventually the train appears on the platform – a nice porter takes the luggage in hand – some chaps appear who are willing to sell tickets, but not in the usual place – the porter explains that several essential people aren't back yet. This he thinks is a bad show. But there are enough back to make the train start blowing the trumpet which it continually blows – passing through stations – or when about to leave. And it finally got off at 1.10 a.m. Not bad. One can see too how useful a strike is symbolically – particularly this kind of token strike. It reminds everyone (what everyone tends otherwise to forget) that the Railway can't be run without railwaymen. At 11.59 the railway is dead – at 12.0 it becomes alive again – and the

chaps who a minute ago were just observers are prepared to start serving the public again – but they don't serve the public unconditionally. In this particular case the strike – so far as I can understand it from talking to the very friendly porters, under-station-masters left-luggage-office-superintendents, etc. was a strike of 'solidarité' with the 'auxiliaires' – the daily-paid workers – to try to get them absorbed in the permanent staff. But I must check on this. Certainly this seems a community well adjusted to strikes. It seems taken for granted that, as soon as the strike is over, the train will go.

But, as you see, I never got this off at Dakar. But instead kept falling asleep in the interval between 12 and 1 a.m. This I might post at some intermediate station – but maybe Bamako would really be best now. I've had a somewhat wild night – sleeping on hardish 2nd class seats – till the end of my spine got so sore that I transferred to 1st class (further up the same coach) – more comfortable – and no one seemed to care much. What was dreams and what was reality during the night I found it hard to tell – I was very much aware at one moment of a woman in what seemed to be great distress, praying (it seemed) to Hussein ibn 'Ali – and decided she must be a *Shi'a*. But on reflection I think it may have been Hassan she was apostrophising – and perhaps it was just one of the Lebanese women in the carriage talking to her husband. I was vaguely aware too of a beautiful pink dawn – and at about 8 pulled myself together sufficiently to come along to this comfortable restaurant car and have a nice breakfast of coffee and bread. And here I think I will in fact stay for most of the journey since there's this admirable table to write on. We're in the region of Tambacounda now – I think – I'm not sure exactly where. We've stopped beside one of these villages of round huts – mud or rush – with thatched roofs – encircled with fences of more plaited rushes: it's this beautiful kind of 'open parkland' (?) – plenty of trees, but not real forest. Usually one gets to Tamba in the middle of the night – so I don't suppose I've seen this particular stretch of country before. I'm back in the carriage now – very empty – more boys going home for the holidays – indeed there's a nice group of lads from the *Cours Normale* at Boutilimit whom I've picked up again (one of them travelled from St Louis with me – oldish – he smokes) – they have fearful distances to travel – to Nema – 'Ain-el-'Atrous – Walata even – and they have to go this fearful roundabout way to get there. They are good-looking brown Moors, mostly, wearing Khaki shirts and trousers.

Now this is really an opportunity for catching up on all the past history you haven't had. I also feel I owe the *Daily Herald* another article – in view of their £100 – and might try to write something about Boutilimit. Since I'll be in this train, I should guess, until 6 or 7 a.m. tomorrow morning there should be plenty of time. I'd better assume that you will get the letter that I left behind in Dakar, and start from where I left off there – so that this one will have to be fitted onto that – I hope it'll make sense that way.

It now appears that I am the only European passenger on this train – which is incredibly empty – no-one having any confidence in when it was going to depart. So lunch is – I gather – going to be entirely for me and the staff.

I left myself – in the last letter – talking to Sheikh Abdullahi ould Sheikh Sydia[318] over tea and orange syrup and wafers. He warmed up a lot towards the end, and invited me to a *Meshwa* (Roast Sheep) that night – but I explained I had to go back in the *camion*. Actually I was rather a fool over this. If I'd thought more I'd have realised that it didn't really matter a damn when Malik the driver started – or finished (see later part of this story) and that Sheikh Abdullahi as the most powerful holy man in the Trarza could perfectly well command him to start whenever was convenient for me. The trouble is that there is a kind of correlation between the degree of tiredness and the tendency to miss opportunities. And the *meshwa* was certainly a missed opportunity, so about midday I said good-bye – ending up with Sheikh Abdullahi saying he disapproved of Allal-al-Fassi[319] and his claim that Moors were Moroccans – Sheikh Abdullahi's view being (crudely) that the Moors had in the past *ruled* Morocco (Almoravids) – and wouldn't

318 The Ouled Ibiri tribe in south-western Mauritania included as temporal and spiritual leader the scholar Shaikh Sidiyya al-Kabir (1775–1868), whose descendants and kin formed one of the major socio-economic groupings in the modern Islamic Republic of Mauritania. One of Thomas's doctoral students, Charles Stewart, later produced a definitive study on the Sidiyya brotherhood, published as *Islam and Social Order in Mauritania* by C.C and E.K. Stewart, 1973.

319 Allal al-Fassi, Moroccan nationalist leader, founder of Istiqlal (Independence) Party in 1943.

mind doing so again, but they wouldn't *be ruled by* Moroccans. But then Sheikh Abdullahi is a 'grand ami de la France'.

Still Wednesday June 27
After a magnificent lunch – pate and salami – nice fried fish with capers, chicken, fried potatoes and watercress, cream cheese, orange, red wine and coffee. Indulging myself this far since I have saved over Fr. CFA 1000 (=£2) by not buying a couchette. More important, I explained to the French manager of the Wagon Lits Restaurants, to eat and drink well – one can sleep anywhere. The country changing very little – rather dryer looking here and smaller trees.

Boghenil-Bamba – No we don't seem to be stopping here. Too small. Hottish – some difficulty in staying awake at the moment. To return to Boutilimit. At about midday the young interpreter and I moved slowly (since it was very hot and sandy underfoot) back to the house of M. Méchain, director of the *Cours Normale*. We drank (I having said good-bye to the young interpreter – I couldn't give him any money it was explained, since he was a chief's son – but I took his photograph – and promised to send it to him – I really must) – and had an excellent lunch. He didn't seem to know a very great deal about the Sheikh's College – although just next door – except that the lads there were on friendly terms with the lads of the *Cours Normale* – and that when the latter moved over to Rosso, as was planned, the Sheikh's lads would move out of the tents in which they now live and occupy his buildings. He also said that Sheikh Abdullahi was extremely rich – thanks to all these *ziaras*[320] and gifts – though it was true that he used his wealth mainly for his flock: that he could get more or less what he wanted out of the Govt: and that Boutilimit pretty well belonged to him. He confirmed what Leriche[321] had said – that the old social inequalities remained more or less unchanged – except that marabouts had tended to become more powerful than *guerriers* (the latter having less to do), *serviteurs* were still, in effect, slaves – though not officially admitted to be such. Occasionally they ran away – their

---

320 *ziaras* – visits accompanied by gifts from the visitors.
321 Albert Leriche (1901–57) was in the French colonial service till 1950 when he left to become Directeur de Centre IFAN, Senegal-Mauritania. He was author of many studies on Mauritanian history and society.

masters would then bring a charge – that they had pinched some cash, or suchlike – which was as a rule false – and drop the charge provided they could get the *serviteur* back again. He was very honest about the influence of nationalist ideas – from Morocco, etc. 'If they are thinking along those lines, they wouldn't tell us Europeans.' But I think anyway the probability is that Boutilimit and the South is much less influenced from Morocco than the Atar region. Of course a lot of boys (more than half) in the *Cours Normale* aren't Moors but Negro peoples (Wolofs, etc.) from the South of Mauritania – the region of the Senegal river – since they have so many more schools – (difficulties over schools of the French type among nomads are obvious) – hence (as in N. Nigeria) a higher proportion of them become teachers and go into black-coated jobs.

Stopped at a station beside the Senegal river – beautiful buildings much more in mud brick here – and landscape more Sudanese. It's a great wide river, winding away. It's something to be going East at last, a feeling of moving in the right direction + regarding Khartoum as more or less 'home'! + A beautiful bright blue bird has just darted past the train.

Méchain was extremely kind – got his driver to drive me back over the burning sand (temperature is said to get up to 47° in the shade at this time of year) – via Malik (to make sure the *camion* took me back in the evening). I then slept for about 2 hours in this comfortable fortress-campement – admirably looked after by its *gardien* – and went out for an hour at 4.30 to look at the town and take photographs – also to buy some cigarettes – in order to repay the kind Postmaster – N'Diaye Abdoullaye – for all his that I had smoked on the journey – I meant to find a present for his family too – but Boutilimit isn't much of a shopping centre – in fact it isn't much of a town at all. Just a cluster of houses in the sand – I was followed round by a horde of (friendly) children – wanting to be photographed – and wanting (as always) to *have* the photograph at once. They talked good French – some of them. The circuit of the town took longer than I'd meant – and I thought I'd better hurry back up the hill to collect stuff and catch the *camion* (quite unnecessary, of course) – the result was that I was in a state of extreme thirst when I eventually got back to the campement – and drank two large bottles of fizzy lemonade almost straight off. Then Méchain's car (jeep) turned up and we went down to the starting-

place of the lorry – the house where Malik slept. The *gardien* and
N'Diaye Abdoullaye sweetly came too – to see me off – N'Diaye
did much more than that. He sat me down inside Malik's house –
full of small children of various families – and gave me fizzy orange
mixed with fizzy lemonade (an excellent drink – though Toby
wouldn't think so) – which quenched my thirst a bit further – and
the children finished up what I couldn't drink. (The country here
is changing now – much more open – red earth, bushed and low
trees – and hills away in the distance. I think I remember this
region.) N'Diaye also insisted on buying me 4 loaves of bread and
a tin of sardines for the journey – he said I would need it
(absolutely correctly) though I assured him I wouldn't – and
refused to be paid back.

We took of course an enormous time to get started – our main
cargo being about 2 tons of boys and their luggage, going home for
the holidays from the Cours Normale. But there seemed many
more boys who wanted to get on board than the 35 who were
allowed for – hence a scramble. Anyway on our first visit to the
Cours Normale we didn't take any boys – just prospected and came
back again. Then we collected an elderly *marabout* (whom I came
to dislike a good deal) and his younger disciple (looking a bit like
a Preraphaelite – or pseudo-P. – Christ) and dropped the old boy
with the blue beard who had insisted on my giving him his pen –
at this point we settled down to a bit of chat – the nice Postmaster,
N'Diaye, being still around. Then back to the Cours Normale to
collect our 35 lively boys, who all piled into the back somehow –
leaving Malik, the driver, myself and the two marabouts 1st class in
front. It was at about this point that the older marabout began to
get interested in my Thatcher's Arabic grammar. Unfortunately he
noticed that it contains – among the exercises – the 1st Sura of the
Koran – and so forth – he clearly thought it improper that I, an
infidel, should possess this book – or at any rate much more proper
that it should belong to him, a marabout. So he kept asking me to
give it him – and I kept trying to explain how indispensable it
was – and how I read it every night before going to bed – and every
morning on rising. But he didn't give up. Eventually I became
afraid that he might even try to pinch it – since he kept explaining
to everyone who turned up that I had a book which contained parts
of the Koran – I was therefore extremely suspicious when on the
journey, he kept pressing me to put the Koran on top of the

camera instead of – as I had them – the camera on top of the Koran. This, I thought, was to make it easier for him to pinch Thatcher at some moment when I had dropped off. However – I misjudged the poor old boy over this at any rate – he only thought it was blasphemous to have verses of the Koran lying *under* something else.

Also this marabout kept anointing himself with perfume – also praying under his breath – also giving me a rap whenever I fell asleep – also continually unwinding his enormous turban and enveloping me in it. I admit these were all quite inadequate reasons for disliking him – and even the fact that he tried to increase his room on the seat and reduce mine continually – these were none of them good reasons for dislike. Anyway I won in the end – I thought. Since after about 12 shots he got tired of trying to wake me up – had to accept my sleeping as a brute fact.

The journey (I may have told you) from Boutilimit to Rosso – 190 Kilos – took 15 hours. Much longer than coming – and it soon became dark after we left – so I couldn't see much of the country – except that it was semi-desert – if one tried to sit down there were crum-crums that stuck into you – and everywhere thorn-bushes. After 50 Km we stopped at the *campement* where we'd stopped coming up. But the ex-schoolmaster chief wasn't there – Malik took us into the tent and left us – the tribesmen, he and I (mainly they to be honest) quickly ate the bread and sardines with which the far-sighted N'Diaye had provided me – then tea arrived – but oddly others, not I, got it in the first round – including the marabout and his disciple who sat with their backs turned to us all the time – in saintly meditation – when I did get some, after about an hour, it wasn't very good. Soon about a dozen of the *cours normale* lads turned up – and gatecrashed into the tea – very sensibly, being by now cold and hungry. We had some pleasant conversation. They asked me what I was doing at Bouti – and I explained the fact that I taught as well as wrote. What did I teach? Philosophy? What is philosophy? Well, it's about what you ought to do, and what rights people ought to have, and what are valid methods of reasoning, and what we mean by 'soul' and 'body' and 'God' and suchlike. But this – they said – is a very dangerous sort of subject – it makes you doubt and lose faith. We had a schoolmaster, they said, who was a philosopher. He was very clever and used to wave his arms about when he taught us – and he went mad. As a rule philosophers do go mad. And what – I asked – do you do with philosophers who go mad? They are shut up in a Lazaret at Dakar – they said. So would you – I asked – agree with syllogism:

'All philosophers are mad – I am a philosopher – ∴I am mad'.

No, they said – we only said '*Some* philosophers are mad' – not *all*. But anyway it is a subject that it is safer to have nothing to do with.

Bamako [French Soudan] – *Thursday, June 28th.* Sorry. At this point this letter got overtaken by sleep – and I never roused myself enough during last night's fairly uncomfortable train journey to finish it. So there'll have to be another series – I want to post this at once. Nice to be back in Bamako – friendly and sometimes familiar faces (particularly the waiters in the *Majestic* Hotel) – and I've managed already to see Cardair,[322] Amadou Ampateba[323] – So feeling on the whole well and cheerful – and not much over a month to go!

To DFH
1 July [1956]

Hotel Terminus – Niamey [Niger] AOF
Quite what is the terminus that this hotel is called after I don't know. It might be the railway which is supposed to be coming here one day – either the little railway from Wagadugu – or the big railway from Algeria, which has been intending to cross the Sahara for the last 50 years or more. But its prospects don't look very bright at the moment. However there is said to be a stationmaster here – in readiness for when there will be a station. It's quite a pleasant hotel – except for these awful American tunes that they will play on the gramophone – I can't think why, when there's plenty of nice French ones. However it's cool out of doors – so I sit here and bear the music – and the wind which blows papers away. I've been spending a lazy day – mainly (when awake!) writing to Dorothy – giving her the main news of the past few days – particularly

322 Marcel Cardaire, published many works on 'Islam noir', including. *L'Islam et le terroir africain*, 1954.
323 Amadou Hampaté Bâ (c.1900–91), historian, collector of Fulani oral traditions, at that time attached to IFAN. Published many works including *L'Empire peul de Macina*.

Bamako, which was very useful and interesting – so I won't repeat that here.

I really had enormous luck – getting onto this Pilgrim Plane (a special – next stop Mecca) yesterday, when I feared I was stuck for 3 days at Bobo-Dioulasso. Tomorrow I must try to get on to Sokoto, after seeing the Administration, and then to Zaria and Kaduna – where I'll find more letters (and I've warned them to keep them this time). Small winged flies keep going down my neck, and can't be recovered. They want to pack up here – so I'll have to move. This is quite a friendly, relatively modest, hotel – with a patron who talks Greek, among other languages. Below is the Niger – unfortunately not visible from here. It was looking beautiful at sunset – an island in the middle – crowded canoes setting off to cross it – people coming down to the water's edge to wash their horses, or their clothes, or their children, or themselves; an occasional fisherman, goats; donkeys; a sort of low escarpment across the river rising out of the plain.

I'm continuing now on Monday. There was a great storm in the middle of the night: lightning, thunder, and a wild wind – eventually rain. At about 3 I and the other chap sleeping in our courtyard decided that it wasn't any good staying out longer – and helped each other in with our beds. Result – I slept longer than I'd meant. The first rain I've had fell on Friday – leaving Bamako in the bus – a very English sort of cloudy sky.

And now I have accidentally picked up a *camion* for Borni-N'Kami, on the road to Sokoto – so I must quickly collect goods – and be ready to start in zero-ish hours – That's the way one travels – sometimes too much time to spare sometimes too little

To DFH
29 July 1956

Khartoum [Sudan]
This is only a scrap – since it's late. But if I don't write now you'll get nothing for a week – as I'm going early in the morning to Bahr-al-Ghazal – Wau – and that neighbourhood – and there's only a weekly aeroplane, more or less.

Saturday, 21st – On the way south to Wau – stopped at Al-Obeid half an hour ago. Now the country is changing noticeably – becoming increasingly green – after the almost desert red, thorny country of Kordofan from which we've just come. (Oh dear I accidentally stuck a cigarette on this paper – sorry. Not a good thing to do in an aeroplane.) (Somewhat sleepy at this point.) Also, of course, it's a green time of year – which helps – the rain having just begun – a kind of spring. Quite a bit of cloud too – having begun in ones and twos, there are now masses – we're just (I think) passing over the Nuba mountains – a part of the Sudan I should much like to visit. (They've brought a cup of coffee – welcome – as I was up at 5 – but there was also a kind old Arab, with two pretty children, at Al-Obeid Airport, who gave us all coffee or tea out of two thermos flasks he had thoughtfully brought with him.

I hope this journey south is going to turn out to be worth while – it's a bit of a speculation – but the MG[324] specifically wanted it – so I thought I'd better do it. Anyhow it's the last major undertaking. If all goes well, I return in a week – then have 3 days in Khartoum again (too much time in capitals really) and a couple in Cairo – and so home.

. . .

A marvellous great mass of clouds – but there are enough gaps to be able still to see the ground below. People in Khartoum as usual very nice and friendly – and comfortable living in the University guest house – with meals provided and all. Not having got this letter finished last night I'll try to send it back to Khartoum by one of the crew – for posting. Fortunately, I have a stamp.

It was lovely to find two letters from you here – one forwarded, efficiently, from Dakar

I see from the papers here by the way that there's a proposal to build a Hodgkin memorial lecture hall in Khartoum in honour (rather than memory) of Robin – the fact that he refused a gratuity is continually brought up in conversation – apart from all his other qualities. I spent one and a half hours this morning at Khartoum airport (while the aeroplane was delayed because – as the Captain explained – "it hadn't enough volts and amps" – a condition familiar in one's own experience) – talking to the Chief

324 MG: the *Manchester Guardian* newspaper to which Thomas was contributing.

Butcher of Khartoum (and the first Educated Butcher) who had been taught geography by Robin at the Gordon College – he also breeds horses and plays polo – on the way to Al-Obeid for a business deal – his eyes lit up when I said I was Robin's cousin . . .

To DMCH
July 1956

[Sudan]
[Editors' Note: This letter starts on page 3 – pages 1 and 2 missing.]
Later – 3 p.m. At this point the D/C Wau – Osman En-Nan[325] – another friend of Da'ud Abd-al-Latif's[326] dropped in for a chat – and stayed 3 hours – which was very nice, and extremely interesting.

He was one of those who evacuated Wau with Da'ud (and other senior Northern officials) at the time of the troubles in August last year – and thus prevented bloodshed (there was in fact no killing in Bahr-al-Ghazal). Since then, I'm afraid, the situation hasn't been too good – and the exact causes of this aren't easy to understand – points of view and stories are so different. 'Federation' has certainly become a popular demand – but what 'Federation' really means seems more uncertain. Osman-En-Nan was arguing that it was often in fact understood as meaning secession – and hence was dangerous. This point was in a way confirmed a few minutes ago when I was talking to a tall Dinka driver, who explained that he talked 14 languages – Dinka, English, Arabic, and Swahili being the first four (he was in the Army during the War, and spent some time in Kenya). His attitude was a gloomy one – 'Federation or else' – and as he put it (when I asked him what he meant by Fedn) – 'It means being ruled by our own people – then if we want

---

325 Osman en-Nan, a Jai'li from Shendi and a former pupil of Robin Hodgkin, had been serving in Southern Sudan for three years. See letter of 17 March 1948 and note on Robin Hodgkin.
326 Da'ud Abd al-Latif, the Governor of Equatoria, had a reputation for straight dealing with Northerners and Southerners alike and when removed early in 1955 was thought to have been taken from Juba at the instigation of Northern merchants upset by his impartiality.

outside experts we can have them.' On the other hand, according to Osman the advantages of Federation (= self-govt, getting rid of Northerners, etc.) were being discussed – it would mean better educn, roads, social services, etc, – and someone asked 'How would you pay for all these improvements' – to which the answer was 'We would get the money from Khartoum'. My conversation with the Dinka, by the way, was interrupted by his suddenly seeing a large dark shape in the river, followed by an excited crowd on the bank. I thought it was a crocodile or hippopotamus – but when we got there, it turned out to be a poor ox, who had fallen in, and was drifting rapidly down stream, with a chain round its neck. Fortunately it was soon fished out again.

I don't know whether it's sensible – but I've gone a bit of a bust on this expedition – and have agreed to spend £35 on a car (new!) to take me for the next 5 days to Yambio, the Zande capital, via Tombora and back. I like Osman – (he, like almost everyone, was taught by Robin) – he seems honest and serious-minded – and he's been in the South for 3 years – so he should know what he is talking about. He's worried about rumours (which he says can travel quicker than administrators in cars) – and we discussed the possibility of adult education here – which doesn't seem to exist as yet – but might be useful for the generation of young Southerners working as clerks and so forth who never had the chance of 2ndary education. (The noise of heavy rains and the croaking of frogs, a rather gloomy combination.)

Aeroplane to Khartoum Saturday 28th July My darling, It seems absurd that I haven't written to you at all for these last 5 days – but conditions haven't been very favourable. I'd better try to begin from where I left off, last Sunday. Later that evening Osman-en-Nan returned with a Southern MP – Sayed Akee Khamis Rizgallia – a Dinka Moslem – NUP, and a supporter of the Administration clearly.[327] MP's in the South I've now learned, having met a good many of them, can pretty well be divided into Federationists and Anti-Federationists – 'Liberal' MP's belonging on the whole to the former, and NUP MP's to the latter, category.

---

327 The National Unionist Party (NUP) evolved from a movement founded in 1942 by Isma'il al-Azhari and was identified with the Khatmiyya Sufi order led by Sayyid 'Ali al-Mirghani. It was the governing party in Sudan from December 1953 to July 1956.

Federationists, like Stanislaus,[328] tend to be suspect to the Administration. Anti-Federationists, like Akee, tend to be suspect to and disowned by educated Southerners (at least in the areas which I've visited), and probably a fair proportion of uneducated Southerners as well. I don't think, to be honest, I learned a lot from Akee – his English was a bit difficult for one thing. And there are various stories about how he became an MP (he was elected unopposed, endorsed, he says, by the Dinka chiefs in his constituency) – other possible candidates (or one possible candidate anyway) not having received letters addressed to them asking them to stand. According to Akee he was opposed actively by the Church (Catholic), as a Moslem, but not chiefs and people don't bother about religion when it comes to elections.

Akee was anxious to insist, anyway, that the Dinka having lived in close contact with the Arab Sudan all this time, were less 'Southern' – or separatist – in their point of view than peoples further South, like the Zande – regarded Arabs as brothers. Not having had the chance to travel much in Dinka country, I don't really know how true this is. The elderly President of the Liberal Party, a Dinka, and deposed chief from Wau[329] a sweet character of military appearance, who came to visit me last night and again this morning with the LP Secretary[330] who spoke English – he didn't – assured me that both the LP and Federation feeling were strong among the Dinka. Hassan – the very nice Leftish Provincial Educn

---

328 The Southern Party was formed in Juba in 1951 and renamed in December 1954 as the Liberal Party open to all Sudanese, but remaining effectively an exclusively Southern political party with a federation programme. The Liberal Party's initial vice-president was Stanislaus Paysama, of Dinka origin from Bahr el Ghazal province although born 1903 in Darfur and a founder of the Southern Party. He accepted a ministerial post in 1956 in the central government of Isma'il al-Azhari.

329 The Liberal Party's initial president was Benjamin Lwoki, a Pojoulo born 1918 and from Loka in the Yei River district of Equatoria province. He had been a primary school teacher earlier in his career. He went into central government in 1956. Lwoki was replaced in the party presidency by Stanislaus Paysama.

330 The Liberal Party Secretary was Buth Diu, a Nuer from Upper Nile. He had been a civil servant, helped form the Upper Nile Political Association in Malakal in the 1940s and was a founder of the Southern Party. He went into central government in 1956.

Officer– said that the Dinka having been more conservative and opposed to Mission Education in the past than other smaller tribes in Bahr-al-Ghazal, were much less strongly represented in Govt jobs – and tended therefore to have less use for Federation than the Non-Dinka – since Federation, as they saw it, would mean more power in the hands of the non-Dinka elite – not themselves.

Two things, I think, are clear. First the fact that during these 3 weeks Bahr-al-Ghazal was actually governed by Southerners (The Southern Police Officer called every morning at Hassan's house to make sure that he was still there and all right.) without a single Northerner left in any administrative post (in Wau anyway) must have stimulated this Federation idea (in the sense of 'Home Rule' for the South) – and pretty clearly the groups represented by the Junta didn't want the Northerners back. Second, it seems a pity that when the Northern administrators returned (apart from the Governor, Da'ud, the people that had gone away), there wasn't a general amnesty declared for all offences committed during the 3 weeks interregnum – since Northerners' lives and property had been protected – and the 'offences' seem to have been pretty minor ones as a rule.

Now – 3.45 p.m. – we're back in familiar Sudanese sort of country – rain cultivation, I suppose – red sandy country, with patches of fields here and there. It's a grey, rather misty kind of day.

One hour later – coming down – flying between one Nile and the other. Everything looks very wet – great puddles all over the land. It's been fairly bumpy lately – lots of storms, I suppose – but not actually raining.

On land again, now, sitting in the Sudan Airways bus – my only companions seem likely to be a gaunt Indian and his wife – opposite is a youth leaning against the wall, holding an enormous red balloon.

I have rather moved away from Akee. But I don't think I learned much more from him than I've told you – NUP, his party, hasn't much of an organisation in B-al-G, as far as I could gather. Then I went to dinner with the Acting Governor Ibrahim at-Tahir– who unlike most, is a good Moslem – so we drank *Tamar* – but ate well – I can't remember what. The conversation was, for me, very useful – mainly about why there is this strong Anti-Northern feeling among Southerners and of course about the mutiny and its causes (another aspect of the same question). Of course there is a strong, and justified, tendency to regard the British 'Southern policy' as a good deal responsible – which treated North and South as almost separate countries. So that Northerners (in the South) and Southerners were on different salary scales – lived in separate locations – used different clubs – and were treated as distinct castes.

Monday 30th – 1.30 p.m. Oh dear – I must post this inadequate uncompleted scrap, or it will never get to you. But I'll go on with the story tonight insha'aalah. Life is interesting but full. All dear love – blessings Beloved – always Thomas.

Index

Index by Christine Shuttleworth